'Enquire not, if the fairy race,
Shed kindly influence on the place.

Enough, that all around is fair,
Composed with nature's finest care'

From *A Guide to Conishead Priory & the Surrounding District*
by Dr Philp, 1880

'It's situation on the west coast gives it the advantage of the mild temperature characteristic of that part of the country, while the rainfall is low, and therefore unlike the lake district proper'.
Newcastle Chronicle c. 1880

'...It is not alone the home of one fortunate family, but the alternate abode, with all the comforts of a well-regulated home, of a rational, well-to-do combination of people in search of health or pleasure ... surrounded by all the externals which created nature, artistically developed, can contribute'.
Lakes Chronicle c. 1880

'One of the finest buildings in the North of England'
Nikolaus Pevsner

About the author

Sarah Elizabeth Holmes was born in East Yorkshire in 1969. She works as a fine artist and writer, living in Cumbria with her husband John Griffiths. As a child she began researching her geneaology, which culminated in her writing and printing a book about her family – *Famous Relations: My Wilberforce Family from Yorkshire* (2004). Sarah has also had articles published in the BBC's *Who Do You Think You Are?* magazine and in the academic research journal of the Bronte Society, *Bronte Studies*.

Her love of history prompted her to bring the beautiful and historic house of Conishead Priory to the attention of a wider public audience by thoroughly researching and writing this fascinating first full-length history of the house and the people who have inhabited it.

The Paradise of Furness

THE STORY *of* CONISHEAD PRIORY *&* *its* PEOPLE

Sarah Elizabeth Holmes

Handstand Press

For my husband
John Griffiths
for his support and encouragement

&

In memory of my father
Ernest F Holmes
who inspired me with a love of history

HANDSTAND PRESS

Published by Handstand Press
East Banks, Dent, Sedbergh Cumbria. England
LA10 5QT

First published in 2012

Designed and set by Longhouse Publishing Services, Broughton Mills, Cumbria.
Printed in Great Britain by Short Run Press, Exeter, Devon

978-0-9552009-8-4

Contents

Illustrations

Acknowledgements

I would like to thank staff at the following offices for their help in locating documents:

Cumbria Record Office, Barrow in Furness
Local History Library, Kendal
Lancashire Public Record Office, Preston
Durham County Records Office
Public Records Office, London
Public Archives Office, Kendal
Archives at Conishead Priory

I would also like to express my grateful thanks to Jack Layfield for his kind assistance and local knowledge, Susan Ritson for permission to use documents and photographs in her care, which belonged to her parents Matron and Superintendent Gray of Conishead Priory; Geoffrey Roe for his great help and support throughout my research; David Cross for allowing me to quote from a family letter and his invaluable guidance in bringing the book together and Carol Bennett and Peter Lowe at the Ulverston Heritage Centre Archives. Lastly, but by no means least, I would like to thank those who have anonymously contributed their precious memories to the history of such a remarkable house.

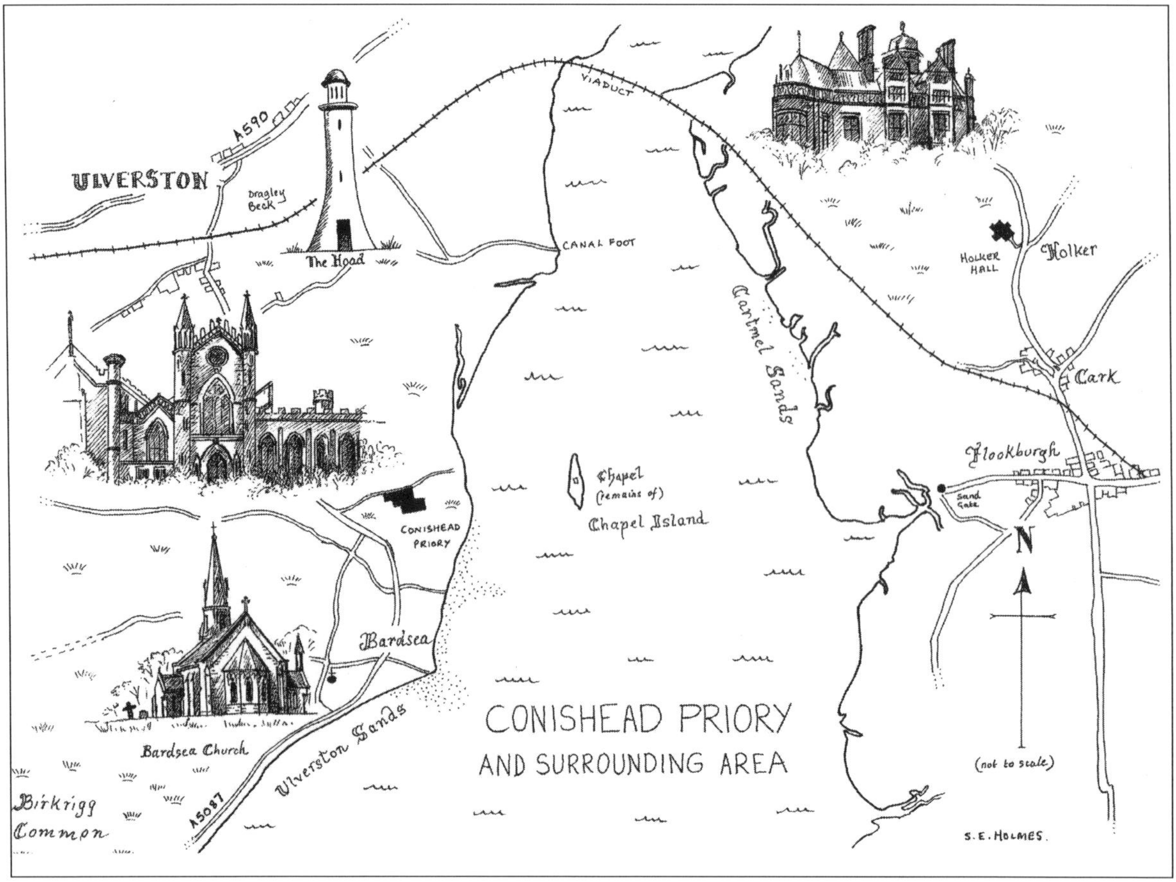

Map of Conishead Priory and surrounding area

(Drawing by the author)

Introduction

Two miles from the market town of Ulverston in Cumbria, and occupying an elevated position on the western shore of Morecambe Bay, Conishead Priory stands as a testament to one man's vision for his family home. During the eighteenth century a local historian and Jesuit Father, Thomas West, described the house and its surroundings as 'the Paradise of Furness' and since that time other writers have used similar euphuisms.

Conishead is magnificent and beautiful, but other adjectives also come to mind: eccentric, curious and palatial. Inside, the house is a warren of endless rooms and corridors with a cornucopia of architectural details and nuances of design. Bearing in mind that the present house was re-built during the early nineteenth century and since then has been adapted for various residents, it is still possible to see that it is a treasure house of artistic and architectural designs, planned and executed by some of the most eminent artisans of the nineteenth century. An amalgamation of styles, it favours the Tudor manor house, combined with the fine, delicate carvings and stained glass of a Medieval Gothic cathedral.

At its core the Priory is a place of refuge, spirituality and healing, but for centuries it also acted as host to royalty, men of eminence, artists and writers, and witnessed bloody feuding and an uncertain and often tragic history, encompassing the rise and fall of the many families who lived there. It has had more distinct and varied phases in its history than the majority of stately homes, from being a family home, then a hydropathic establishment, to a military hospital and convalescent home.

Since 1976, it has been the spiritual home of a Buddhist community. Today, through their tremendous endeavours of restoration and conservation, Conishead Priory is open to all as a place of historical interest, architectural delight, and a haven of peace and tranquillity.

Sarah E. Holmes
Cumbria, 2012

Plate 1 'A view of Conishead Priory, the seat of Colonel TRG Braddyll', by John Wilson Carmichael c. 1840 (location of original unknown)

One

'IN GOOD STATE & PLIGHT'

1154 – 1548

The main purpose for you having come together is to live harmoniously in your house, intent upon God in oneness of mind and heart.
(The Rule of St Augustine)

Conishead was first built as a hospital between 1163 and 1167 during the reign of Henry II, England's first Plantagenet king, on land known as 'Coningsheved', a word derived from the ancient 'Cyning' or 'Conyings' ('Kingshead'). Tradition has it that this denoted a royal burial place, and later, a Saxon boundary marker. Conishead Priory was established to take care of the 'poor, decrepit, indigent and lepers' of the surrounding areas of Ulverston, Furness and Kendal by Gamel de Pennington, whose descendents resided at Muncaster Castle near Ravenglass in Cumbria[1]. Early documents relating to Conishead Priory are vague and contradictory due to the irregularity of early English records. Some claim that a Norman nobleman, William de Taillebois of Lancaster[2], entrusted Gamel with establishing the hospital. Later medieval manuscripts, however, name Gamel as the sole founder. In *A History of the County of Lancaster*, William Farrer writes:

> *'Possibly the true explanation of these contradictions may be found in a remark dropped by a visitor to the priory in 1535. After stating that it was founded by Gamel de Pennington in 1167 he adds: 'It was in strife for some time, being built upon the land of William Lancaster, baron of Kirkby Kendal and Ulverston.'* [3]

The land which William of Lancaster gave to Gamel de Pennington on which to build Conishead was originally part of the land granted to Furness Abbey by its founder Stephen of Blois (the future King of England). Eight miles from Conishead Priory, the Abbey of St Mary of Furness had been established in 1127 and was administered

[1] Gamel founded Pennington Church near Ulverston.

[2] Also known in early manuscripts as William Fitzgilbert (William, son of Gilbert).

[3] From: *Houses of Austin Canons: The Priory of Conishead, A History of the County of Lancaster: Volume 2*, pp. 140-143 (1908) by William Farrer.

Plate 2 William of Lancaster who gave the land on which Conishead Priory was built.

(*Detail from the main stained glass window in the hall at Conishead Priory*)

by Benedictine monks belonging to the Order of Savigny from northern France. It was the first Savigniac monastery to be established in England. By 1150, the Abbot of Savigny had changed the Priory order from Benedictine to Cistercian rule and under this new regime, St Mary of Furness became the second richest Cistercian Abbey in England after Fountains Abbey.

In 1163, a dispute arose between the Abbot of Furness Abbey and William of Lancaster regarding Furness Abbey's claim over the Furness Fells. The matter was settled by thirty sworn men who decided that the Fells should be divided between the contending parties. William of Lancaster acquired the western side between Coniston and the Duddon Estuary, along with Ulverston and the land upon which the hospital of Conishead would be built. The Abbot of Furness had opposed the establishing of a second religious house within the boundaries of Furness to protect its unrivalled influence in the area (at about this time, the abbey possessed a total area of 55,000 acres)[4]. The idea of founding a hospital at Conishead rather than a priory may have been a way of circumventing this embargo.

When construction of the hospital was complete, Gamel de Pennington gave instruction to the order of Augustinian monks to take care of the inhabitants.

The canons of the Augustinian Order lived by the rule of St Augustine of Hippo (354 AD-430 AD), which provided a sound and practical basis for the religious life. The simple daily routine of preaching, praying and pastoral care based on the lives of the Apostles attracted a huge following. By medieval times, over two hundred Augustinian priories had been founded in England and Wales[5].

The canons' dress, still worn by Augustinians today, consisted of a long black cassock worn under a white rochet (a knee-length over-tunic generally made of linen), with

[4] *Barrow and District* by F Barnes (1951), p 34.

[5] A 13th century illuminated manuscript of the Epistles of St Augustine belonging to the canons was held for centuries in the library at Conishead, and is now in the Tullie House Museum in Carlisle.

tight fitting sleeves and a hooded black cloak. They grew beards and wore caps to cover their heads.

At Conishead, the canons' chief duty was the care of the sick. In addition, they provided a school for the children of the hospital's tenants and workers. Living on the shores of the treacherous Morecambe Bay, the canons were also entrusted with the important task of guiding travellers across the sands to Cartmel and Lancaster. A guide was employed and granted three acres of land from the Conishead estate at Saltcoats and paid £10 a year for his service[6]. A small chapel was built on Harelside Island (later known as Chapel Island) in the Bay, approximately a mile from Conishead bank, where mariners and travellers, guided by the sound of the canons' ~~bell, would~~ find sanctuary and a place to thank God for a safe passage[7].

Sometime between 1180 and 1184 the hospital of Conishead was raised to the status of a priory and church, dedicated to the Virgin Mary. William of Lancaster's earlier grants had been made to *'the hospital of St Mary of Conishead and the brethren there'*, but later endowments from the early 1180s onwards were made to *'Deo et ecclesiae B. Marie de Conyngeshevede'* ('God and the Church of the Blessed Mary of Conishead').

Surviving medieval manuscripts list the Priors of Conishead from about 1194 until 1536. Not all names are recorded in their entirety. The incumbent between 1194 and 1199 is known only as 'R'. He was succeeded by Thomas in the early years of the thirteenth century and then John, mentioned in manuscripts of 1235 and between 1258 and 1259. The first full name to be recorded is Thomas of Morthyng who held office between 1272 and 1292. He was succeeded by Robert; William Le Fleming (1309 and 1318), John (1343), Richard of Bolton (1373 – 1401), John Conyers (mentioned in 1431), Thomas (mentioned in 1440 and 1452), Robert Godson (c. 1489), John (1505 – c. 1515), George Carnforth (mentioned between 1515 – 16 and pensioned in 1527) and finally Thomas Lord, who was Prior at the time of the dissolution of the monasteries in 1536.

Sadly there is no evidence from the time showing the original appearance of the hospital and priory buildings. We can, however, get some idea by looking at the Priory Church of St Mary and St Michael in the village of Cartmel, Cumbria, which dates from the same period. Founded in about 1188 by the Augustinians, the church, together with the gatehouse, survived the dissolution of the monasteries after villagers petitioned King Henry VIII to allow them to maintain the church as their place of worship. On a larger scale than Conishead, Cartmel Priory Church's basic cruciform layout, building material and decorative details were probably very similar.

[6] In 1256, a Charter was drawn up in which Magnus Olafson, King of Man and the Isles exempted *'his special friends the Prior and convent of Conishead'* from paying toll throughout his land (the Isle of Man), possibly in return for his safe passage across the Leven Sands.
Following King Henry VIII's dissolution of Conishead Priory in the 16th century, the guide charged himself and his successors with the payment of a sum of money.

[7] The island lost the remains of the ancient chapel centuries ago, but it was long reputed that a secret tunnel stretched beneath the sea between it and Conishead Priory.

An archaeological excavation begun in October 1928 discovered the foundations of Conishead Priory's church making it possible to create a more reliable image of its appearance before the dissolution[8].

The excavation focused on an area of raised ground which is now the Priory's south lawn. The foundations, constructed from yellow sandstone, were dated to approximately 1250. About 100 foot in length, the archaeological evidence suggested that Conishead Priory church was slate roofed with a central tower housing four bells, tracery windows, and unusually short transepts. These were no more than nine foot in length and without aisles or pillars[9]. When the hospital became a priory, further building was required to include a church and conventional buildings. As work progressed on the church, space was found to be limited so Conishead remained relatively modest in size compared to other religious houses of the time. Archaeologists agree that the construction of the church would have incorporated a chancel, choir and probably a small chapel on the south side, near the altar.

The chancel was constructed of lime concrete and laid with enamelled 'encaustic' tiles painted with diamond and floral patterns, typical of thirteenth century religious buildings. As with most Augustinian priory churches, the main door was probably at the west end, reached by stone steps. Fragments of 'dog-tooth' moulding from an archway were found during the excavation at the northern end. A carved wooden rood screen separated the nave from the high altar, dividing the lay people from the canons and Prior, who took their place in choir stalls leading up to the altar in the presbytery. Fragments

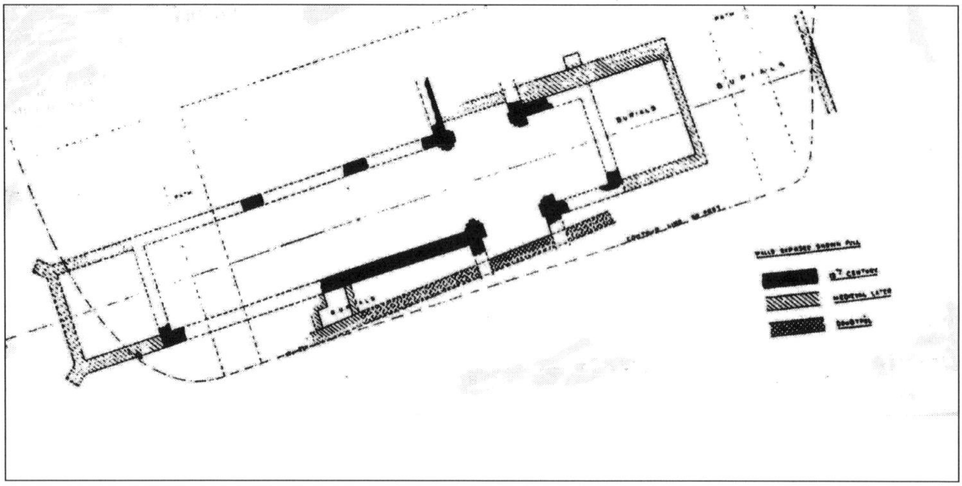

Plate 3 Plan of the excavated foundations of Conishead Priory Church on the south lawn, 1929

('Transactions of the Cumberland and Westmorland Antiquarian and Archaeological Society' Vol 30. 1929, Local History Library, Kendal)

[8] *Transactions of the Cumberland and Westmorland Antiquarian and Archaeological Society* Vol 30. Article by P V Kelly – 11 September 1929 (Local History Library, Kendal)

[9] In 1540, the Churchwarden's petition to the Crown mentioned the fact that *'there are no pyller stones at Conygshed'* because the priory *'hade never no pyllers'*.

recovered also suggested that the interior mouldings, monumental slabs and tombs were made from local red sandstone and the inner walls were covered with plaster.

Sufficient remains of the red sandstone high altar were discovered to show that it had been a rectangular table, 5 foot long, 3 foot wide and 3 foot 6 inches in height. The upper altar stone or slab was carved out in a hollow, perhaps to contain a religious relic, maybe Conishead's 'girdle', which was supposedly worn by the Virgin Mary. The archaeological report described how:

> *'This altar had been in all likelihood executed by some skilful craftsman employed for the purpose, as the quality of the work is much superior to anything else in the church. ... The front face was divided into panels by four flat pilasters rising from the projections of the base slab, and surmounted by capitals with a roll and fillet moulding on the top, and divided from the pilasters by a bead moulding. Between the capitals are three corbels, similar in design but smaller and forming with them a cornice, which supported the upper slab. The bead moulding, which is repeated on the corbels, forms with that on the capitals a continuous string across the top of the panels. ... The front panels ... were ornamented with a diamond-shaped pattern of alternate rounds and hollows. The character of the moulding and ornamentation suggests 13th century work, and probably contemporary with the earlier part of the church.'*

Runic lettering was found hidden on a fragment on the inner face of one of the pilaster capitals which experts believe to be twelfth-century Danish, spelling 'dotbrt' ('Robert'), possibly a stonemason who worked on the building of the church.[10]

The hospital or infirmary buildings, chapter house, library, cloisters, almshouse and dormitories, refectory, kitchen, Prior's house and other domestic offices were located to the north of the priory church on the site of the present nineteenth-century house and evidence suggests that they were constructed from yellow sandstone[11]. There

[10] In 1966, the archivist from the Lancashire Record Office wrote to Dr John Wishart, who had briefly held joint ownership of Conishead at the close of the 1920s and who instigated the archaeological dig on the south lawn. He enquired about the location of the ancient runic stone which had disappeared by the 1920s and Wishart replied that he did not know its whereabouts. The archivist also received the same enquiry from Mr J. Melville, a council member of the Cumberland and Westmorland Antiquarian and Archaeological Society, who regularly provided local history columns for the local evening newspaper. It was Melville who was able to finally solve the mystery of the missing stone. He wrote to Wishart in 1968, reassuring him of its safety:

> *'You may remember I wrote to you in 1966 regarding the runic inscribed stone that was found at Conishead Priory during the 30's* (sic). *I am now able to let you know that it has been recently re-discovered. While the gardener was taking out some bushes he unearthed a number of stones and fortunately he and the Superintendent were interested, as a result of my enquiries some time earlier and they examined these. To their delight they found the missing stone and it now occupies a place on view in the Priory. The inscription still baffles the experts. ...'*

[11] When the present house was erected during the early 19th century, parts of the medieval priory were still visible above ground and these were either removed or incorporated into the fabric of the new build. Three yellow sandstone blocks, carved with a diamond pattern, intersected with roses, were incorporated into the outer lower face of the south wall of the house. It is believed they formed part of a frieze from the priory's chapter house or refectory.

In nearby Pennington Church, the vestry fireplace lintel was constructed from a medieval grave carved with a wheel head cross, and this, together with the shaft of a yellow sandstone sundial, is believed to have been taken from Conishead Priory church when it was dismantled during the dissolution of the monasteries in the 16th century.

Plate 4 A stone fragment from Conishead Priory Church c. 12th century bearing the runic lettering 'Dotbrt' (Robert), possibly a Danish mason

('Transactions of the Cumberland and Westmorland Antiquarian and Archaeological Society' Vol 30. 1929, Local History Library, Kendal)

would also have been barns, stables and workshops nearby in which to store produce, animals and tools.

Amongst the artefacts discovered during the excavation were roofing slates (with holes for wooden pegs), medieval pottery, large numbers of broken iridescent-coated glass flagons, carved bone handles and the teeth of various wild and domestic animals. These fragments provide only a partial window on the life of the canons at Conishead, but their existence would have differed little from other religious houses in the country. Except for the times when rent was due from the estates, a canon's life was passed within the closed precincts of the priory.

The Prior kept a 'fish house' at Conishead, a standard feature in most medieval priories. Fish, as well as meat, was part of the canons' staple diet. Fish supplies were salted for storage and quantities were given out to the poor and the children of the area every Maundy Thursday. An underground watercourse was discovered in the twentieth century running in three channels from under Conishead Priory, each covered with a barrel vault. A vertical shaft lined with masonry connecting with the stream was also found and this probably served as the main drain from the kitchen and other domestic buildings. The canons were granted permission to bring water from a spring at the nearby hamlet of Trinkeld by means of a 12-foot wide channel, so they were never short of water.

Building work carried out during the nineteenth century uncovered many skeletons and pieces of gilt coffin-plate by the south wall, near the high altar and further to the west of the church building. These tombs are likely to have belonged to the wealthy benefactors of Conishead, such as the Harringtons of Gleaston Castle, near Aldingham, and the Bardseys of Bardsea Hall, near Ulverston, who had their family vaults and memorials in the priory church. In his will of 1528, Christopher Bardsey requested that his body should be buried *'within the priory of our Blessed Lady of Conyshed'* on the south side of the church.

The archaeological report of 1929 describes another burial area that was uncovered:

'To the east of the gable wall of the chancel there are foundations of rough masonry, enclosing a rectangular space of 18ft 6ins by 24ft. These are difficult to account for, as the only building permissible here would be a small Lady Chapel with a roof sufficiently low, as not to obstruct the light to the east window of the church. These foundations therefore can only be those of what was probably a low wall surmounted by a rail or other fence, which enclosed a special portion of the cemetery nearest the church, reserved for the burials of priors or other persons of distinction.

Still further to the east, in spite of the unfavourable nature of the ground, the slope had been used as the cemetery, and here were found many burials. Great care was taken to disturb these as little as possible beyond noting the general appearance of the tombs, although the ground had been clearly disturbed before. The tombs were large chambers of rough masonry containing several interments, and were covered with undressed slabs of stone. The cemetery seemed to have been enclosed in a roughly built wall, and there were also partition walls of similar character. The partition walls probably enclosed a special part of the cemetery which was reserved for the burial of lepers.'

When the excavations were complete, the area was re-covered leaving the bones undisturbed. Eventually the site was transformed into a rock garden.

As a hospital and priory Conishead depended on the support of wealthy local patrons and benefactors, such as the Harringtons and Bardseys. The large list of gifts including land, properties, rents, and privileges, show that they gave generously. William of Lancaster's family patronage of Conishead ended with his son,William, who died without an heir in 1246. His sisters' sons inherited the patronage along with their family's lands, which passed by marriage into the Couci family[12].

Along with his gifts of land, William of Haverbred, another wealthy donor of Conishead, granted the privilege of grinding the canon's corn at his mill with as much sand as they pleased and the means of erecting a salt-house *'betwixt the two roads below the woods'*. Valuable as a food preservative, salt was procured from sea sand by evaporation with boiling water. These bequests and benefits from local landowning families, together with the developing local iron industry, provided a regular source of income for the canons. As with many other priories, Conishead housed a holy relic

[12] By 1343, the patronage of Conishead passed to the Crown through lack of a Couci heir. The last patron before the dissolution of the monasteries was Henry, Duke of Richmond, the illegitimate son of King Henry VIII.

which augmented their income. While the canons made claim to the Virgin's girdle, Cartmel Priory was known to make twenty shillings a year from pilgrims flocking to see a piece of the Holy Cross. Furness Abbey, surprisingly, had no relics. Perhaps their comparative wealth made such enticements unnecessary.

The Harrington family of Gleaston Castle had a chapel in Conishead Priory church named after them, where their family were buried. This may have been sited on the south side.[13] In March 1458, William Lord Harrington, who had been a standard bearer at the Battle of Agincourt in 1415, donated a large bell for the church tower which was inscribed with his and his wife's names: *'Wilelmus de Haryngton Dominus de Aldyngham et Domina Margareta Uxor eius.'*[14] A sixteenth century manuscript from Conishead mentions their gift of the bell along with

> *'three sets of vestments and copes ... two glazed windows in their chapel and a lead roof, an altar with alabaster reredos and marble image of St Mary, a missal and a churchyard cross'.*

In return for these gifts, the canons were required to practice daily intercessions and an annual requiem mass for Lord Harrington and his Lady.

Through the generosity of the descendants of the Penningtons of Ravenglass and William of Lancaster, Conishead was given the Chapel of Drigg near Ravenglass and the churches at Ponsonby, Muncaster, Whitbeck and Hale in Cumberland; Pennington and Ulverston in the Furness district, and Orton in Westmorland. A canon from the priory was appointed as vicar for each of these churches.

In 1281, the new Bishop of Carlisle, Ralph of Ireton, restricted the activity of the Conishead canons by stipulating that outside the confines of the priory they should be accompanied by a fellow canon and a secular chaplain. They were also forbidden to administer the sacraments. The Bishop's instruction suggests that the canons had perhaps become prey to the temptations of the outside world.

Regular disputes over the legality of their bequests and endowments were a constant source of irritation to the canons of Conishead. Sometime during the thirteenth century the Abbot and monks of St Mary's in York made claim to the church at Whitbeck. The Archdeacon of Richmond stepped in to mediate between Prior Thomas of Conishead and Robert de Longo Campo (the Abbot in York). Finally, the Abbot and monks of York, *'considering the poverty of the house of Kuningesheved'*, agreed to grant the canons at Conishead all rights to the church at Whitbeck 'for ever', for an annual payment of five shillings, which the canons would make to the church of St Bega in Cumberland.

Closer to home there was animosity between the canons and the Cistercian monks at Furness Abbey. The monks of Furness, threatened by Conishead's increasing wealth and

[13] An elaborate tomb belonging to one of William's ancestors stands near the high altar of Cartmel Priory. The canopied effigies of John, 1st Lord Harrington, who died in 1347 and his wife Joan, originally came from Conishead Priory church and may have been located in the south side chapel above the Harrington vault

[14] 'William Haryngton Lord of Aldingham and Lady Margaret his wife.'

status, returned to their earlier grievance that Conishead had been built on land which rightfully belonged to Furness Abbey. Furness Abbey also claimed that the churches at Ulverston and Pennington which had been granted to Conishead were originally chapels belonging to their church at Urswick. Conishead's right to Hawkshead chapel as dependent on the church of Ulverston was also contested. In 1208 a commission which included the Archdeacon of Richmond, Gilbert Reinford Lord of Ulverston and Furness Abbey's Abbot, was appointed to arbitrate between the two houses. It was decided that the canons at Conishead should have the right to nominate a person to hold church office and collect the tithes of Ulverston and Pennington. The canons also agreed they would accept

'grants of land over which the monks (of Furness) exercised control, excepting within their own territory of Ulverston, and that even such grants must not exceed in total one-third of the whole manor without the consent of the abbot. Furthermore, by the same agreement they bound themselves not to allow the number of canons at the priory to exceed thirteen'.

It was also settled that the canons would make an annual payment of fifty shillings[15] to Furness Abbey and that no women would reside at Conishead Priory. We have to assume that before this time women were living at the priory either as lay sisters, servants or poor dependents. The commission resulted in an improved relationship between the two religious houses.

Ownership of the land on which Conishead was built was finally settled in 1307 when King Edward II confirmed the endowments of land and tithes granted to Conishead Priory by William of Lancaster. These included St Mary's Church in Ulverston, all the lands on both sides of the road which lead from Bardsea to Ulverston, forty acres of land in Ulverston and a salt works between Conishead and Ulverston. The endowments of St Mary's in Ulverston were given to the Prior and canons for their own use who, in turn, promised to perform divine service and all parochial duties.[16]

In 1338, King Edward III bestowed a Royal Charter upon Conishead. This important document confirmed all grants and rights belonging to the priory, leaving no doubt as to the ownership of lands.[17]

Despite its relative isolation Conishead was not immune to events in the outside world. The thirteenth and fourteenth centuries had seen recurrent skirmishes with the Scots. In 1316 and 1322 Scottish invaders reached Furness

'and burnt that district ... taking away with them all the goods of that district, with men and

[15] In 1230, this sum was massively increased to 120 shillings a year.

[16] During the next five hundred years subsequent owners of Conishead inherited the perpetual curacy of St Mary's Church, Ulverston, and served as lay rector and patron.

[17] A century later however, ignoring the Royal Charter, a Kendal nobleman, Sir Thomas Parr, claimed the right to St Leonard's Leper Hospital in Kendal through an inheritance of part of the Lancaster estates. The Prior of Conishead William Tunstall and his canons were forced to turn to the law to recover their ownership of the leper hospital, which had originally been granted to them by William of Lancaster's son on his deathbed.

women as prisoners. Especially were they delighted with the abundance of iron which they found there, because Scotland is not rich in iron'.[18]

When Robert the Bruce and his armies seized Carlisle in 1322 and arrived in Furness, the Abbot of Furness Abbey met with him and paid a ransom to prevent further assaults on the land and its people. Robert the Bruce stayed at the Abbey and accepted the deal, however the Abbot's efforts to negotiate peace in the area were not entirely successful and the Scots continued to pillage and burn, rendering land uncultivable.

Between 1348 and 1349 the epidemic known as 'The Black Death' ravaged the world and decimated approximately half the population of Great Britain. It is inconceivable that Conishead Priory escaped this catastrophe and it is likely the disease spread through the community. For those canons spared to care for the sick and the dying, there would be the additional strain of working the land and attending the livestock with depleted numbers.

The dawn of the sixteenth century heralded the final days of the religious community at Conishead. In 1525, storm clouds began to gather. Pope Clement VII authorised Cardinal Thomas Wolsey to place Conishead, along with another twenty-eight religious houses in England, into the hands of King Henry VIII to provide funds for an Oxford college. At the final hour Conishead was saved by the efforts of the Marquis of Dorset, Lord Harrington of Muchland and the Duke of Suffolk, who argued that *'the house is of great succour to the King's subjects, and the Prior of virtuous disposition'.* The 'virtuous' Prior at this time was George Carnforth, who was pensioned in 1527 with £10, and with food and drink to the amount of £5 a year.

In 1533, following an inspection of the monasteries of England and Wales, Thomas Legh, a Lawyer and official of Thomas Cromwell, accused the new Prior of Conishead, Thomas Lord, of murder. Legh alleged that the Prior had ordered the death of his cousin, John Bardsey, a wealthy neighbour. Local man, Richard Johnson, corroborated his story in a petition to the Chancellor of the Duchy of Lancaster. He claimed that the Prior had maliciously sacked him as the *'Carter or Guyder* (Guide) *of Levyn sands in Furness'* because he had arrested a man named Edward Lancaster for stabbing his master, John Bardsey, eleven times, on the authority of the Prior. The report of the incident came before the Lancaster Assizes but no charge was made as the matter was *'colourably borne by divers gentlemen'.* The Prior seems to have escaped indictment, an indication perhaps of his power and influence.

Two years later Prior Thomas Lord would meet with Thomas Legh again when King Henry VIII commissioned a survey to evaluate the wealth of church properties in England and Wales. Called the 'Valor Ecclesiasticus' ('Church Valuation'), it was the instrument which governed the decision to dissolve the monasteries in 1536. Thomas Legh was one of the inspectors commissioned to carry out the survey of Conishead

[18] Excerpt from the 'Chronicle of Lanercost' quoted in *Barrow and District* by F Barnes (1951), p 36.

Priory and it would have been surprising if his previous dealings with the priory did not influence the findings in his report.

Listed as residents at Conishead with Thomas Lord were George Carnforth (the ex-Prior with a pension), and eight canons (one who was *'keeping cure'* - or acting as vicar at Orton church). Forty-eight lay people also lived in the Priory, including nine waiting servants, fourteen common officers of household and sixteen servants of husbandry (working the land) and there were two poor people, including a widow living on charity. The Priory's net income was estimated at £97 with a debt of £87 17s 3d and it was noted that alms were distributed to the poor on a daily basis:

'- Alms given to seven poor persons every week day, formerly called 'Lady Moneys' of the institution of the founders – £6.13s.4d
- Similar alms given to the poor every day called 'Purse Alms' of the foundation of the founders – 16s.8d
- To seven poor persons during the whole of Lent every day called 'Maundy Money' – 13s.4d
- Similar alms given to children every Monday in bread and drink, immediately after the Mass of St Mary to 20 shillings at the dictate religious.
- Alms given on Maundy Thursday in bread, salt fish and money to children and other poor - £2.6s.8d
Total – £11.10s'

During their inspection on behalf of the King, Legh and another of Cromwell's officials, Richard Layton, found five of the eight canons at Conishead guilty of sexual incontinence with women, two in an aggravated form. Although this seems shocking it was not an exceptional incident. The inspection of religious houses in England and Wales revealed many alleged incidents of 'self-abuse' and sexual misconduct, some no doubt true but others probably exaggerated in order to justify the King's antipathy towards the religious houses. At Conishead, however, Layton and Legh's report may have been accurate. Previous reports from visiting Archbishops had found the canons' ways of living questionable. Many of the Priory's residents were described as being of low birth, 'worthless' and 'foolish', with morals considered equally low. Abusive language, stealing and moneymaking was commonplace. As early as 1302, the Vicar of Orton Church, who had been appointed by the Prior at Conishead, had been fined for 'unchaste behaviour'.

Following this survey, Conishead Priory was included on the list of religious houses to be dissolved by Parliament, with the property and land to be given over to the King's treasury. The structure of the priory buildings of Conishead were inspected and judged to be in a *'good state and plight'*. A valuation of the priory contents was undertaken between the 9 and 13 September 1536 by Sir Marmaduke Tunstall, Sir James Leybourne, Thomas Sherbourne, a group of Lancashire Knights and gentlemen; the auditor Thomas Burgoyne and the receiver Thomas Armer. Two images of Lord and Lady Harrington and an alabaster tomb were marked on the inventory as *'not valued, because it is thought no man will give no money for them'*.[19] Realising Conishead's vulnerability, Prior Thomas Lord had written a begging letter to the auditor Thomas Burgoyne a fortnight before the commissioners arrived. He entreated Burgoyne to be as good to him *'as you are unto the Prior of Burscough and others'* and requesting he buy the tithe corn of Ulverston and the corn on the priory land. He sent Burgoyne two gold angels *'for a remembrance of the same'* and added *'you know my Lord Admiral is good lord to me'*.[20]

The ex-Prior George Carnforth asked to be allowed to continue receiving his pension of £10, together with *'one honest chamber and garden'* and food at the Prior's table for himself, two servants, and two horses, which had been paid by the priory. The commissioners granted him his pension only. The canons were allowed to keep their bedding and personal effects at the discretion of the commissioners, together with their wages. The value of goods allowed to each canon averaged £1. 5s. 1d.[21]

After two attempts to seek exemption from dissolution, the priory was at last closed in September 1536 and the canons ejected, despite fierce protest from local people. The Prior, however, was determined not to relinquish Conishead without a fight. A month later he and the canons returned to the priory. From there they wrote on the 16th October to an army of Northern rebels, who were part of a religious and social uprising in the North of England, known as the 'Pilgrimage of Grace', asking their help to defend the priory. Led by a London Barrister from Yorkshire, Robert Aske, and with approximately 40,000 northern men, the rebels mounted insurrections throughout the country, defending the monastic cause and calling for an end to the King's reformation. One of Aske's objections to the Act of Suppression had been the fact the religious houses in the North of England gave generous alms to the poor. He also deplored the loss of divine services which the abbeys and priories provided for the people. Ultimately, the uprisings were quashed following the King's betrayal of a promise of a general pardon. Aske and his followers were executed and the *'the whole Convent of Conishead'* was included on a list of those to be tried for their part in the rebellion. Luckily the canons escaped trial. The priory was stripped and dismantled and the canons allowed to disperse in peace. Thomas Lord was appointed vicar of Orton church and the canons each received pensions of £1 17s 8d. At the dissolution the priory's outstanding debts totalled a little less than £88. The furniture, cooking equipment, window glass and choir stalls were estimated to be worth £288 and the *'goods and chattels, lead, bells and timber'* were sold for £333 6s 3d. Some lead was removed to Lancaster Castle and the churchwardens of St Mary and St Michael's Church in Urswick purchased the 'Haryngton Bell'[22]. A large quantity of stone was taken from Conishead Priory church and used to re-build part of

[19] R. J. Mason *The Income, Administration and Disposal of Monastic Lands in Lancashire from the Dissolution to 1558 (1962).*

[20] Ibid.

[21] Public Records Office, Kew (PRO DL29/2313).

[22] Other bells are thought to have gone to St Cuthbert's Church in the nearby village of Aldingham. The Aldingham church tower has three bells which were acquired in 1550. One or more of them are believed to be from Conishead

the church and tower of St Mary's Church in Ulverston, which had been devastated by a severe storm.

The dissolution of the religious houses freed great tracts of land for purchase from the Crown and old priories were converted into domestic homes. Thomas Burgoyne, the auditor of Conishead Priory, attempted to purchase the site and the surrounding land. He appealed to King Henry, but negotiations were never finalised. The remaining fabric was used in the building of a manor house on the site, which retained the name Conishead Priory. For the next three years profits from the priory were paid by order of King Henry VIII, as Duke of Lancaster, to the Receiver-General for the Duchy.

In 1539, Thomas Stanley, 2nd Lord Monteagle[23] leased Conishead and the surrounding land from the Crown and farmed the estate until King Henry VIII died in 1547. On the succession of Henry's son, the boy-King Edward VI, Conishead Priory was granted to the Right Honourable Sir William Paget and his wife Anne and heirs.[24]

By the end of November 1547, having received a Licence from the King, Paget had transferred his lease to John Machell, a cloth worker of London, his wife Joan and son, William. The Licence, granted by King Edward VI gave details of the estate of *'our well-beloved and faithful counsellor William Pagett'* and provides a glimpse of the sixteenth century Conishead Priory. Paget was licensed to:

> *'give, grant, sell and dispose to ...John Machell ...all that his close, confines and liberty lately belonging to the Priory of Conyshedde otherwise called Conyngshedde, in the County of Lancaster, and all and sundry houses, buildings, erections, orchards, gardens, pools, fishing waters, fishing lands, soil, commodities, profits and hereditaments thereof whatsoever within the site of the said late Priory of Conyshedde ...and also all those Mains, cloisters, meadows, pastures and other hereditaments thereof...'*

The mention of the ancient monastic 'cloisters', suggests they were still intact following the dissolution and had been incorporated into the build of the new Tudor mansion house.

A year later, Conishead Priory changed hands once again, when William Sandys, a descendent of an ancient Cumberland family, purchased the house and the estate from the Machells. A new and intriguing period in the history of Conishead Priory was about to begin.

Priory or Furness Abbey. One is inscribed in Latin *'Christ, King of Heaven, may this sound please thee'* and the other with a triple 'S' ('Sanctus').

[23] His son was to expose the Gunpowder Plot of 1605.

[24] Sir William Paget had served King Henry VIII, who had employed him on several important diplomatic missions. Appointed Clerk of the Privy Council, he was also Secretary to King Henry's fourth wife, Queen Anne of Cleves, and at the time of his brief tenure at Conishead Priory he was Chancellor of the Duchy of Lancaster.

Two

'ALL THE PRETTY COMPANY'

1548 – 1687

When William Sandys came to Conishead Priory in 1548, he was moving into a house built within the last ten years from the stones and timber of the original priory and church. Remnants of the medieval buildings, which included the cloisters, lay close-by in ruins. Whilst there are no known images or descriptions of the appearance of Conishead Priory from this time, written accounts and an engraving produced two centuries later show that parts of the priory buildings were incorporated into the west side of the new house. East and west wings supported the castellated north elevation and the main entrance. To the front of the house there was a courtyard or piazza in the fashionable Italian style, supported by Gothic pillars. The windows, variously constructed from timber and grey sandstone, were quatrefoil and arched, probably re-used from other parts of the original priory. According to a twentieth-century archaeological report, the Tudor house had a large, arched and slightly domed brick oven, 4 foot wide and 2 foot high, which was probably located in the kitchen.

It was to this house that William brought his wife Mabel and their two daughters, Margaret and Barbara[1]. Shortly after the move, Mabel died and William rapidly married again, no doubt in hope of an heir. His second wife, Agnes Strickland, swiftly performed her duty and a son, Francis, was born in 1549. Francis would have much to inherit. His father, one of King Henry VIII's bailiffs, had inherited vast family wealth and the appointment of Receiver General of the Lordship of Furness. With this post came the responsibility of collecting the rent and tithes on behalf of the Crown which, before the Dissolution, would have gone to Furness Abbey. William, however, was greedy and unpopular, ruthlessly extracting rent from his tenants, many of whom struggled to pay.

[1] The Sandys family were descended from the 13th century Le Sandes family, originally from Burgh by Sands near Carlisle.They settled through marriage at Rottington Hall near St Bees in Cumberland. William Sandys was the second son of Margaret (nee Dixon) and William Sandys of Esthwaite and Hawkshead, who was a Justice of the Peace and Receiver of the Liberties of Furness. William and Margaret had six sons and a daughter; their eldest son and heir George was killed at the Battle of Musselbrugh in 1547, and William junior (of Conishead), who initially resided at Colton Hall in Lancashire, inherited his father's Esthwaite estate in 1548. His younger brother Edwin Sandys became Bishop of London and Archbishop of York during the reign of Queen Elizabeth I.

Anger and discontentment grew and on 10 September 1558, he was met at Conishead by a crowd of about fifty tenants, who had come to protest their ill treatment. Their complaints fell on stony ground. When William threatened to deal even more severely with defaulters a riot broke out on the south lawn and William was *'very riotously and wilfully'* butchered to death.

John Rawlinson of Furness Fells, a witness, stated at the inquest in Preston in 1559:

> *'William Sandys was murdered on account of certain tythe corns which were in his possession and which the sons and servants of William Bardsey Esq., attempted to carry away. The sons were Nicholas and Robert and the name of the servant was John Trogheton* (sic)[2]'.

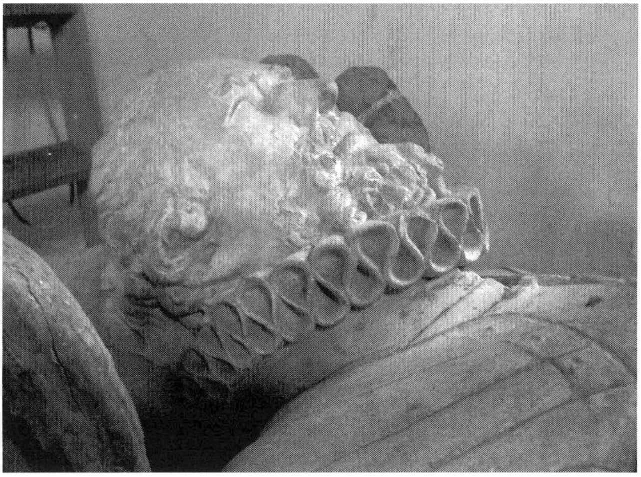

Plate 5 The effigy of William Sandys on his empty tomb in St Mary's Church, Ulverston (photograph by the author)

Unfortunately, Rawlinson was unable to say who dealt the mortal blow.

Sandys had accused his neighbour, William Bardsey of Bardsea Hall, of *'concealing a piece of land from the Queen'*. The Bardseys in return were angry that Sandys held the tenure of tithes of corn and grain from which he was making a considerable income at their expense. It is also possible that religion paid a part in the tension; the Sandys were Protestants and the Bardseys staunch Catholics. Later evidence suggests that Nicholas Bardsey struck Sandys with a mattock, described at the time as a *'certain heinous offence'*. Soon after the murder, Nicholas and his brother fled to Scotland where they lived in secret until they received a pardon from Queen Elizabeth I. William Sandys had died a brutal death. His body was reportedly thrown into the water of Morecambe Bay and never recovered[3].

Francis Sandys was only nine years-old when his father died. He inherited Conishead Priory but was held in ward to Queen Elizabeth until 1571, when he was twenty-one and able to take possession of the estate. In the meantime his mother, Agnes, remained at Conishead and married Henry Sandford, with whom she had a son, Alan.

As soon as Francis Sandys was twenty-one he took possession of Conishead and

[2] John Broughton.

[3] During the 18th century, an altar tomb was placed in St Mary's Church, Ulverston, bearing the recumbent effigy of William Sandys wearing a suit of armour. When the tomb was moved for refurbishment in recent times, it was found to be empty, substantiating the belief that Sandys went to an unceremonious watery grave.

married. His wife was Jane Dalston. They had no children and when Francis died in 1583, Conishead Priory was left to his elder half-sisters, Margaret and Barbara.

In 1560, Margaret Sandys had married Myles Dodding, a Chief Clerk of the Crown of Kendal and heir of William Dodding, of Colton Hall, Lancashire[4].

Margaret's younger sister, Barbara, had married Myles Philipson, a wealthy magistrate of Thwatterden Hall, a fifteenth century farmhouse in Crook near Kendal in Cumbria. When their half-brother died, the sisters agreed to divide the tenancy of Conishead between them, signing a deed of partition on 21 March 1593.

Barbara and Myles Philipson moved to Conishead with their two eldest sons Robert and Christopher, and eight other children, whilst Margaret and Myles Dodding returned to London.

When Myles Philipson died, Christopher remained at Conishead and his brother, Robert, took over Thwatterden Hall and Calgarth Hall near Lake Windermere. Christopher married Bridget Kirkby and had sons Myles, Thomas and Christopher, but his tenure of Conishead was short-lived. He died in 1600 and his young widow Bridget left the area with their sons, married again and settled at Heversham.

The death of her nephew brought Margaret, her husband Myles Dodding and their two surviving sons Myles and Henry from London to live at Conishead Priory. Margaret and Myles Dodding were to remain at Conishead until their deaths within months of each other, in 1606.[5]

Myles and Margaret's eldest son, Myles, born in 1572, married Ursula Davill, the daughter of Christopher Davill from Coxwold, in Yorkshire[6]. Their first child was a daughter, Beatrice, born in 1602, followed by a son George, born in 1603; Margaret in 1606 and Isabella in 1609.

By 1603, it came to light, through a search of concealed lands, that estates belonging to Conishead had been illegally transferred from the crown, a common occurrence after the dissolution when leases lapsed and rebels forfeited. Under a 'Commission for Defective Titles', (issued by King James I to enable his subjects to *'quietly and privately enjoy their private estates and possessions'*, and to prevent prying into land titles caused by the search for concealed land), the manor of Conishead was given in trust to Messrs Brownrigg and Hooper, to be held by the Crown *'as part of the Duchy of Lancaster, by*

[4] Before his marriage Myles had lived in London, where he attended court and won favour with Queen Elizabeth. On the yearly payment of 12d to the Queen in 1593, Myles Dodding was granted all the rents from two London men, William Typper and Robert Dawe. The rents came from the lands of the old hospital of St Leonard in Kendal, the marsh and common with salt water that ran between Conishead and Plumpton, the land at Crake and *'a certain Isle called Harelesyde* (Chapel Island) *of the late dissolved monastery of Conyngshed.'*

[5] They were buried in St Mary's Church, Ulverston; Margaret (*'Old Mrs Doddinge'*) on Christmas Eve. A brass memorial depicting their full-length portraits was placed above their resting place near the east end of the south aisle in the side chapel.

[6] A post nuptial settlement was made between the prospective bride and groom's fathers. Upon the marriage in 1601, Ursula's father was granted areas of land which Myles Dodding had owned in Chancery Lane, in the Parish of Dunstan's in West London.

HERE BEFORE LYETH BVRIED THE BODIES OF MYLES
DODDING ESQ: & MARGARET HIS WIFE WHO DIED IN THE
YEARE OF O^{R} LORD 1606 AFTER THEY HAD LIVED MARIED
43 YEARES & HAD ISSVE TENNE CHILDREN OF WHOME
THERE ONLY SVRVIVED THEM. MYLES DODDING & HENRYE.

Plate 6 Myles and Margaret Dodding, 1606 from their brass memorial in St Mary's Church, Ulverston
(Conishead Priory archives)

military service, of the fortieth part of a Knight's fees and a rent of 16s. 8d. per annum'[7]. In March 1613, Brownrigg and Hooper conveyed Conishead in these terms, and in equal share, to Myles Dodding and his Aunt Barbara Philipson's grandson, Myles Philipson.

During his time at Conishead, Myles Dodding was appointed Bailiff of the manor of Neville Hall in Ulverston and Receiver General of Furness for King James I. A year after his death in 1629 his heir, George, purchased the half share of the Conishead house and estate from Myles Philipson for £1,200. The Doddings were now the sole proprietors of Conishead Priory.

In 1631, aged twenty-eight, George Dodding married seventeen-year-old Sarah Backhouse in London. They had five daughters[8] and a son Myles, born in 1641. Family life at Conishead however was disrupted by the onset of the English Civil War in 1642. Together with neighbouring families at Swarthmoor and Plumpton Hall, the Doddings of Conishead gave their support to Oliver Cromwell's Parliamentarian cause. George Dodding was made a Deputy Lieutenant by the House of Commons and joined forces with another local man, William Rawlinson, to form a local troop of seventy horses over which he was appointed Colonel. He also commanded a regiment of men in Cromwell's army under General Lord Fairfax, known as 'The Hundreds' and fought in several battles, including Marston Moor (where he lost many men). He saw the defeat of the Royalists, led by Colonel Sir William Huddleston of Millom Castle, at Lindal near Dalton in Furness in 1643, and garrisoned Greenhaigh Castle, the last Royalist stronghold in Lancashire.

In 1643, the Royalist Earl of Derby took George Dodding and a fellow Captain, George Tolson, prisoner from aboard a ship carrying ammunition for the Parliamentary forces[9]. They were imprisoned at Oxford for many months until the House of Commons ordered an exchange and their release.

A year later, George (a Governor of Lancaster Castle) ordered the construction of defences in Lancaster in anticipation of Prince Rupert's advance on South Lancaster. The expected advance never happened and

> *'in 1645, Parliament made an order for the payment of compensation to the town to the amount of £8,000, to be taken from the estates of 'Papists and delinquents' when the war should be ended'*[10].

A local broadsheet, commented on George Dodding's bravery:

> *'...the Lord Ogleby and Colonel Huddlestone* (sic) *marching towards Latham House in Lancashire, encountered with Colonel Doddington* (sic) *not far from Preston, and the first*

[7] *Antiquities of Furness,* Thomas West, William Close, 1805.

[8] Elizabeth, who married Alexander Mawdesley, heir of Mawdesley Hall in 1657; Sarah; Ursula, who married Richard Patrickson of Calder Abbey in Lancashire in 1665; Mary, who married Sir Thomas Preston of Holker Hall near Cartmel, Lancashire, and Jane.

[9] The Earl of Derby had ordered the ship to be burnt. The Parliamentary troops however, managed to rescue most of the ammunition on board.

[10] *A History of the County of Lancaster: Vol 8* Farrer and Brownbill, 1914.

dispute was very difficult, but Colonel Shuttleworth received an alarm upon his engagement, his quarters being near, delayed not any time to rescue the first undertakers, upon whose approach Colonel Doddington's men were put in great courage and these two valiant Colonels joined together, charged the enemy with such brave resolution, that they were put into disorder and many of them slain in the place.'

'Valiant' George's regiment was disbanded in 1645 and he returned to Conishead Priory, where he died safely in his bed in 1650. His wife Sarah outlived him by twenty-nine years. When she died she left an endowment of £30 a year for St Mary's Church in Ulverston. Their son, Myles, took over Conishead Priory and was to be the last of the Doddings in the direct male line to occupy the estate. A lease document dated 1657, shows that part of the ruins of the Augustinian priory and church still survived near the sixteenth century house at this time, for it lists the *'late dissolved Priory of Conishead, Conishead Hall etc. in Ulverston'*.

Myles Dodding was educated at St John's College, Cambridge, and married Margaret Kirkby, the daughter of Roger Kirkby and Agnes Lowther of Cross Hall, Kirkby Ireleth in 1662.[11] They had four children – Agnes, born in 1664; Sarah, born 1665; George, who was born in 1666 but died a year later; and an heir William, born in 1668.

Documents and letters in the Dodding family archive reveal aspects of everyday life at Conishead during the seventeenth century. Letters written by Myles Dodding contrast his business and personal life. One written in 1672, is apologetic and written on behalf of the tenants on his estates to the local Justice of the Peace and Deputy Lieutenant of Lancaster, Sir Robert Bradshaigh of Haigh Hall near Wigan:[12]

'Honoured Sir,

I was desired by Mr Sawry and Mrs Fell to kiss your hand with this enclosed, the contents whereof they did communicate to me, desiring (at your convenience) you will please to signify your intentions in a line to me. I doubt I and my partners may have justly forfeited your noble kindness through our neglect in paying the two last years duty; but that we may no longer incur your censure of being forgetful and ingrateful (sic) *for so great a favour we have desired Will Kirkby to pay all that's due from your most obliged servants, humbly requesting a continuance of this kindness to us so long as you think fit, and we shall for the future be more punctual.*

I beg you will make my most humble service acceptable by presenting it to your noble Lady, son and daughter and that you will believe I am, Sir,

Your most faithfully devoted servant,
Miles Dodding.'

[11] The Lowthers were related by marriage to the ancient Le Fleming family of Aldingham and the Prestons of Holker Hall. During the 17th century these families, together with the Doddings, Dicconsons and Braddylls intermarried and were among Lancashire's wealthiest families.

[12] Bradshaigh's daughter was to become the second wife of Myles's brother-in-law, Sir Thomas Preston of Holker Hall, after Myles's sister Mary Dodding died.

Sometime during 1680, Myles began to have problems with his neighbours, the Anderton family of Bardsea Hall. The Andertons were Catholics; their ancestors had been charged with 'recusancy' (resistance) to the established Protestant faith and this, together with political differences, lost them Bardsea Hall. In a letter of January 1681 to his local Magistrate, Clerk of the Peace, and wealthy landowner Sir Roger Kenyon of Peel Hall, Lancashire, Myles wrote:

> *'If Madam Anderton of Bardsey, with her sons Mr Thomas Polewheele and Baskervill, and the rest of their family be convicted* (of recusancy), *it would not be amiss to humble them, for they are very ill neighbours and highly injurious to me. When you send any officers on this side, let them call at my house and I will put them in a way how to get something, for though they have few goods, yet rather than go to gaol they will assign part of their estate to pay the King's due. Good Sir, do not forget this whereby it will oblige me.'*

By contrast, another warm and domesticated letter shows Myles' affectionate side. It is addressed to his eldest daughter, thirteen-year-old Agnes[13], staying at Wrightington

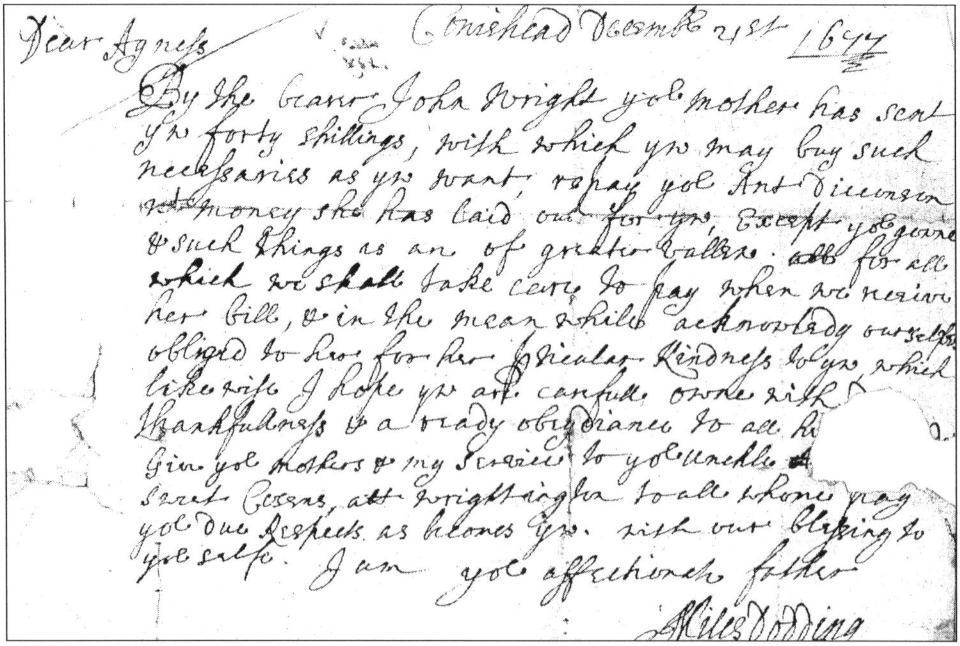
Dear Agnes   Conishead Decemb 21st 1677

By the bearer John Wright yor mother has sent you forty shillings, with which you may buy such necessaries as you want, repay yor Ant Dickinson the money she has laid out for you, Except yor geare & such things as are of greater valew. all for all which we shall take care to pay when we receive her bill, & in the mean while acknowledg ourselfs obliged to her for her perticular Kindness to you which likewise I hope you are carefull to owne with thankfulness & a ready obedience to all hi[illegible] Give yor mothers & my Service to yor Unckle & Sweet Cossens, att Wrightington to all whome pay yor due Respects as becomes you. with our blessing to yor selfe. I am yor affectionate father

Miles Dodding

Plate 7 A letter from Myles Dodding to his young daughter Agnes, 1677
(Lancashire County Record Office)

[13] On 25 November 1686, Agnes Dodding became the second wife of widower Sir Richard Atherton of Atherton Hall near Warrington in Lancashire and mother to his young children. The marriage was short-lived. Richard died a month after their marriage, leaving his son John Atherton from his first marriage to Isabella Holt as his heir. Poor Agnes contracted smallpox and died a short time later.

Hall, near Wigan in Lancashire with her Aunt and Uncle Hugh Dicconson[14].

'Dear Agnes
By the bearer John Wright your mother has sent you forty shillings, with which you may buy such necessaries as you want, repay your Aunt Dicconson that money she has laid out for you, except your gown and such things as are of greater value; for all which we shall take care to pay when we receive her bill, and in the meanwhile acknowledge ourselves obliged to her for her particular kindness to you...
Give your mother's and my services to your Uncle, Aunt and sweet cousins at Wrightington, to all whom pay you due respects as becomes you.
With our blessings to yourself
I am your affectionate father
Miles Dodding'.[15]

A short, but charming note written by Myles, whilst he was staying in Dalton in Furness in September 1682, is addressed to his second daughter Sarah Dodding:

'Dear Sarah
This comes to let thee know the company that are here will not dine at Conishead today; therefore you need make no preparation. Whether they will call as they go over, I do not yet know. I will be at home this afternoon. For the meantime give my service to all the pretty company with thee.
In haste
I am thy loving father
Miles Dodding'.[16]

Myles Dodding died a year later in 1683, at the age of forty-one, and was buried in woollen *'brought within 8 dayes'* in St Mary's Church, Ulverston. His memorial commemorates a *'faithful son of the Church of England'*, a solicitous father and benevolent to all. In his will Myles had given specific instruction as to the future education of his son, William. He required that William receive a *'competent maintenance and good education'* and be

'committed to the tuition of my Reverend and worthy friend Mr Marseden of Walton, who I hope will be careful to instruct my son in the principals and fundamentals of the true

[14] Her aunt Agnes (nee Kirkby) was the sister of Myles Dodding's wife Margaret. The Dodding's cousins were Hugh and Agnes's children Agnes Dicconson, Edward Dicconson (who became a Catholic Bishop), William Dicconson and Roger Dicconson, who were staunch Roman Catholics and were later implicated in the plot to overthrow the Government of King William III and Queen Mary II and bring back the exiled Roman Catholic King James II back to the throne. William and Roger Dicconson were put on trial at the Manchester Assizes, but were acquitted. They were exiled to the ex-King James's side in France, where Roger Dicconson became Tutor to James II's grandson Charles Edward Stuart ('Bonnie Prince Charlie').

[15] Letter from Myles Dodding to Agnes Dodding – 21 December 1677 (DDX 41/11) Lancashire County Record Office

[16] Letter from Myles Dodding to Sarah Dodding – 30 September 1682 (DDX 41/12) Lancashire County Record Office

Protestant religion as it is now settled and established by law … and insure his learning as is proper and fitful for a Gentleman and as may qualify him to serve his King and country.'

William Dodding complied with his late father's wishes and went to be educated at Walton-on-the-Hill, three miles north of Liverpool, under the care of his tutor Mr Marseden. Only two letters are known to exist from the young scholar, written to his sister Sarah Dodding at Conishead:

'Dear Sister
I received thine (letter) *on Monday last, for which I do give thee my most heartful thanks and doth hope that thee will pardon me for not returning thee an answer, but my indisposition … did hinder me. I pray thee give my duty to my honoured mother whose blessings I do earnestly beg and withal I desire her that she will send me some black buttons for my riding coat which I do intend to turn and face up anew and if my mother please, I would have thee to send me another periwig for the Sundays, being that this doth grow red at the ends. …*

I pray thee give my true love and service to her (his mother) *and accept of the same to thyself, born from him who is thy real affectionate brother 'til death,*
William Dodding.'[17]

In May 1685, William wrote another letter to his sister Sarah, contemplating his future education at Oxford or Cambridge and relishing details of a recent murder near Liverpool:

'Dear Sister
I received yours and am glad to hear that you are all in good health, which I praise God I have had in very great measure since I came hither. My tutor and myself do both of us wonder that we have not an answer of that letter we'd sent by my uncle Preston, for now the time draweth on that we should make ready, if my mother thinks fit that I should go. My tutor was mistaken in one thing, that is he'd thought my father had begone of Oxford, which made him mention that place, but when I did inform him how the mater was, he said that Oxford was the better air and the place where he thought I might do full as well, but because my father was at Cambridge, he'd thought that my mother would be unwilling to go to Oxford, but if I go to Cambridge this year, I should be there about Midsummer's Day, which I fear can scarce be done.

My tutor and myself are about to go to hear the examination of a man who murdered another, and indeed my heart doth bleed to give you the narrative of the murder, but this is it, which follows. About nine or ten of the clock in the evening of Friday last, this man was murdered and his throat was cut, his arms cut off, his legs and thighs cut off about the groins, his head dinted, his face pricked full of holes and his bowels were taken out of his body and were sewed up in his shirt with a great stone about fifteen or 16 pound weight, and were thrown into a pit together with all the rest of the parts of his body, and was miraculously

17 Letter from William Dodding to Sarah Dodding – undated (DDX 41/16) Lancashire County Record Office

found by two masons who went on Saturday morning to drink at that pit; this was about a quarter of a mile from Liverpool that this murder was committed, though the man was a constant inhabitant in the town, and the man that murdered was a lodger in his house, and after the murder went and robbed the murdered man's house.

I am in haste for my tutor is just now come down the stairs, and therefore I pray desire my mother to give me her blessing to whom I give my humble duty, and desire that you too will accept of my most humble service, and so commending you all to the protection of God Almighty, I subscribe myself to be what may.

Dear Sally thy loving brother, whilst that I am give my service to all my friends,
Will Dodding.'[18]

Sadly, William never fulfilled his father's hopes and ambitions. Like his older sister Agnes, he too fell ill with smallpox and died on 23 June 1685 at Mawdesley Hall, Lancashire, the home of his aunt Elizabeth Mawdesley,[19] leaving his one surviving sibling, Sarah, as the heir to the Dodding family's estates, including Conishead Priory.

In 1687, Sarah Dodding married John Braddyll, the son of Thomas Braddyll and Jane Rishton of Portfield, near Whalley in Lancashire, in a quiet ceremony. According to Sarah's cousin, Sir Daniel le Fleming, her mother Margaret was unhappy with the match. On 7 April 1687, Daniel recorded in his account book:

'This day my cousin Sarah Dodding was privately married without her mother's consent at Conishead'.[20]

It is difficult to know why Margaret Dodding disapproved of her daughter's marriage. The groom's family were not lacking in wealth or status. Originally known as 'Breddale', 'Bradhull' or 'Braddal' the ancient family took their name from the manor of Bradhull, near Whalley and Brockhall in Lancashire, from where they originated. By the reign of King Henry II, they had become an established and influential family, related by marriage to distinguished families in the North West, including the Flemings, Nevilles, Talbots, Ashetons and Harringtons. The same Harringtons had been benefactors of the original Conishead Priory and church. Throughout the fourteenth, fifteenth and sixteenth centuries the Braddyll family held high office under the crown and several of John Braddyll's ancestors were Receivers General for Queen Elizabeth I and commissioners for surveying the Queen's woods in Furness. An uncle of John Braddyll, also named John, was, like the Doddings, a loyal Parliamentarian and an Officer during the English Civil War, when he fought and lost his life.

There is, however, the possibility that one of John Braddyll's cousins, Thomas Braddyll, was the reason behind the Dodding family's displeasure. Thomas was a printer

[18] Letter from William Dodding to Sarah Dodding – 18 May 1685 (DDX 41/13) Lancashire County Record Office

[19] 'Willm Dodding Esq., from Maudesley Hall, buried 25 June 1685' (Eccleston, Lancashire Christening, Burial and Wedding Registers 1603 – 1694).

[20] Sir Daniel le Fleming's Account Book (Public Archives Office, Kendal)

in London during the 1680s and 90s and known to be a radical Whig, a member of a group who sought to separate politics from sectarian conflicts and reduce the power of the Crown. Amongst Thomas Braddyll's publications printed in 1678 was *An Account of the Growth of Popery and Arbitrary Government in England*, by the Whig poet and MP Andrew Marvell. The book was a daring and controversial attack on the monarchy, religion and Parliamentary practice:

> *'There has now for divers years a design been carried on to change the lawful Government of England into absolute tyranny and to convert the established church into downright Popery'.*

In the book Marvell described the elections to Parliament as 'debauchery' and 'lewdness':

> *'... So that the vice and the expense are risen* (sic) *to such a prodigious height, that few sober men can endure to stand to be chosen on such conditions. From whence also arise feuds and perpetual animosities, over most of the counties and corporations, while gentlemen of worth, spirit and ancient estates and dependences see themselves over-powered in their own neighbourhood by the drunkenness and bribery of their competitors ... While men ... care not thus how they get into the House of Commons, neither can it be expected that they should make any conscience of what they do there, but they are only intent how to reimburse themselves (if their elections were at their own charge) or how to bargain their votes for a place or a pension'.*

The book provoked outrage but fellow booksellers came to Thomas Braddyll's defence:

> *'Mr Braddyll is a first-rate Printer, and has always been a very active, diligent man. He is religiously true to his word, and faithful to the Booksellers that employ him ... But Mr Braddyll has met with back-enemies, as well as other men; and upon that score he is very tender of giving wounds to others in the same place where he himself has suffered, which is certainly a good improvement of those ill practices. I dealt with him for many years, and have not only found him just, but as well accomplished for all the parts of his business as any other Printer I can name'.*

It is possible that Thomas Braddyll's radical views and the fact that he was in trade provoked Margaret Dodding's displeasure. Whatever the reasons, Sarah and John were prepared to marry without parental consent and create a future home for the Braddyll family at Conishead Priory.

Three

A 'DELIGHTFUL VILLA'

1687 – 1776

The Braddylls' tenure of Conishead Priory, as the seventeenth century ended and the eighteenth century began, coincided with a period of huge social, industrial and economic change. It was an era of greater religious tolerance and enlightenment, and an age of elegance, which was nowhere more apparent than in those great emblems of wealth, status and power – the houses of the gentry.

Whilst there are no known images or written accounts of Conishead from the time, we know that alterations were made during the late seventeenth century, which we must assume would have been influenced by the vogue for the 'Palladian' style of architecture introduced by Andrea Palladio. His style echoed the perspective and symmetry of the formal classical temple architecture of the Ancient Greeks and Romans. Visitors during the eighteenth century would describe Conishead as elegant and charming. However, there were still elements of its Tudor structure visible in the piazza, Gothic tracery windows and battlements.

John and Sarah Braddyll's marriage seems to have been successful despite the objections of Sarah's mother. Until the end of her life, Sarah kept a lock of her *'dear Mr Braddyll's hair'*. For the first time Conishead Priory became a family home, cared for by a 'constant and sincere' landowner, magistrate and benefactor who enjoyed the esteem of those who knew him.

As Protestants, a difficult religious life under the Catholic rule of King James II came to a welcome end when both the English Parliament and an invading army led by the Dutch Protestant William of Orange forced James into exile. In 1688, just a year after John and Sarah began their married life at Conishead, King James died and was succeeded by William of Orange and his wife Mary. Rivalry in the district between Protestants and Catholics continued to disrupt local life but the Braddylls could now feel more secure in practising their chosen religion.

Domestically, John and Sarah were fortunate that in a time of great infant mortality, ten of their twelve children survived childhood. Sadly, their first son Dodding, died at four months, but another son who arrived a year later in 1689, also named Dodding, was strong enough to live to be the next Braddyll heir. Siblings followed in quick succession.

A third son, Thomas was born in 1690, and died in infancy. His namesake, born in 1691, became the first Governor of Calcutta and Fort William, in Bengal. Jane, the eldest daughter was born in 1693 and remained a spinster until her death at eighty-five[1]. John, born in 1695, became a West Indian Merchant. Margaret was born in 1696[2], followed by Sarah, in 1698; William in 1700; Roger in 1702; Agnes, in 1705 and finally Anne in 1709.

When John Braddyll died in March 1728, his life was celebrated on a memorial tablet in St Mary's Church, Ulverston:

> *'He was a pious member of our excellent church, a zealous friend to our happy constitution, an hearty lover of his country, a painful and impartial Magistrate, an affectionate husband & tender parent, a constant and sincere friend, a sober and upright man in all his conversation. With these qualities he lived beloved by the good, feared and respected even by the bad.'*

Sarah survived her husband a further sixteen years. According to her memorial

> *'calm was her closing scene as reposing innocence, such is the end of those who spend the few moments allotted them here in the unwearied exercise of the duties of virtue and religion'.*

John and Sarah's son, Dodding, inherited Conishead on the death of his father[3], but from the start, it was clear that the house would no longer enjoy the pattern of domesticity established by his parents. In comparatively few years, the structure of the house began to suffer.

As a young man, Dodding Braddyll had spent most of his time living in London. It was there that he met his future wife, Mary Hyde, an encounter possibly contrived by brother-in-law Christopher Wilson who was employed by the East India Company, where Mary's father, Samuel Hyde, was a Director.[4] They married in October 1711 at St Peter-Le-Poer Church in Old Broad Street, London, and lived in Hart Street, where Dodding and Mary's three sons were born: Roger in 1719, Robert in 1727 and Thomas in 1730. Unlike Dodding's parents, however, their family life was ill-fated. In 1726, the eldest son Roger died, aged only seven, and then in 1742, Robert died at the age of fifteen. This left their only surviving youngest son, Thomas to inherit Conishead Priory, a house that was now unoccupied and slowly deteriorating through neglect. Dodding's burgeoning political career in Parliament and his role as Director of the East India Dock

[1] At Jane's death in 1777, she left a clause in her will stating that £40 be distributed in bread amongst the poor of the parish who attended church regularly, and over a hundred years later, this act of charity was still being carried out.

[2] In 1728, Margaret Braddyll married Christopher Wilson, a Sea Captain in the East India Company. They lived for a short time at Conishead Priory with Margaret's parents and their two daughters Sarah and Margaret (who were born there), until Christopher Wilson purchased Bardsea Hall a few years later from Lord Molineux, whose family had resided there since 1720.

[3] During the 1960s, a discovery was made which brought the past alive again. A resident of Cheshire contacted the owners of Conishead Priory stating that she owned a bible that once belonged to Dodding Braddyll as a boy. In the frontispiece of the book, the ten-year-old had written *'E Libris Doddinge Braddyll, Hunc suis addidil 1699'* ('The book of Dodding Braddyll, this added in his own name, 1699').

[4] The Company was established in 1600, as a challenge to the Dutch-Portuguese monopoly of the spice trade and went on to make large profits from its trade with India in cottons, silks, spices and tea.

Plate 8 The former 'Braddyll Chapel' in St Mary's Church, Ulverston, now dedicated to soldiers of the World Wars *(photograph by the author)*

Company engaged him permanently in London,[5] so Conishead Priory was left to the housekeeper and a handful of servants and labourers working on the estate. Henry James once remarked that *'happy occupants in England are almost always absent'*. This was certainly the case during the early eighteenth century, when many owners of country houses remained absent from their estates for years at a time. In *A Country House Companion*[6] Mark Girouard explains that the people who lived in these country houses

> *'had enough money to do nothing, and many of them did nothing. Doing nothing is not a recipe which produces interesting people. Staying in country houses could be a highly enjoyable or even idyllic experience, but it could also be, as numerous letters or descriptions testify, a dull or disillusioning one.'*

For Dodding Braddyll, London was the centre of the world, where politics and trade took precedence, and his wife could take pleasure in society. Conishead Priory was little more than a quiet, country retreat; a holiday home rarely visited.

On retirement, Dodding and Mary moved to the house they had kept at Woodford in Essex, joining a number of their children. They did not return to Conishead, perhaps because they found the house unfavourable in size or appearance, and they had lived in the south for so long.

[5] From February 1715 to 1722, Dodding Braddyll was Whig Member of Parliament for Lancaster. In 1719, he was listed as one of the MPs who voted for the Peerage Bill.

[6] Magna Books, 1992 p. 9.

Dodding Braddyll died in December 1748, leaving a loving testimony to his marriage in his will of September 1747, in which he described Mary as *'my tender and indulgent wife'* who showed *'tenderness* (to him) *in a tedious disorder'*. He left instructions that she look after their estates, including Conishead, and the welfare of their son Thomas, until he reached the age of twenty-one. When Mary died in 1771, Thomas was still a bachelor, having completed his studies at Kings College, Oxford and become High Sheriff of Lancaster.

Thomas Braddyll seems to have been a landowner who was neither frivolous with his fortune nor uncaring of his tenants, employees and estates. He had begun to make improvements to Conishead in 1763, before his mother's death, instructing John Hird, a joiner-turned-architect from Cartmel, to renovate, make minor alterations and make good the deterioration of the past. On inheriting Conishead, Thomas divided his time between Woodford, Conishead Priory and his town residences in Halfmoon Street, Piccadilly and Stratton Street, in Mayfair. He seems to have been a quiet man, *'much esteemed for his private virtues'* and whose charitable work *'he was... studious to conceal'*.

In 1772, a local Furness writer, topographer and Jesuit Father, Thomas West of Tytup Hall near Dalton, contacted Thomas requesting information about the history of Conishead Priory for his forthcoming book *Antiquities of Furness*. A number of letters passed between them and Thomas appeared very amenable towards the writer and his appeal. He wrote from Stratton Street, allowing West permission to examine the deeds of the Dodding and Braddyll families, and include extracts from Dodding and Braddyll family documents:

'I received your favours of the 31 December by this days post and am very happy it is in my powers to contribute in the least towards your laudable undertaking for which purpose I shall give orders to my steward Mr Cottam for you to have the inspection of such deeds and grants at the Priory, as may be of service to you, and as I may remember there are some that may be so.

If I recollect the Doddings became possessors of the Priory by marriage with one of the co-heiresses of Sandys, as you mention and as the quartering in my arms testify. The other sister married a Phillipson (sic). *I apprehend the minor son of Christopher, who you mention to be living the 42nd reign of Eliz; died unmarried, therefore his moiety came to the Doddings, but trust you will find deeds that will clear this point.*

As to the Braddylls, my grandfather John Braddyll of Portfield in the County of Lancaster, Esq ... married Sarah, sole heiress of Myles Dodding of Conishead Priory in the County of Lancaster, Esq. My father Dodding Braddyll inherited from them and I from him. I do not recollect the year my grandfather married but you will find that at the Priory, at which place I shall be happy to pay my respects to you, and am

Sir, Your most humble servant

Thomas Braddyll.

If there is any further information in my power you will be so good to command it'.[7]

[7] Letter from Thomas Braddyll to Thomas West – 9 January 1772 (Lancashire Record Office, with permission of Fr Luiz

West made his notes, returned the documents and requested a list of the Priors of Conishead Priory to assist him further in his research. It appears that Thomas Braddyll took an interest in West's work and a genial acquaintance developed between the men. A note, which Braddyll directed via his Steward, Richard Cottam shows evidence of this hospitable informality:

'...Mr Braddyll's compliments to Mr West; is sorry he cannot wait upon him to Furness Abbey this afternoon, but shall be glad of Mr West's company on Monday to dinner and afterwards to shoot rooks at the Abbey if the day is fine.'

On 3 March 1772, Thomas Braddyll wrote again to West, offering further suggestions:

'Sir,
I am greatly obliged to you for the compliment you intend to pay my family in your laudable work. There are some little alterations I could wish, which will point out to you, if you will suffer me, when I have the pleasure of seeing you at the Priory, which hope will be soon in May.
Leland and Willis I have, the other books I cannot as yet get. Those I have, will either send or bring down with me, and if you want any further information from the Duchy Office and can appoint any proper person to inspect for you, I think I can get you permission for so doing. I'd be very happy to assist you all in my power and am
Sir, your most obedient, humble servant
Thos. Braddyll'

Thomas West's book was published in 1774. Chapter Seven gives an account of *'The Priory of Conishead, near Ulverston, in Furness, belonging to Thomas Braddyll Esq'*. It describes the early history of the priory and church, through to Thomas Braddyll's ownership of the estate. In his chapter 'The Furness Families', West presents family histories of the Braddyll and Dodding families. More importantly, he describes for the first time the appearance of Conishead Priory as it looked in the eighteenth century, famously praising it as 'the Paradise of Furness':

'The house stands on the site of the Priory of Conishead ... the north front is in the Gothic style; this and a piazza supported by clustered Gothic pillars and three series of ox-eye windows, crowned with a battlement, give to the whole an elegant and respectable appearance ... The numerous views from this pleasant seat are delightful, and the approach to it from Ulverston is enchanting.' [8]

Ruscillo, St Mary's Church, Hornby).

[8] In 1906, eighty-seven-year-old James Wilson recalled that as a boy at Stewnor Bank farmhouse near Ireleth, Robert Ashburner, an Ulverston builder, informed him that when he built the farmhouse in 1830, he used oak window frames and windows from Conishead Priory. A window in the attic at Stewnor Bank was described as a plain pointed arch with rectangular panes, in an oak frame, with the upper panes arranged to imitate early English tracery, and an 'ox-eye' (quatrefoil) window, 4ft 3in high of grey sandstone, which also came from Conishead. This would be one of the windows from the series of three described by West in his book, which were part of the 16th century building. (*Transactions of the Cumberland and Westmorland Antiquarian and Archaeological Society*, Vol VI – 1906).

The south front was of white rough cast render and extended by an arcade, bordered with yellow stucco. It was designed in the neo-classical style, introduced during that period by Robert and James Adam. Thomas Braddyll would have seen this graceful style of design embodied at Leighton Hall in Lancashire, where Hird had begun work in 1759.

When Thomas West published *A Guide to the Lakes in Cumberland, Westmorland and Lancashire* in 1778, he once again praised the qualities of Conishead:

'The Paradise of Furness – a Mount-Edgecombe in miniature, which well deserves a visit from the curious traveller. ... The apartments are elegantly furnished and the house is good and convenient'.

It appears that remains of the mediaeval priory were still visible above ground at this time. An eleven-year-old Ulverston schoolboy, William Fell, later described in his 1777 manuscript *History and Antiquities of Furness* how

'there is near Ulverstone (sic) *a Priory of ancient form, but one side built anew by the curious Architect Hird'.*

Although Thomas Braddyll never married he saw that the fabric of the house and its ancient monastic history were preserved.

On his death in July 1776, Thomas Braddyll left Conishead Priory and the Braddyll estates of Brockhole, Portfield, Salmesbury Hall, Burneside Hall and Osmotherly to his twenty-year-old cousin, Wilson Gale[9]. He was buried, as he had desired, in linen and in a leaden coffin in St Mary's Church, Ulverston. The local *Cumberland Pacquet* for 8 August 1776, described how:

'A few days ago died at his county seat at Conishead near Ulverston, Thomas Braddyll Esq., a gentleman much esteemed for his private virtues. In him, the polite Gentleman and good Christian were united. His good qualities raised some degree of emulation in those of his own rank, and his memory will be held dear by numbers who experienced the various effects of that charity he was so studious to conceal. We hear he has left his delightful villa of Conishead and the bulk of his large fortune to Wilson Gale Esq., of this town (Whitehaven)'.

Plate 9 The bust of Thomas Braddyll above his memorial tablet in St Mary's Church, Ulverston
(photograph by the author)

[9] Thomas Braddyll was known to suffer severely from gout for many years, a victim no doubt to a rich 18th century diet of meat, sweets and alcohol.

Four

'A TOLERABLE GENTLEMAN'S HOUSE'

1776 – 1819

When Wilson Gale inherited the *'delightful villa of Conishead'* and the bulk of his cousin Thomas Braddyll's fortune at the age of twenty, he was already a wealthy man.[1] His affluence came from two sources. In 1774, Wilson had inherited £500 from his great-aunt Susanna Richmond, a sum no doubt welcomed by a *'profuse bachelor'* who had *'lived much at taverns.'*[2] Two years later, he married his second cousin, Jane Gale, at St Marylebone Church in London and acquired a substantial dowry. Jane was the daughter and sole-heiress of Matthias Gale and Jane Bennett of Egremont in Cumberland. Her family were well known merchants from Whitehaven whose wealth had come from the tobacco trade. One of her great-great uncles was stepfather to Augustine Washington, the father of America's first president, George Washington.

In accordance with the conditions of his cousin's will, Wilson changed his surname to 'Braddyll' and adopted the arms of the Braddyll family, incorporating details from the arms of the Braddyll, Dodding, Rishton, Sandys and Rawson families, by Royal Sign Manual on 15 August 1776. Thomas Braddyll's will had requested that Wilson and his family should

> *'take and use the surname and arms of Braddyll only and ...call and write themselves by the said surname of Braddyll and not by any other surname whatsoever.'...*

In November 1776, Jane gave birth to their first child, Thomas, at their London home in Bruton Street, near Berkeley Square. In February of the following year, Wilson celebrated his twenty-first birthday choosing Conishead as the venue for the joint celebration of his birthday and his son's baptism. The local newspaper, *The Cumberland Pacquet* described the festivities:

[1] Wilson was the eldest child of John and Sarah Gale. His two sisters, Margaret and Sarah married well. Margaret Gale became the wife of Colonel Richard Greaves Townley (he was responsible for introducing Sunday Schools into Lancashire), and Sarah Gale married George Bigland of Bigland Hall, Cumbria. Wilson's brothers were William and Henry Richmond Gale of Bardsea Hall.

[2] Lord Farrington on Wilson Gale Braddyll.

Plate 10 A portrait of Wilson Gale Braddyll age nine by Sir Joshua Reynolds, which was originally in the morning room at Conishead Priory (location of original unknown)

'On Monday last, the son of Wilson Braddyll Esq., of Conishead Priory was baptised by the name of Thomas, by the Rev Dr Scales of Ulverston. The sponsors were John Gale, Esq., and Thomas Hunt, Esq., of London, Mrs Gale of London and Mrs Wilson of Bardsea. The same day Wilson Braddyll Esq., came of age. A great number of ladies and gentlemen came from Whitehaven and different parts of the country, met by invitation at Conishead to celebrate the day, the entertainments of which were at once polite and liberal, as they related to the different qualities of the guests, and happily united the magnificent entertainment of a gentleman with the hospitality of an Englishman. The morning was ushered in with a round of cannons from eight ships lying in the river, which washes the boarders (sic) *of that delightful seat; their colours were displayed. A large ox and a sheep were roasted and served up in a large barn, to an amazing number of tenants, labourers, etc., a band of music (the performers of which were placed in barrels suspended from the roof of the building) playing all the time of dinner; at the conclusion of which a number of fireworks were played off, beautifully disposed and well conducted. This part of the company then proceeded to different kinds of rural amusements, when the ladies and gentlemen were ushered into a spacious apartment where the ceremony of baptism was performed; after which they adjourned to dinner. It is unnecessary to describe the elegance, which presided at table, or to mention the toasts, which were drank* (sic). *The company were next entertained with a concert; several of the performers were from Lancaster. To this succeeded a ball, which continued til twelve o'clock, when supper was served up. This is only a faint sketch of this jubilee, which suspended for a time the cares and labours of a multitude, and spread over the adjoining country the pleasing smiles of innocent amusement.'*

The Cumbrian Chronicle was more succinct:

'Monday last week, Wilson Braddyll Esq., celebrated the joint festival of his coming of age and the christening of his son, with such generous hospitality, at his seat of Connistone Head (sic) *Priory, as did him much honour'.*

At the end of the year their daughter, Jane, was born. Six more children followed in close succession; Margaret Sarah in 1780; Sarah, born in 1783 and who died soon afterwards; Charlotte in 1785, Henrietta Maria in 1786, and Harriet and Georgina, both of whom died in infancy[3]. Wilson and Jane's children enjoyed similar privileges to those born into the wealthy echelons of society and at their 'coming of age' their daughters were presented at Court.

In July 1804, in Kingston upon Thames, Surrey, Margaret Sarah Braddyll married Gordon Forbes, the son of Lieutenant General Gordon Forbes of Skellator in Aberdeenshire. Following the marriage and the death of a son in infancy, the couple went to live in the East Indies, where Gordon served in the East Indian Civil Service in Bengal. Sadly, their marriage was short-lived. On 6 October 1807, Margaret *'fell an early sacrifice to the climate of Indostan'* and died at Calcutta aged twenty-seven from fever. She was buried in the North Park Street Cemetery, Bengal where a memorial was erected as *'a tribute to exemplary merit and a record of the tenderest conjugal affection'.*

Wilson and Jane's youngest daughter, Henrietta Maria (once described by a female contemporary as *'a young lady so elegant and refined'),* was married at Hampton Court in October 1808 to George Vernon of Clontarf Castle near Dublin. They lived at Clontarf in the early years of their marriage and presented Wilson and Jane with ten grandchildren. Not long after the birth of her tenth child, Henrietta Maria died whilst staying at Cantley Hall near Doncaster. Her death was followed a year later by that of her husband, tragically leaving their young children orphans.

Heartbreak came again, in December 1811, when Wilson's unmarried daughter, twenty-six year old Charlotte Braddyll, died when staying with her paternal aunt and uncle at Bigland Hall, near Ulverston.

In November 1813, the eldest of the sisters, Jane became the second wife of Rear-Admiral Frank Sotheron[4] of Kirklington Hall, Nottinghamshire. The couple lived at Darrington Hall in Yorkshire, which Frank had inherited. They had one daughter, Lucy Sarah. Jane survived her husband by two years, dying in London in 1841.

Wilson and his family moved regularly between their properties in the town and country; common practice amongst the wealthy. In the early years of their marriage, as well as enjoying the fashionable London season, Wilson's progression through the ranks at Court meant that for most of the time he and his family lived at their Mayfair addresses in Bruton Street and Savile Row. Whether they saw Conishead as the 'delightful villa' described by the local newspaper is hard to say, but it appears that

[3] The Braddyll children were taught by a Governess Elizabeth Ann Dove. Years later, when Dove published a book of stories for young children in 1823, she dedicated it to Jane Braddyll:
'The permission to dedicate these Tales to my first pupil, adds to the many obligations I have received from your family, through a long period in my life employed in the tuition of yourself and sisters, and the earlier part of your brother's education. It greatly increases my present happiness to know that my endeavours, under Providence, and the anxious care of a kind parent, have been crowned with success.'

[4] Frank was believed to be a relative of General James Wolfe, the British Army Officer who led the British to victory over the French in Canada. At the age of eleven, he joined the Royal Navy as a Midshipman, becoming Captain in 1793. A prestigious career followed which saw him join Lord Horatio Nelson in the Mediterranean in 1802 where he was entrusted with the defence of the Bay of Naples. He was made Admiral in 1830. Southeron stood as a Tory Member of Parliament for Nottingham for nineteen years.

Plate 11 Bigland Hall near Ulverston, Cumbria where Charlotte Braddyll died in 1811 (photograph by the author)

the house was used primarily for celebrations and entertaining. With its impressive art collection including paintings by Reynolds, Romney, Gainsborough and Lely, and priceless furniture and ornaments, Conishead lay uninhabited for much of the year with only a skeleton staff to look after the house and grounds. When the London season was over, a large section of society converged in Bath to take the spa water and continue the social life. Others returned to their country estates or visited friends. Despite his long absences, Wilson gradually began to develop a connection with his northern country estate. When they were there, life at Conishead would have seen the family and guests enjoying the pastimes of the eighteenth-century elite. They were part of a society that

> *'rode to hounds, talked politics, farmed and watched over tenantry, drank copiously and ate too much. Once or twice a year they would pack up and go to spend a month or so at some friend's estate where there would be much hunting, dancing and gambling'*[5].

In 1778, Wilson was elected High Sheriff of Lancashire and Commissioner of the Peace for Lancashire, an office he held for thirty-nine years. These positions brought power and influence and Sheriffs often abused their authority. Evidence suggests that Wilson was a fair and generous man who understood the needs of those less fortunate. As the owner of considerable land and estates himself, he had experienced unavoidable legal wrangling of indentures, bonds, rents and leases.

Wilson was made Colonel of the 3rd or Prince Regent's Own Regiment of Royal Lancashire Militia and was patron of several local causes, including the new charity school on the Green in Bardsea. He contributed five guineas towards the building of the Town Bank Sunday school in Ulverston, and he signed a grant with the Rev John Hartley, the vicar of Whalley, to donate £10 a year to place poor children as apprentices.

In 1780, turning his attention to the organisation of Conishead, Wilson instructed

[5] *Life* Magazine, 13 September 1948.

a Yorkshire land surveyor, a Mr Cottam, to carry out a complete survey of the estate. Cottam contacted the Headmaster of the Town Bank Grammar School in Ulverston to request the help of two students with sound ability in arithmetic and geometrical calculations. The Headmaster offered the services of a young Zaccheus Walker and John Barrow. In later years, John Barrow would recall:

'We remained at the Priory as well as I can recollect about two months, in which time we completed the survey to the satisfaction, as I was afterwards informed, of Colonel Braddyll and I may add, for my own part, to my incalculable benefit derived from witnessing the practical methods of conducting a survey of the various description of surface, for it contained all – level, hilly, woodland and water; audit was not the less useful to me for the practical knowledge acquired of the theodolite and of the several mathematical instruments in the possession of Mr Cottam; in fact during our sojourn at the Priory I so far availed myself of the several applications of these instruments that on arriving in London some years afterwards I extended my knowledge of them so as to draw up and publish a small treatise to explain the practical use of a case of mathematical instruments, being my first introduction to the press, for which I obtained twenty pounds'.

On John Barrow's eighteenth birthday, in honour of his special day and in recognition of a young man he considered *'so clever and active for his age'*, Wilson procured a 'dashing flag' from Conishead Priory and hung it outside John's home in Ulverston, in the rowan tree which John had planted as a boy. The youth became Sir John Barrow, founding member of the Royal Geographical Society and Secretary of the Admiralty who famously promoted great exploration and voyages of discovery, notably in the Arctic Seas[6].

Wilson's wealth and status brought him into the political arena. He succeeded Lord Richard Cavendish as Whig Member of Parliament for Lancaster between 1780 and 1784, and was elected Member of Parliament for Carlisle and Horsham in Sussex between 1791 and 1796.

In August 1791, Wilson was one of thirty-eight men in Ulverston who agreed to build a canal. With his wife he was a shareholder in the scheme. Progress was halted, however when Wilson objected to the idea that the canal should be carried through to Conishead Bank where a deeper entrance could be secured. It would of course encroach on his estate. In due course, he was able to use his influence as a Member of Parliament to thwart the plan.[7]

[6] When he died in 1848, the people of Ulverston honoured his memory with a lighthouse monument, placed for all to see on Hoad Hill.

[7] The company petitioned Parliament, and an Act of Parliament was obtained and took effect in June 1793, stating that the *'Canal should be made from a place called Hammerside Hill in the parish of Ulverston ... to a certain other place in the same parish called Weint-end, with a Dock or a Basin at, or in some convenient place thereof'*. The Scottish civil engineer, John Rennie's design, however became something of a white elephant when the canal silted up at the entrance soon after construction. It is worth wondering if this would have happened if the mouth had been located nearer to Conishead, as originally planned. When it eventually opened in December 1796, the Ulverston Canal claimed to be the deepest, widest and straightest canal in the United Kingdom. Materials such as iron and copper ore, limestone, charcoal, grain,

Wilson was a man who indulged in expensive hobbies. He patronized the arts and literature, inviting dedications from aspiring painters, musicians and poets[8]. He also enjoyed sporting activities, such as pugilism, and became the patron of Richard Humphries, known as 'the Gentleman Boxer'. Boxing was an entertainment for all classes of society when it gained popularity during the eighteenth century.[9] Wilson continued to follow Humphries' career, and when he retired from the ring, helped establish him as a coal merchant.

Breeding racehorses was another enthusiasm. As well as owning his own stock, Wilson rode the King's horse at several racing events. In 1785, a number of the nobility were conspicuously absent from the already declining numbers attending the Dalton Mayor Hunt. Whilst it was reported in the newspapers that the Earl of Derby was not likely to go again (as his time was 'taken up' with a Miss Farren, a well-known actress at Drury Lane), Wilson was staying in apartments in Carlton House attending '*the Prince in his Frolicks*'[10].

The Prince Regent was infamous for his pleasure-loving lifestyle, his excessive consumption of food and wine and his pursuit of women. His courtiers, including Wilson Braddyll, were required to be on attendance whenever and wherever he demanded. Wilson became a close confidante of the Prince Regent, and as part of the King's inner sanctum, Wilson and Jane were regularly featured in the court circulars listing royal events. For convenience, they were granted a Grace and Favour Apartment at Hampton Court by the Prince Regent's father, King George III and the rent-free accommodation was settled in recognition of Wilson's great service to the Crown and his country[11].

In keeping with their status, the Braddylls posed for eminent artists including George Romney, Thomas Gainsborough and Sir Joshua Reynolds who appears to have been their favourite[12]. He painted Wilson and Jane separately, and in 1789 was commissioned to paint a family portrait of Wilson and Jane, with their young son Thomas[13]. The portrait cost Wilson approximately 200 guineas (£210) and is believed to be the last

malt, gunpowder, leather and wood products were exported and coal, timber and general merchandise were imported for the trades people of the district.

[8] Wilson Braddyll was a member of the 'Noblemen and Gentlemen's Catch Club' in London, which was initially a male music and poetry society, founded in 1761 '*to encourage the composition and performance of glees, catches and canons*', a society that was involved in reviving Renaissance vocal music in the 18th and 19th centuries.

[9] In 1787, Wilson Braddyll commissioned John Hoppner to paint a portrait of Humphries in anticipation of his famous match against Daniel Mendoza on 9 January 1788.

[10] Carlton House was the town residence of the Prince Regent for several decades from 1783 until about 1820. It faced the south side of Pall Mall, and its gardens were adjacent to St James's Park.

[11] King George III had introduced the Grace and Favour arrangement on his accession in 1760, when he and the royal family decided not to live at Hampton Court. From the 1780s onwards, King George and his family regularly resided at Windsor Castle.

[12] Sir Joshua Reynolds was elected Principal Painter to King George III in 1784, succeeding the King's previous favourite, Alan Ramsay. Wilson Braddyll was already acquainted with Reynolds from the time he sat for his portrait as a young boy.

[13] Reynolds's group portrait of the Braddylls was later displayed in the corridor of Conishead Priory, facing the grand staircase, before Christies sold it at auction in 1846. The catalogue described the painting as '*a family group of a Gentleman and lady with their son in a garden scene, the lady seated, holding a spaniel – an important and capital picture.*' It is now part of the Fitzwilliam Museum collection.

Plate 12 A portrait of Wilson Gale Braddyll by Sir Joshua Reynolds, 1788 *(private collection)*

Plate 13 A portrait of Jane Braddyll by Sir Joshua Reynolds, 1788

(By kind permission of the Trustees of the Wallace Collection, London)

Plate 14 A portrait of Wilson Gale Braddyll, his wife Jane and son Thomas by Sir Joshua Reynolds, 1789 *(© The Fitzwilliam Museum, Cambridge)*

portrait painted by Reynolds before he retired, due to deteriorating eyesight, in July 1789. The portrait was probably commissioned to coincide with the visit of the Prince Regent and his brother Frederick the Duke of York, who stayed at Conishead Priory in September 1789[14].

Impressive in size and appearance compared to the family's London residences, Conishead served its purpose when entertaining royalty. The *World* Newspaper declared

'Mr Braddyll has much credit for his superb preparations for the Prince and the Duke of York. Conishead Priory, always a charming place, never was so charming'[15].

A travel writer, Henry Skrine described in his 1795 *Three Successive Tours in the North of England and great part of Scotland* how he

'...visited Connishead (sic) *Priory, the elegant seat of Mr Bradyll* (sic) *who has fitted up his house and laid out his grounds with much taste. It stands on an elevated spot above the coast under a pyramidical hill of wood, and commands an uninterrupted view over Cartmel, the sands and the whole coast of Lancashire...'*[16]

Henry Kett, a writer, poet and Fellow of Trinity College, Oxford, used the word 'charming' again, in 1798, when he visited Conishead, although he was not so complimentary about the appearance of the house:

'In the afternoon, walked to see Conishead Priory, the seat of Mr Bradyll (sic). *This house is a disgrace to the noble scenery around it. It is of white rough cast in front, with gothic battlements and an arcade bordered with yellow stucco. The plantations around look too artificial, and are too minute when compared with the picturesque grandeur around it. At the end of the gravel walk and the plantations, the view extends over a wide bay terminated by craggy rocks or fringed with wood, with pastures and cornfields and a background of vast and bold mountains: from another point of view, not far distant, opens an extensive sea view, seen between the lofty sycamores and bounded by a dim prospect of land. Nature has done much for this charming place, but the builder of Mr Bradyll's house caught no enthusiasm from the scene; for never was there an edifice reared in a more contemptible style.'*

By the end of the eighteenth century, there was nothing left of the mediaeval priory and church, which adjoined the house. A *Journal of a Tour in Westmorland* from 1786 noted the lack of ruins, the 'neat and comfortable' house, and that Wilson resided there 'very little'.

A lawyer and artist, Richard Holden, from Rotherham in Yorkshire, visited Conishead

[14] Queen Adelaide, the wife of William IV (successor to George IV), stayed with the Braddylls at Conishead some years later. The rooms used by members of the royal family became known as the State Room, the King's Bedroom and the Queen's Bedroom.

[15] 10 September 1789.

[16] *Three Successive Tours in the North of England and great part of Scotland* by Henry Skrine, 1795, p17.

during a touring holiday of the North. The Braddylls were absent at the time, and according to his travel journal, Holden was as equally unimpressed as Kett:

'In the evening having a little time to spare, we went to see Conishead Priory of which Mr West speaks in such rapturous terms. We found it a tolerable Gentleman's House with a fine Park well wooded and the ground finely varied by nature, but nothing remarkable about it. Much of this way he ascribed to the absence of the Master (Wilson) *Braddyll Esq. The house is not usually shown but an old woman let us in by the power of the all-opening key. A few good portraits of Mr and Mrs Braddyll and their children by Sir Joshua'.*

The 'old woman' was probably the housekeeper. The house's finest ground floor rooms were not usually open for viewing during the family's absence, as would be the custom in later years.

On 10 March 1812, Wilson was one of eleven members of the aristocracy granted the prestigious role of Groom of the Royal Bedchamber. It would be a duty he served for the ailing and increasingly eccentric King George III for the next six years[17]. The grooms of the bedchamber waited in the King's Chamber during his dressing, waited at dinner when the King dined privately, took wine or food from the servants to give to the Lords to serve to the King. This office was in the gift of the Crown and the number of grooms fluctuated considerably. The salary attached to the office, payable at the exchequer, was £500 and Wilson received food and lodgings when the court was in progress around the country. In 1813, it was noted that at the Prince Regent's 'Ball and Supper' at Carlton House

'Colonel Braddyll was selected for the honour of presenting tea to the Princess Charlotte, which he did in the most graceful manner, on gold plate'.[18]

In 1814, Wilson took possession of Bardsea Hall on the death of his brother Henry. In October of the same year, his father John Gale died and the Braddylls inherited the Gale estates of Highhead Castle, Cleator Hall, Haswell in County Durham and Burneside Hall. With these additional houses came additional expense and debt.

It is not known whether it was Wilson who decided to embark on building work at Conishead, or if the idea originated from his son Thomas, but in April 1818, George Webster, an architect from Milnthorpe near Kendal, was commissioned to produce plans for additional first and second floor chambers.[19] The decision to improve the appearance of Conishead may have been influenced by tourists' recent criticism of the house.

Webster's drawing for the 'first principal chamber floor' shows that the rooms were designed to be built adjoining existing bedrooms over the 'cloister' and 'Mrs Braddyll's

[17] Newspaper reports regarding the details of King George's psychological and distressing illnesses (believed to have been the symptoms of Porphyria) were printed daily, and under such difficult circumstances, Wilson was obliged to perform his role.

[18] *The Morning Chronicle* 8 February 1813.

[19] Cumbria Record Office, Barrow (Z/1019/1).

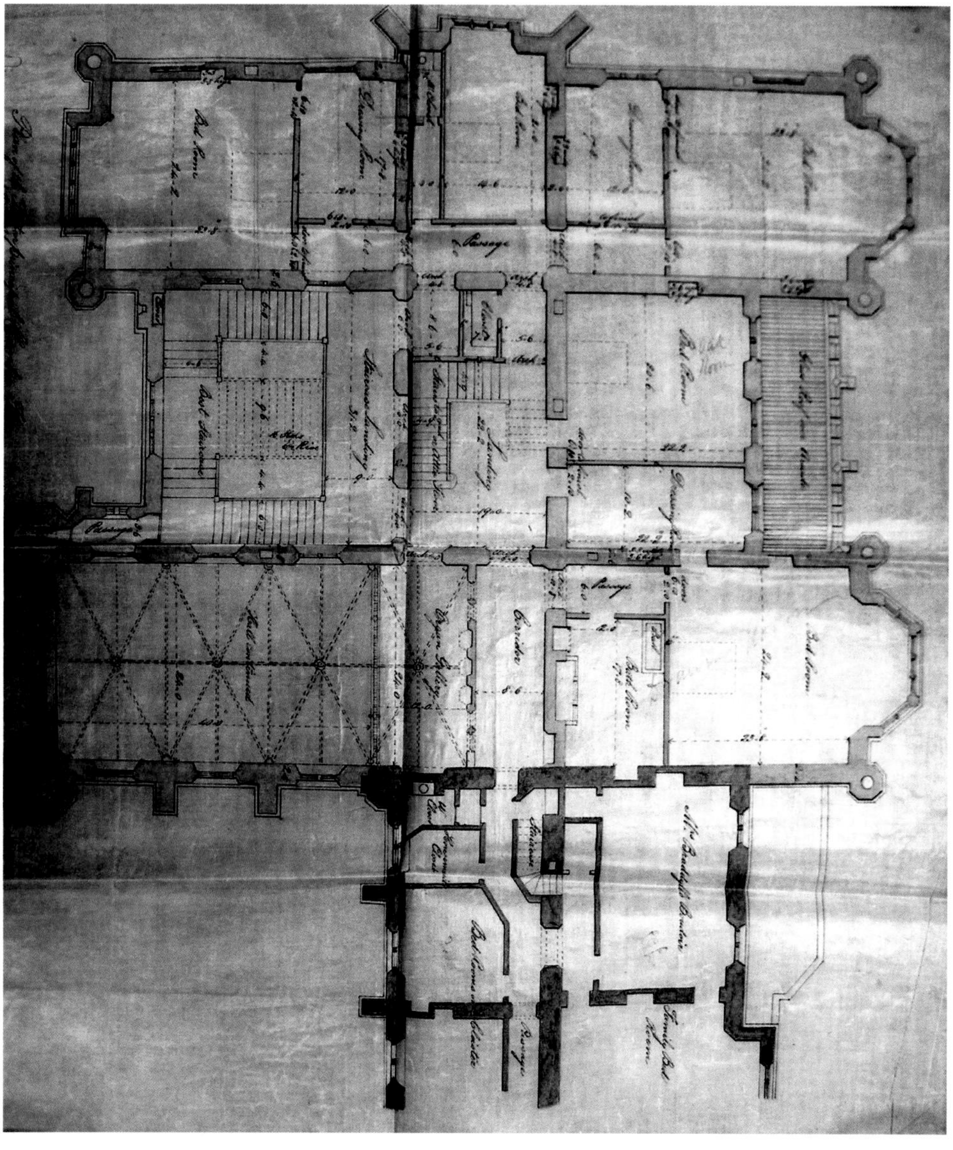

Plate 15 First floor plan of Conishead Priory by George Webster, 1818 (Cumbria Record Office, Barrow)

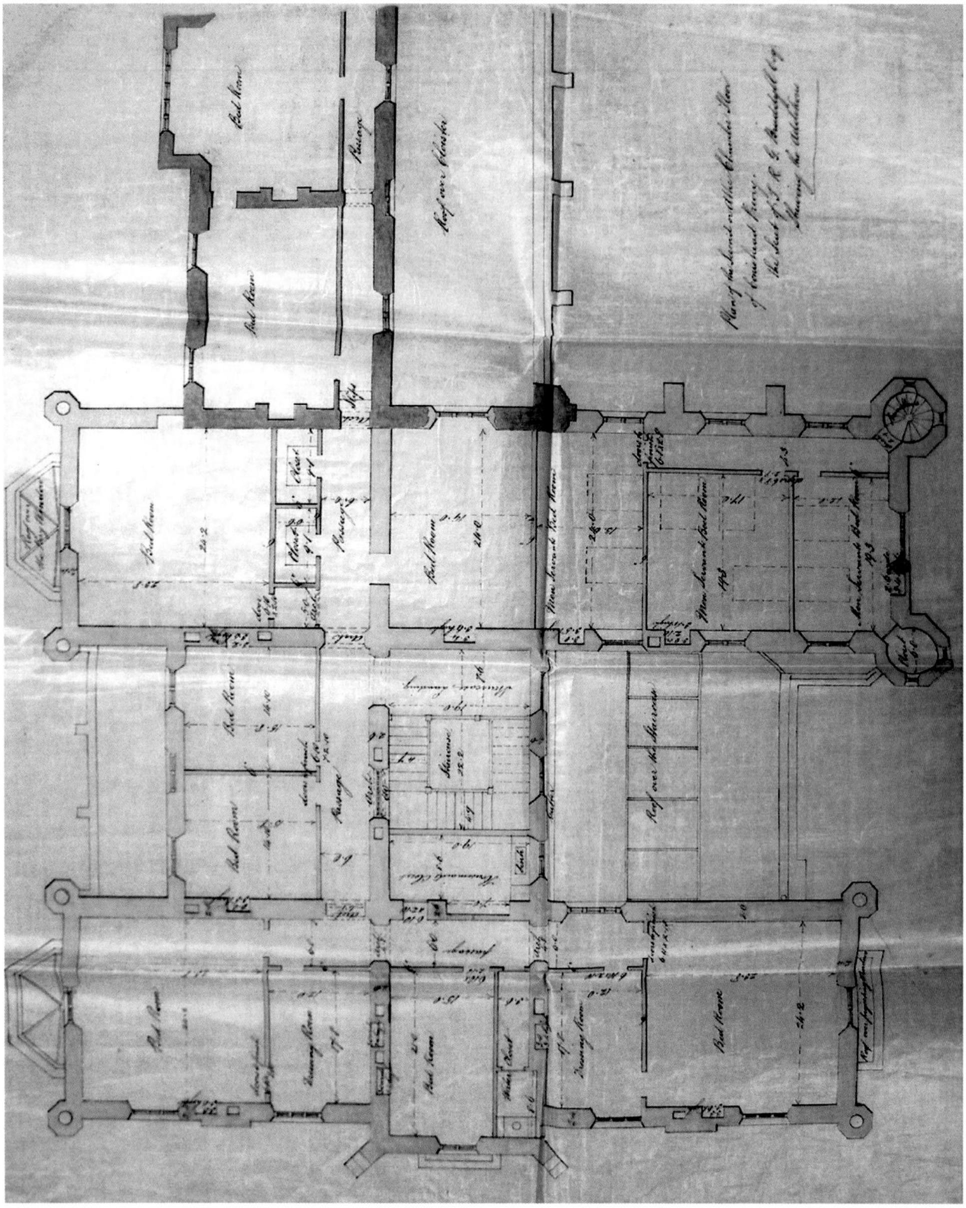

Plate 16 Second attic floor plan of Conishead Priory by George Webster, 1818 (Cumbria Record Office, Barrow)

boudoir'. Five bedrooms, three adjoining dressing rooms, a closet and a bathroom, were to encompass a great 'best staircase'. The 'Second or Attic Chamber Floor' was probably intended for visitors. It provided seven further bedrooms with two dressing rooms, five closets, including one for a housemaid, and three men servants' bedrooms. There would also be bay windows and turrets housing closet and staircases, and a glass roof above the arcade. By this time, Wilson's son Thomas Braddyll had begun to explore the possibility of investing in the Durham coalfields in order to raise money for the general upkeep of the family estates. He seems to have been sufficiently confident in this venture to sanction a building programme at Conishead, which would expand the premises, improve the deteriorating fabric and bring a new, fashionable appearance to the house. Plans were drawn up and agreed but work failed to start. Seven months after Webster had produced his drawings, Wilson Braddyll was dead.

One of Wilson's last duties as an intimate member of the Royal household had been to arrange a celebration for the Prince Regent's birthday at the Sun Inn in Ulverston. But on 17 November 1818, the nation was plunged into mourning when King George III's wife and consort Queen Charlotte died at Kew. As a member of the Royal household, Wilson would have been obliged to attend the state funeral in London. Whilst on his way there, and intending to visit his daughter Henrietta Maria Vernon in Doncaster, he collapsed and died whilst staying at the Duke and Duchess of Devonshire's coaching house, The Devonshire Arms Hotel, near Skipton. His carriage had arrived at the hotel at about six o'clock on the evening of Thursday 19 November, accompanied by his valet and footman. Shortly afterwards, he complained of feeling unwell. While the waiter was preparing the table for dinner, Wilson reportedly said

"You are giving yourself much useless trouble, for I don't think I can eat anything".

According to newspaper accounts, he managed to eat a little, and then retired to his bedchamber, where his valet later discovered him on the floor, seized with an apoplexy. Medical assistance came too late and Wilson died the following morning.

William Fleming, a local man of Rowe Head in Pennington near Ulverston recorded in his diary on 28 November 1818:

'…I am informed that Mr Braddyll of Conishead Priory is departed this life on Friday 20th at Skipton on his way to visit his son in law Mr Vernon. …' [20]

Wilson's body was brought back through Kendal to Conishead, in preparation for his burial in Ulverston, which coincided with Queen Charlotte's a few days later. On the day of the funeral, William Fleming wrote:

'Tuesday 1st December 1818 – We had some showers of rain during the day … and was extremely cold. This morning preparations were making (sic) *in the burial ground in*

[20] William Fleming's Diary (Cumbria Record Office, Barrow)

Plate 17 The Devonshire Arms, Skipton, where Wilson Gale Braddyll died on his way to Queen Charlotte's funeral in 1818
(Photograph by the author)

Ulverston Church belonging to Conishead Priory, for the internment of Wilson Gale Braddyll of the Priory. There is no vault, but a deep grave was dug and the sides and ends neatly lined with green sods and stuck with flowers.

Wednesday 2nd December 1818 – Was tolerably fine but continued damp and cold with some fog. This day was fixed for the funeral of our good old Queen. This afternoon about 2 o'clock Mr Braddyll of Priory was interred in Ulverston Church. The crowd of people whom curiosity drew together there was very great.'

On his death Wilson left his wife

'500 guineas – all the money that at the time of my death be in my houses at Conishead Priory and Hampton Court ... and in the hands of my agents or bankers for her own absolute use and benefit' (and) *'the use and enjoyment of my mansion at Conishead for life'.*

Jane Braddyll survived her husband by only a year, dying *'universally lamented and beloved'* in November 1819 at their Grace and Favour Apartment at Hampton Court. Her obituary in the *Cumberland Pacquet* described her as

'beloved and admired by all who knew her; one of the most amiable of her sex, fitted at once, from her accomplishments and the graces of her person, to adorn the first circle of fashion, yet exhibiting through life the most engaging pattern of every domestic virtue'.

Leaving £15,000 each to her daughters Jane and Henrietta, she bequeathed the residue of her estate and belongings to her son Thomas, who not only inherited Conishead and other family estates, but the massive debts that went with them. Undeterred, Thomas returned to the priory to continue his project to create a residence which would rank amongst the most splendid and striking buildings of the nineteenth century.

Five

'A MONUMENT OF EXPENSIVE AND THOUGHTLESS FOLLY'

1819 – 1843

(*James Losh*, 1831)

The death of Wilson Braddyll in 1818 began an important chapter in the history of Conishead Priory. His only son, Thomas Braddyll, now having full rein over the future of the house, decided a complete re-build would be necessary to create a home that his family would occupy more frequently than his forebears.

Following an Eton education, Thomas Braddyll had served as an Officer and Lieutenant Colonel in the Coldstream Guards.[1] In 1803, he married twenty-six-year-old Frances (Fanny) Bagot Chester, a twin, and fourth daughter of fourteen children born to Charles Bagot Chester and his wife Catherine (nee Legge)[2]. Thomas and Frances's early married life was spent at their grace and favour apartment in the Lord Treasurer's Lodgings at Hampton Court, where Thomas's parents and siblings lived[3]. Thomas became a close friend of the Prince Regent and was involved in social activities surrounding the Royal Court. His first child Frances, known in the family as Fanny, was born at Hampton Court in 1805, followed two years later by a son Edward Stanley Bagot Braddyll. Margaret Frederica was born in 1808; Louisa Mary in 1810 (who died a year later); Sarah Jane in 1811, and Clarence in 1813[4].

Thomas followed his father into politics and stood as Member of Parliament for Bodmin. In 1819, a year after his father's death, he was appointed to command the

[1] This was the oldest regiment in the Army. Thomas Braddyll was a prestigious member of their Nulli Secundus Club. ('Nulli Secundus', meaning 'Second to None').

[2] Brought up at the Chester family seat at Chichley Hall in Buckinghamshire, Frances's paternal grandfather Sir Walter Wagstaffe Bagot was a Baronet. Her mother's grandfather was the 1st Earl of Dartmouth. Her father Charles Bagot, a friend of the poet William Cowper, had assumed the name of Chester in compliance with the will of Sir Charles Bagot Chester of Chichley, from whom he inherited the estate. The Bagots were one of the oldest established families in Staffordshire where they resided at Blithfield and Little Hay near Lichfield.

[3] As well as residing in their Grace and Favour Apartment at Hampton Court, Thomas and Frances were also tenants of the 'Old Court House', facing Hampton Court. It was, in the early 18th century, rented and almost entirely re-built by Sir Christopher Wren, who is believed to have died in the house in 1723. Wren's footsteps are believed to echo in the house on the anniversary of his death, although whether Thomas and Frances were ever troubled by such phenomenon is not recorded. Having passed through the hands of Wren's son and grandson successively, it was then rented to others, including the Braddylls.

[4] Clarence Braddyll was named after his royal godfather, William Duke of Clarence (later King William IV), who was the third son of King George III.

Plate 18 A portrait of Thomas Richmond Gale Braddyll c. 1779 by John Hoppner (location of original unknown)

Ulverston and Furness Yeomanry Cavalry, which he generously funded. In 1821, he was installed as High Sheriff of Lancashire for the year.

Thomas took an interest in the culture of his neighbourhood and many remembered him as a 'liberal and kindly man' with a 'uniform kindness of manner'. Elected Patron of the Theatre Royal in Ulverston[5], he was also a distinguished member of the oldest fellowship in Furness, the 'Book and Card Club', and allowed an annual race meeting to be held regularly in the park at Conishead, known as 'The Furness Cavalry Races'.[6] He was also a very able artist and provided sketches for the famous political cartoonist of the day, James Gillray.

In October 1819, Thomas applied by licence to be granted the additional surnames of Richmond (originally spelt Richmund) and Gale. The name Richmond was in honour of his paternal great-grandmother Margaret Richmond and her family of Highhead Castle. Gale derived from his father and mother's family of Whitehaven. From this time, Thomas and his family would be known by the name of Richmond Gale Braddyll.

Following the amendment to his surname, Thomas pursued his plan to transform Conishead Priory into a house worthy of the name 'Paradise of Furness'; a spectacular country house, which would embody the latest in architectural taste and honour the house's monastic origins. By the time he inherited Conishead, any ground level vestiges of the medieval priory had disappeared, and the out-dated and worn appearance of the

[5] Thomas enjoyed acting in amateur theatricals. In April 1805, he played the leading role in the tragedy of 'Tancred and Sigismunda', a military theatrical at the Rochester Theatre in Chatham. A news review commented that *'Mr Braddyll gave a promising specimen of his theatrical talents, by his just conception of the part he enacted'.* (*The Lancaster Gazette and General Advertiser*, 20 April 1805)

[6] One year, the local newspaper reported that the spectators included a good proportion of the *'fair nymphs of Furness who appeared to vie with each other in the neat simplicity of their attire'.* This annual event continued until 1846, when it was transferred to Swarthmoor Heath near Ulverston.

Plate 19 A portrait of Thomas Richmond Gale Braddyll (private collection)

house gave no hint of its religious history apart from the name. How far Thomas had been involved in the decision to commission major building work at Conishead seven months before his father's sudden death is not known, but clearly he had ideas of his own, for it appears that Thomas did not return to the original plans submitted by George Webster in April 1818. There were perhaps several reasons. Webster might have been unavailable or perhaps Thomas disliked his designs. Instead, Philip William Wyatt, an architect from a prestigious family in the trade, who was known in the business to be 'charming' but feckless, was selected. He was the youngest son and pupil of James Wyatt, an architect reputed to have a colourful personality, who had attracted controversy with his drastic refurbishments of several major cathedrals.[7]

We have a striking image of Conishead Priory, shortly before the re-building work began. An engraving was published in the 1822 issue of the *Lonsdale Magazine and Kendal Repository* and depicts a couple, probably Wilson and Jane Braddyll, walking in the grounds of the priory. The house has the 'elegant and respectable' appearance noted by Thomas West, and the battlements and extended arcade, which was probably added by Hird in 1763. The accompanying article described the house:

'The South front is in the modern taste, extended by an arcade. The North is in the Gothic style, with a piazza and wings. The apartments are elegantly furnished and conveniently arranged but what recommends itself most to the curious is a plan of a pleasure ground on a small scale, containing beauties equal in number to gardens of the greatest extent in England. The prospect from the Priory of the sands and the sea is extremely fine. ... A late writer says of Conishead Priory – "Among the various picturesque spots in the neighbourhood of Ulverston, Conishead Priory, the seat of Mr Braddyll is the most remarkable. The present mansion is built on the site of the Priory of Conishead and the West wing is part of the ancient edifice ...

The interior of the house is extremely elegant and contains a few excellent paintings... (The) *Music Room ... is a large and lofty room and contains an exceedingly well-toned organ. ...* (In the) *Library* (there is a painting) *'A schoolmaster and his pupils' by Watson – it is possibly the best painting we ever saw ... At the same time we should recommend any who feel anxious to attain the same excellence, to visit this painting and study it attentively, for we are confident that Mr Braddyll's uniform kindness of manner would afford the artist every facility in such a study.*

It is expected in a few years that Conishead Priory will be one of the most splendid buildings in the North of England, being now rebuilding after a plan by Mr Wyatt. A Conservatory is already erected ... The road which led so near the South front has been diverted and a fine open park spreads round it on every side.'[8]

[7] Amongst over 130 buildings listed as designed by James Wyatt are Oriel College Library in Oxford, Downing College, Cambridge and Fonthill Abbey in Wiltshire. One of Philip Wyatt's cousins, Sir Jeffrey Wyattville, remodelled Windsor Castle for King George IV. His brother Benjamin was a favourite architect of the Duke of York.

[8] Cumbria Record Office, Barrow

Plate 20 The earliest known image of the original Conishead Priory c. 1820

(an engraving from the 'Lonsdale Magazine and Kendal Repository' of 1822)

Plate 21 The south west aspect of Conishead Priory epitomising Philip Wyatt's distinct style

(photograph by the author)

Plate 22 Design for a conservatory alcove at Conishead Priory by George Webster, 1840

(Cumbria Record Office, Barrow - courtesy of Mrs S Ritson)

Philip Wyatt decided to construct the new Conishead Priory on the medieval foundations from Bath stone, which required shipping from the south of England at great expense. Work began slowly. Within a year of accepting his commission from Braddyll, Wyatt had also begun work for Charles Stewart, the 3rd Marquis of Londonderry, at Wynyard Park near Durham. In 1828, he was also commissioned to design the alterations and enlargement of Mount Oswald House in Durham. In both projects, Wyatt integrated elements of the original house in the design and constructed the new additions in a simple Grecian style of architecture. He probably intended a similar approach at Conishead; his plan at Conishead integrated the Grecian classical with the battlements, square towers, arches and narrow windows of its former Tudor design[9].

Whilst work progressed, the new west wing of the house was allocated to the domestic staff and was also temporarily occupied by the Braddyll family, when they were not in London.[10]

[9] Philip's father James Wyatt also used a castellated style particularly when he remodelled Belvoir Castle in 1801, and Philip used similar elements in his designs for Conishead.

[10] The romantic novel of 1820, *De Clifford or, A Passion More Powerful Than Reason*, mentions the Braddylls, alluding to the stresses and strains of a family during a time of upheaval. In a letter to her daughter, the Dowager Lady Pemberton writes from her house in Grosvenor Street: *'The Braddylls are with us at present, and we shall have them here until their own house is prepared for them. Mrs Braddyll is as tiresome as ever; but I put up with her caprice, for the sake ... of that dear good creature, the Colonel.'*

In May 1821, the completed conservatory was the scene for King George IV's birthday celebration, when Thomas and his family were host to 'several neighbouring gentlemen' and the Ulverston and Furness Yeomanry Cavalry Corps, over which he was Colonel. The day began with the corps assembled at Conishead:

'At this time all the beauty and fashion of the town and its immediate vicinity had collected in the grounds fronting the house and shortly after the corps was seen filing from the woods on the right, and having formed upon the rising ground opposite, advanced in line, and halted within a short distance of the spectators.'[11]

The local vicar pronounced a 'short but impressive' prayer upon the consecration of a standard, which Frances Braddyll then presented to the corps. The company then went through

'several manoeuvres, with a rapidity and precision that would have done credit to veteran troops ... About four o'clock, the whole corps, and several neighbouring gentlemen dined in the Gothic Conservatory at the Priory; after which several loyal and constitutional toasts were given, and appropriate songs and music introduced at intervals, and admirably performed by the Ulverston Musical Society ...'[12]

Frances Braddyll and her children later entertained the gathering with their singing.

By 1828, Conishead was still only half-complete, but this failed to disrupt family celebrations. In January of that year, the local newspaper noted that Thomas's eldest son Edward would come of age, *'on which occasion there will be right joyous doings at the Priory'!*[13] Unfortunately, however, the planned festivity was postponed, due to the death of a relative.

Parson and White's *History, Directory and Gazetteer of Cumberland and Westmorland* for 1829 noted the

'delightful grounds of Conishead Priory, where Thomas Richmond Gale Braddyll Esq, has been re-building his mansion on a scale of great expense and splendour. ...The mansion of this 'Paradise of Furness' is not yet completed. It is in the Gothic style of the fifteenth century, from plans by P W Wyatt Esq, and constructed of Bath stone. The gardens are extensive and beautiful and the walks through the park are finely shaded with trees and command beautiful views of the bay and mountains.'

A visitor to the house, James Losh, (a relative of the wife of Thomas's cousin William Gale) commended the house, but was rather uncharitable towards its owner:

[11] *The Lancaster Gazette and General Advertiser, for Lancashire, Westmorland, &c.*, Saturday 19 May 1821

[12] Ibid

[13] *The Lancaster Gazette and General Advertiser, for Lancashire, Westmorland, &c.*, Saturday 12 January 1828

'... when the new house is finished it will in all respects be one of the finest places in the Kingdom ... Mr Braddyll, the owner, shewed (sic) *us everything himself and was abundantly civil, but he is a shabby fellow notwithstanding, and one cannot help lamenting that such a stately and delightful place should be in such hands.'*

Losh's disdainful comment about Thomas's appearance may be an indication of diminishing finances caused by increased expenditure on the house and a precarious speculation in mining.

Before his father's death, Thomas Braddyll had been exploring ways of generating further income to pay off his inherited debts. Between 1822 and 1825, Thomas sub-rented a limekiln for selling burnt lime at Scale Haggs, leased lead and copper mines at Caldebeck Falls in Cumberland and expended a large sum of money in his endeavours to obtain coal, copper ore and iron ore in Ulverston, but all attempts proved failures.

He became attracted to the prospect of exploiting the rich reserves of coal in Durham, along with men such as Lord John George Lambton, 1st Earl of Durham and Charles Stewart, the 3rd Marquis of Londonderry, who had shared Braddyll's architect Philip Wyatt. A chance meeting in London with Dr William Smith (1769-1839) 'the Father of English Geology', who challenged the belief of mining engineers that coal deteriorated when it lay under limestone, led to Thomas commissioning Smith to prepare surveys of his estates in Lancashire, Cumberland and Durham, to determine whether coal existed beneath. The 700 acres of land on his Haswell estate in Durham, situated on magnesia limestone, was judged poor, and reduced its value in the eyes of Thomas's agents. But Smith's surveys reported the existence of a good body of coal beneath the limestone, which could be worked at an attainable depth. Thomas attempted to sink a shaft at Haswell but the operation had to be abandoned. Smith's accuracy however, in determining the location and quality of the coal seams was eventually verified when shafts were carried down through limestone years later.

At home, both Braddyll and the 3rd Marquis of Londonderry were having problems with their architect. In September 1828, a letter written by mining engineer and coal owner John Gregson to a colleague cast doubt on Wyatt's position as architect for Londonderry and Thomas Braddyll:

'I have just seen a copy of his Lordship's long letter to Braddyll, which in many respects is very indiscreet, as it is however we cannot help it, but I wish he had not so written.

Can you with certainty inform me whether Mr P Wyatt the architect is taken into any degree of favour or employment at Wynyard? Is he in any way authorised to go on with any business for Lord Londonderry or is he absolutely dismissed from the works? I wish you would inform me accurately as to this fact for I understand from Mr Forster (one of Braddyll's partners in his mining company) *that Wyatt has written a letter to Col. Braddyll ... in which he states that Lord Londonderry has taken him again into favour and requests a similar indulgence from the Colonel, from this letter certain inferences are drawn by Sykes which are unfavourable to his Lordship's motives...'*[14]

The letter implies that Wyatt was no longer welcome at Conishead and that he had appealed to Thomas for another chance to complete his work.

The matter came to a head in 1829, when Thomas decided he had waited long enough for the work on the house to be completed and was not prepared to grant Wyatt further 'similar indulgence' of favour. The work had taken ten years, with little progress to show. Wyatt was over-stretching his energies, simultaneously working on Conishead, Wynyard Park and Mount Oswald, and his extravagant use of Bath stone at Conishead had over-reached the budget. Unable to rely solely on his mining investments, Thomas resorted to borrowing large sums of money in order to continue paying for the materials. Between 1829 and 1840 alone, he borrowed £115,000 from local bankers. Deeply dissatisfied, Thomas dismissed Wyatt from Conishead[15].

James Losh's opinion was damning:

'...had the house been completed the place would have been one of the best worth seeing in the Kingdom. As it is, one can only consider it a monument of expensive and thoughtless folly.'

After several years of non-productivity, Thomas returned to George Webster, to complete the work Wyatt had begun. The son of Francis Webster, a mason and architect from Kendal, George had designed his first country house at the age of twenty-one. The house he designed, The Croft near Windermere, built for Liverpool sugar merchant James Brancker in 1830, was described as a 'strange Gothic fantasy mansion'. Shortly before starting work on Conishead, he had been commissioned to re-build Whittington Hall, near Kirkby Lonsdale. The design of Whittington Hall was in the same Gothic style he applied at Conishead and it seems likely that Webster was working between Whittington, Conishead and Holker Hall at the same time, since records show that Whittington's owner Thomas Greene had complained about Webster's slow work. In his defence, the architect pleaded ill health and the fact that he was also *'fully engaged designing for Lord Burlington at Holker.'*[16]

It is possible to identify the difference in styles between Wyatt and Webster's later work on the house. Philip Wyatt's work came to a halt at the east end of the downstairs main corridor. Webster continued with the corridor through to the east door, installing a huge double cantilevered staircase to the north, a hall and a suite of rooms on the ground, first and upper floors to the south, as he had originally proposed in 1818. Instead of Bath stone, Webster chose less expensive red brick, stone and cement; however, although this reduced the outlay on materials, his intricate designs did little to reduce

[14] Letter from John Gregson – September 1828 (Durham County Records Office – NCBI/JB/594 B)

[15] Philip Wyatt continued his work at Wynyard for Lord Londonderry, but did not live to see the house completed. In 1833, he was declared bankrupt and sent to the debtor's prison, where he died two years later.

[16] *The Websters of Kendal* by Angus Taylor (2004)

Plate 23 The south front of Conishead Priory completed by George Webster
(photograph by the author)

the overall cost. In true Gothic revivalist style, they were richly decorative, combining *'imitations of a fortified house with ecclesiastical structure and modern ideas of convenience'.*

The north, south and east elevations display the Gothic intricacies of spires, finials, minarets, carved gargoyles and animals, and other ecclesiastical and flamboyant details, which were typical of Webster. They were in keeping with the demand for 'true Christian Architecture' and the revival of all things medieval, which was beginning to sweep through late Regency and early Victorian England.[17]

By 1835, external work on the house was nearing completion, and apart from periods of residence in London and business excursions to Durham, Thomas and his family were able to stay more frequently at Conishead Priory. A year later, work on bedrooms was complete, including the installation of a hot and cold water system and bathrooms supplied with salt water at a cost of £140,000. The house was now habitable and fit for entertaining guests. Queen Adelaide, the wife of King William IV, stayed at the house about this time, possibly in what became known as the 'State Bedroom'.[18]

[17] There were originally 193 of Webster's working drawings for Conishead Priory. Unfortunately, only a handful survive, which display fine draughtsmanship and close attention to detail. (Cumbria Record Office, Barrow – BDX53/10/1)

[18] According to the court circular, Thomas's daughters Frances, Margaret and Sarah Braddyll had been presented to Queen Adelaide by their aunt Jane Sotheron in 1834.

Plate 24 Detail of interior gargoyle, possibly depicting a Conishead Priory cook

(photograph by the author)

In 1836, the artist, writer and poet Edward Lear paid a visit to the house and afterwards dispatched an enthusiastic letter to a friend:

'I set off with a note from Lord Derby to the finest house in these parts – Mr Bradylls (sic) *– whose family are Saxon & so old, that Adam is supposed to have been brought up in it. Conceive any place so lovely! Enormous sycamores & ash bury it – great rocks shelter it from cold – & all the slopes down to the sea – where the Bay appears on each side & on one hand Hellvellyn – the other far in the distance Pile* (sic) *Castle & the Isle of Man! – the landscape shown was my least pleasure: for the Miss Braddylls are 20 degrees beyond perfection – & what with all sorts of singing & music with them, their father & Brother & Admiral Southeran* (sic) *– a band of 2 accordions, flute-harp-guitar & piano, – we minded not the rain a tittle. Oh dear! oh dear! that splendid priory, – how sorry I was to leave it! ...'*[19]

In his book describing the scenery of the Lake District in 1839, the Rev William Ford declared that

'Mr Braddyll has raised a magnificent edifice, in a style of English architecture tastefully agreeable to its locality and name'.

On a visit to Conishead in the summer of 1839, Lord Burlington of nearby Holker Hall wrote

[19] Letter from Edward Lear to Mrs George – 6 September 1836 (source unknown)

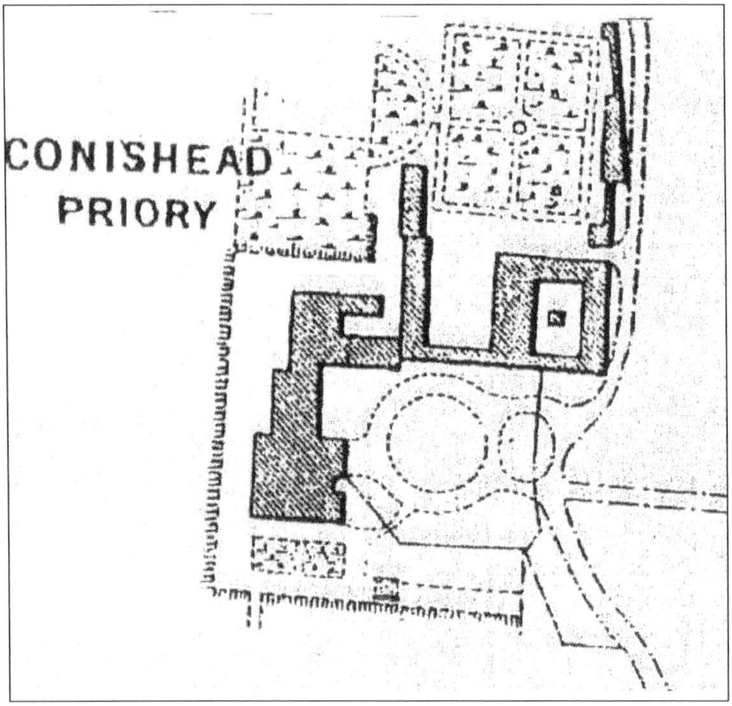

Plate 25 A plan of Conishead Priory and grounds from a 19th century map
(Conishead Priory archives)

'of an immense pile of building at the Priory since I was last there. It will look very well when finished, as there will be a fine set of rooms and a very huge hall.'

In December, he noted in his diary:

'The Priory has grown a great deal since we saw it in the summer. Dining room ceiling finished and looks very well. Entrance Hall also very handsome.'

By 1840, two 100 foot octagonal lantern towers had been built at either side of the main entrance on the northern facade, topped with elaborate spires and ornamented with the carved heads of monks and nuns.

Webster also designed a South lodge, which was situated on the main road from Bardsea that led through Conishead's grounds to the main North gate. The design of the two-bedroomed cottage imitated the medieval Gothic style of the main house and was occupied successively by the Braddylls' bailiff, head gardeners and labourers.

The census for 1841 records the occupants of Conishead and provides a glimpse into the Braddyll household at the time. Thomas was described as 'Independent' (a gentleman of means) and his wife Frances, together with their unmarried daughters Frances, Margaret and Sarah Jane, are listed with him. Their orphaned cousin Charlotte Eliza Vernon, (the twenty year-old daughter of Thomas's late sister Henrietta Maria), was staying with them, and the remainder of the household comprised eleven female servants, five male servants, an upholsterer, a cabinet-maker, a coach driver and head gardener, Joseph Burton. The estate gamekeeper and his family lived nearby. Thomas's wife Frances employed her own gardener, a Mr Garner, and a handful of other servants lived at the Braddylls' nearby property, Bardsea Hall.

One of the gardeners, Jonathan Beck from Bardsea, who had been with the Braddyll family since the late 1790s under Wilson Braddyll's employment, continued working at Conishead until his death aged eighty in 1849. His wife Mary was employed as housekeeper, and their son James as an agricultural labourer on the estate.

Thomas Slaney, who had formerly been employed by the Dukes of Norfolk and St Albans, was House Steward (butler) for the Braddyll family for seven years during the 1840s. His role was to manage the house and servants and ensure the efficient organization of the household.[20]

Another Braddyll employee made the headlines in the local *Soulby's Ulverston Advertiser* when he was the victim of a life-threatening accident:

Plate 26 Thomas Kendall, a domestic servant at Conishead Priory who survived a shooting accident (author's own collection)

'... a young man named Thomas Kendall, a domestic in the service of T R G Braddyll Esquire of Conishead Priory was so seriously wounded by the accidental explosion of a gun, the contents of which entered his body; that although he is still alive, lingers in a very precarious state.'

Miraculously, Kendall survived his ordeal and eventually become the landlord of The Old King's Head in Broughton in Furness.

In 1843, a *Sketch of Furness and Cartmel: Comprising the Hundred of Lonsdale North of the Sands* by Charles M. Jopling was published, which dedicated a chapter to Conishead Priory:

'The present Priory (which is quite modern, having been built by its present proprietor) is erected partly upon the site of the ancient one'.

He noted that a new approach to the house was developing:

... *'by which the visitor will be led along a winding road, at the foot of the Hermitage Hill, through a wood of noble trees, and past some singular limestone rocks. On emerging from the wood, the north front of the building is seen and gradually other parts appear in view. The position of the Priory is commanding.*

[20] When his employment with the Braddyll's terminated, Slaney briefly became House Steward for the Earl of Mansfield. By 1851, he was managing the Furness Abbey Hotel, near Barrow in Furness.

...The north front, with the grand entrance, is a fine design. On either side of the main door-way are two minaret towers, which rise to the height of a hundred feet. To the right of the entrance are cloisters, and on the left the grand staircase and the windows of the drawing-room. Over the door-way there is a fine traceried window, and above it a Catherine wheel. From the court in front, which contains some antique specimens of thorn, a most lovely peep is obtained of the summit of the Old Man mountain; a little to the left of which are seen the Scawfell (sic) *Pikes. The quarterings of the family are displayed on this front in several places.*

On the east front is a noble terraced promenade, with flower-gardens, fountains and vases. The entrance of this side leads, through a vestibule, into the cloisters; and over the entrance there is an oriel window: on either side are the drawing-room windows.

The south front, round which a broad terrace extends, has an entrance leading into the morning room: on the left is the dining room, and on the right the drawing room windows'.[21]

At last, Thomas Richmond Gale Braddyll had transformed Conishead Priory into one of the finest, most flamboyant houses in the country and for the first time, a detailed exploration of the new house and grounds was presented for the public's delectation. But it came at great emotional and financial cost. Before the final touches had been completed, Conishead Priory and the Durham coal mining enterprises, which had helped finance the build, were proving to be massive financial burdens which the Braddyll family could not sustain.

[21] *Sketch of Furness and Cartmel: comprising the hundred of Lonsdale north of the sands* by Charles M Jopling (1843) pp. 145 – 148.

Six

THE 'WORTHY PROPRIETOR'

1843 – 1847

Plate 27 Conishead Priory c. 1842 from Charles Jopling's Sketch of Conishead Priory'

(Conishead Priory archives)

Charles Jopling's *Sketch of Furness and Cartmel*, published in 1843, brought to public attention the architectural and decorative magnificence of Conishead Priory. Thomas Braddyll had, at last, realised his dream to create a true 'Paradise of Furness' at Conishead.

Jopling began his tour of Conishead Priory at the north front of the house, where the principal entrance was flanked by two carved heads, probably portraying King Edward II, who confirmed the foundation charter of the priory, and his Queen Isabella.

On either side of these carvings were the coat of arms of the Sandys, Plantagenet and Lancaster families. A pair of 'Lantern Towers', capped with red sandstone turrets and spires, borrowed details from Webster's Roman Catholic Church in Kendal.

The entrance opened up into the chapel-like hall, sixty feet in length by twenty-four in width and extending the full height of two floors. A carved sixteenth century screen, known as the chapel screen, decked with Braddyll family banners, dominated the far end. Approximately thirteen feet high and twenty feet in width, it had been brought to Conishead from Samlesbury Hall, another Braddyll property near Preston. Above the screen, a groined and decorated forty-one foot high vaulted ceiling with foliated capitals, carved stone shields, gargoyles, carved faces and pillared walls gave the appearance of a fine medieval hall.

Plate 28 *Carved detail depicting Queen Isabella on the front entrance of Conishead Priory* (photograph by the author)

Jopling described the armour of *'mute attendants'* dating from the eleventh century Crusades to the sixteenth century, which ranged on either side of the fireplace. The collection comprised Norman chain mail, a suit of 'Splint' armour from the reign of King Edward IV, two suits of fluted steel armour from the reign of King Henry VII and various implements of war.

But the most stunning aspect of the hall was, and still is, the stained glass windows. Thomas Braddyll had chosen the very best craftsmen for Conishead Priory. In the west wall, opposite the fireplace, three lancet windows designed by Thomas Willement (1786 – 1871) depicted eighteen scenes from the life of Christ. Willement had served as heraldic artist to King George IV, and stained glass artist to Queen Victoria. He was one of the first Gothic revival artists to work with new developments in stained glass when the eighteenth century practice of painting on clear glass with enamel paints was changing to the use of pot-metal glass and lead lines to outline the designs. Thomas Willement's windows at Conishead Priory are early examples of this style of stained glass work.

Plate 29 The hall at Conishead Priory c. 1842 from Charles Jopling's Sketch of Conishead Priory

(Conishead Priory archives)

The large stained glass window above the main entrance, with a circular window above (a stained glass rose within a Star of David) depicted four life-size figures, representing William of Lancaster (benefactor of the original Conishead Priory), Gundred, Countess of Warwick (his wife), King Edward II and St Augustine (the founder of the Order of Canons at the Priory). The window lights on either side of the figures depicted the arms of principal benefactors of the Priory – William of Lancaster, Gamel de Pennington, Richard de Hoddleston, King Edward II, Magnus King of Man, Anselm de Fleming, Margaret de Ros, Roger de Bardsey, Richard de Boyville, Thomas Musgrave, Peter de Lowick and Richard de Ponsonby.

The main corridor, entered through the three-arched hall screen, with its *'charming vista of elegant Gothic pillars and groined roof, ornamented with many beautiful and grotesque designs'*, was described by Nikolaus Pevsner as *'quite a spectacular sight'* and led to the public rooms and main staircase of the house. The nearest of the public rooms was the dining room, forty-five feet by twenty-four, with a magnificent Wilton carpet and a carved white plaster ceiling. The room, wrote Francis Evans in 1842, was *'exquisitely furnished'*.

Jopling noted the dining room's massive pedestal sideboard – *'a fine specimen of carved work'*, made by Gillow and Company of Lancaster, who Thomas had commissioned to provide most of the furniture[1]. The founder, Robert Gillow (1704–1772), came from Leighton Hall near Carnforth. His company brought the first shipments of mahogany to England, inventing the billiards table and providing furniture for Queen Victoria.

Other furniture in the dining room included a large carved oak dining table and twenty four carved chairs. A suite of Utrecht crimson velvet curtains was draped at the windows and the walls were panelled with oak wainscoting in fifteenth and sixteenth century Flemish linenfold design. Above the elaborately carved black marble mantelpiece was a full-length oil painting of Queen Elizabeth I by Zucchero. Through inheritance and purchase, the Braddylls had amassed a large quantity of fine art principally by Dutch, Italian and English masters, and these were displayed in each of the rooms[2].

Adjoining the dining room was the morning room, known by 1848 as the saloon, forty feet long by twenty-four feet wide. Following meals in the dining room, Frances Braddyll, her daughters and female guests would have withdrawn to this room, leaving

[1] In 1841, Thomas commissioned Gillow to create an oak bookcase. This masterpiece of craftsmanship was for sale in London in 2002, and the catalogue stated that it was *'an important oak inverted breakfront bookcase commissioned from Gillows by T R G Braddyll, High Sheriff of Lancashire, for Conishead Priory.'* It was later moved to Whittington Hall in Lancashire, and then most recently to be found in the Judge's Lodgings in Lancaster.

[2] A proficient artist, Thomas Braddyll made copies of old masters, which were displayed in the rooms at Conishead. Thomas later presented his copy of a painting by Guido of Christ's Crucifixion to St Mary's Church in Ulverston, where it formed part of the altarpiece. The painting was mentioned in William Fleming's diary of 19 August 1813:

> *'...The large window at the east end of Ulverston Church was taken out and replaced with beautiful stained glass made by Charles Seward of Lancaster. This was at the expense and by the munificence of Wilson Braddyll of Conishead Priory. Major Braddyll his son has finished a painting, which he will present, to be placed over the communion.'*

Plate 30 Stained glass window above the north entrance (photograph by the author)

Plate 31 Stained glass panel by Thomas Willement from a window in the north hall, depicting a scene from the life of Christ

(photograph by the author)

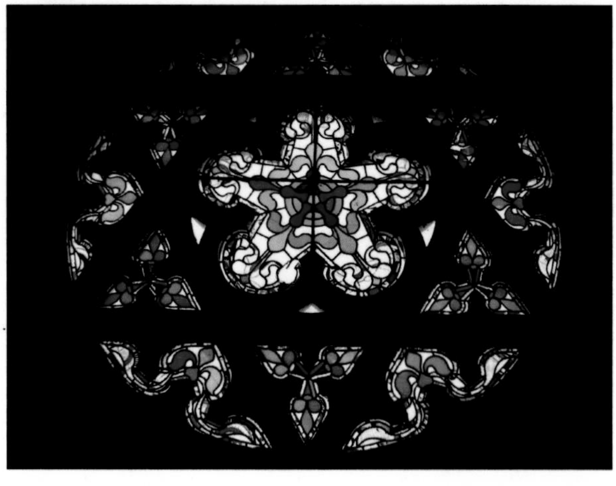

Plate 32 Stained glass window above the north entrance

(photograph by the author)

the gentlemen to talk and smoke in the dining room. Described as *'elegantly furnished'*, it was draped with twilled chintz curtains. The ornate plaster ceiling was carved with the combined arms of the Richmond, Gale and Braddyll families and the Chester and Bagot arms of Frances's family. The Braddyll motto 'Cognoies toy mesme' ('Know Thyself'), the family symbols of the mountain cat (Richmond family), the badger (the Braddyll family), family crests, Tudor roses and Thomas's initials 'TRGB' were included in the design. The fireplace was carved from expensive white Carrara marble. Scattered around the room were conversational and lounging chairs, couches, occasional tables, card tables and inlaid tables. A marble bust of Jane Braddyll by Joseph Nollekens, took pride of place, and Jopling noted a cabinet displaying a pen and ink miniature of King William III surrounded by embroidery made from his wife Queen Mary's hair,[3] and miniature Braddyll family portraits[4].

The morning room opened into the Gothic conservatory of hybrid rhododendrons (including the species *'Rhododendron Ulverstoniana'*), overlooking the south lawn. It was the first part of the new house to be built and during the Braddylls' residence was *'tastefully constructed with Gothic windows filled with stained glass and covered in front with ivy'*.[5] It would have created a dazzling backdrop to the colourful flowering shrubs.

Beyond the morning room was the blue drawing room, forty-five feet in length by twenty-four feet, described by Francis Evans as a *'delicious apartment.'* In 1842, it was unfinished but hung with numerous paintings. There seems to have been some disagreement over the furnishings in this room. Gillow learnt from Thomas's steward, Mr Hayward that he no longer wished to furnish the room in the French Style of Louis XI as originally agreed, and instead favoured the Gothic theme of the overall house. Gillow expressed regret at the decision, but wisely bowed to his client's preference.

From the blue drawing room, across a small vestibule with an elegant porch opening onto a terraced walk and a fountain flower garden, was the north drawing room. Rumour has it that this room had a secret passage down to the basement, used during the English Civil War, and indeed a trap door in the floor is still in evidence. Built over the foundations of the old Tudor house, the passage may have been used to hide members of the family and their most treasured possessions.

[3] Agnes Strickland's *Lives of the Queens of England from the Norman Conquest* (1854) describes the miniature in detail: *'Among the valuable collections of Colonel Braddyll at Conishead Priory, Lancashire was preserved a very fine miniature of William III, delicately executed in pen and ink etching. It is a small oval, laid on a background of white satin, surrounded with a wreath of laurel, embroidered in outline tracery in his royal consort's hair, surmounted with the crown-royal. The frame is wood, curiously carved and gilded, and at the foot is a circular medallion, radiated and enclosed in the riband of the Garter, containing also, under a fair crystal, Queen Mary's hair, which is of a pale brown colour and of an extremely fine and silky texture. At the back of the picture Queen Mary has inscribed on a slip of vellum, with her own hand, "My haire, cutt off March ye 5th 1688". Under the royal autograph is written, "Queen Mary's hair and writing".'*

[4] Amongst the earliest were mid-18th century copies in watercolour and gouache on ivory, after William Larkin from Elizabethan originals depicting Edward Braddyll in 1560, and Margaret Dodding, the wife of Myles Dodding and daughter of William Sandys.

[5] Francis Evans, 1842.

The north drawing room, forty feet by twenty-four feet, remained unfinished, but in 1842 it displayed a fine collection of paintings.

At one end, a carved oak mantelpiece displayed the arms and crests of the Braddyll, Richmond and Gale families together with those of Rishton, Dodding and Sandys, their related families. In keeping with the other rooms on the ground floor, the ceilings were richly plastered with the crests and monograms of the Braddyll and Gale family.

A huge bookcase covered the length of one wall,[6] with a central section of false book spines, concealing the entrance to a secret space. Known as a 'Judas' closet, it is a relic of bygone plots and intrigues.

Further along the main corridor, adjoining the breakfast room was the library, twenty-four feet by twenty-seven, with an architraves of grape vines finely carved in plaster, and a large gilt chandelier. The room was predominantly furnished in crimson, with a Brussels carpet and crimson satin damask curtains, ornamented with fringes and tassels. There was a carved oak sofa, a set of twelve oak chairs and a pair of oak library chairs covered in crimson Utrecht velvet, oak bookcases, a carved oak Davenport desk and an expensive Buhl and tortoiseshell knee-hole writing table. It was here that Thomas Braddyll kept one of the family's ancient treasures – a thirteenth-century illuminated copy of the *Epistles of St Augustine* on vellum and bound in calfskin, which once belonged to the canons of the medieval Conishead Priory.

The walls were hung with a collection of engravings, family portraits, a painting of the interior of a Swiss Castle and a portrait from the school of Rembrandt. As well as housing approximately 4,000 books, including Shakespeare, Byron and Dickens, the library shelves contained numerous volumes of music, portfolios of watercolours and drawings and several maps and charts.

Above the relatively plain stone Tudor-style mantelpiece, stood an elegant Parisian clock in an ornamented case. A large carved Tudor rose ceiling boss, carved rose motifs on the three oak doors, and stained glass windows depicting the arms of the Dodding, Sandys, Richmond, Gale, Braddyll, Chester and Bagot families repeated the Gothic theme of the room.

From the entrance screen in the large hall, the corridor on the right led towards the cloisters, stretching an impressive seventy-two feet in length and eighteen feet in width, and originally set out with wood floorboards. This part of the house was designed to evoke the atmosphere of the medieval priory, reminding the visitor of Conishead's ancient history. Charles Mackay, writing in 1852, suggested that these nineteenth-century cloisters were built on the site of the original priory cloisters, but there is no evidence for this.[7]

The cloister windows were painted with the arms of the Braddyll, Dodding, Richmond, Gale, Sandys and Vaux families (the Vaux family married into the Richmond family during the early seventeenth century).

[6] The bookcase still stands in the room today

[7] *The Scenery and Poetry of the English Lakes, a Summer Ramble* by Charles Mackay (1852)

Plate 33 Detail from the fireplace in what was originally the Braddylls' north drawing room

(photograph by the author)

Plate 34 False book spines in the 19th century library bookcase

(photograph by the author)

Plate 35 Detail of door in what was originally the Braddylls' library

(photograph by the author)

Plate 36 Stained glass window in the cloisters

(photograph by the author)

Plate 37 Detail of Braddyll heraldry in a stained glass window in the cloisters

(photograph by the author)

Along the walls, recesses displayed unusual suits of black armour dating from the early seventeenth century and 'other curiosities', including ancient war spears, a sword used at the Battle of Waterloo and a Waterloo medal. In his book, Jopling noted that a *'place is reserved for an organ over the screen'*.

The breakfast room, referred to by the Braddylls as the little dining room, was twenty-six by sixteen feet and furnished with deep fringed red merino curtains and ornamented gilt cornices. There was a set of mahogany dining tables on pillar and claw frames, a set of mahogany chairs, an oak and marble-topped table and a grand pianoforte cased in Spanish mahogany by Collard and Son. Today, referred to as the servery, this room has a service lift and a stairway giving access to the main kitchen and storerooms below. It leads into what was once the Braddyll's library.

Next to the library was a gentleman's dressing room, usually furnished as a private sitting room, together with a bathroom and water closet. From the corner of this room a winding stone staircase led to the 100 foot north towers which offered magnificent views. Several family portraits and *'ancient pictures belonging to the monastery'* were displayed in the room, presumably once the possession of the Conishead Priory canons.

At the end of the cloisters, steps led up to a small study with an *'exquisitely finished'* oak carved over-mantel dated 1638, probably removed from the old house. Above the

Plate 38 The 17th century carved mantelpiece in what was Thomas Braddyll's study, and came from the old Conisheaad Priory house (photograph by the author)

mantelpiece and at each side of the arms of the Dodding, Sandys, Rawson and Davil families were two sets of male and female figures, possibly depicting mythological or biblical characters. A carved frieze of the same period decorated the upper walls of the room and the plaster ceiling carried the painted arms of the Braddylls, Doddings, Sandys and Dixons (who married into the Sandys family in the sixteenth century).

Further along the corridor, hung with copies of Old Masters and various family portraits, was the housekeeper Mrs Beck's room, and the main kitchen, thirty-three by twenty-seven feet, with a vaulted roof, glazed turret, oak case clock and tin Dutch oven. Nearby there was also a smaller kitchen, the cook's sitting room, a still room[8], two larders, a servant's hall (forty-one by twenty-six feet, where the domestic staff dined), the butler's bedroom and sitting room, a pantry, the housemaid's parlour, a lamp room, various other domestic rooms and five cellars.

Adjoining offices on the ground floor consisted of a knife room, game larder and 'other minor offices', probably lavatories. By 1848, pipes conveyed warm air throughout the ground floor in an early form of central heating, and a 'patent apparatus' warmed and forced water into the baths. Outside, a pump and well drew salt water for use in the household's salt-water baths.

At the foot of the great double-cantilevered oak staircase, with its 3 foot wide Wilton carpet, Jopling noted Sir Joshua Reynolds's full-length portrait of Thomas Braddyll as a boy with his parents. The staircase remains an impressive feature of the house, its size and magnificent construction showing off Webster's skill as an architect. Above the banisters, grotesque masks, frolicking cherubs and Tudor roses, made from papier-mâché and painted to simulate oak, added to the spectacle. The lower newel posts were mounted on either side by a carved badger, supporting a banner depicting the arms of the Richmond, Gale and Braddyll families, and on the next set of posts were a carved mountain cat and a unicorn. A copy of the 'Death of Cleopatra' by Guido hung on the right of the stairway and on the left, a painting of 'the Sibyls' by Guercino. A marble statue of 'Purity' by Ricci stood on the landing, lit by a large stained glass window by William Wailes, displaying the coats of arms of the families related to Conishead and the Braddyll family, including the Lowther, Dodding, Sandys, Vaux and Rawson families. William Wailes (1808–1881), like Willement, was beginning a career in stained glass manufacture when Thomas Braddyll commissioned him to produce the window. Wailes had worked for three years with Augustus Welby Pugin (1812–52), the master of Medieval Gothic revivalism. After his break with the architect, Wailes's work became increasingly sought after and by 1850, he was employing seventy-six workers. In the style typical of Pugin, Wailes's work was unadulterated 'Gothic' and he was known to despise new fashions. Amongst his many commissions was the west window of Gloucester Cathedral.

[8] A 'still room' was commonly found in large houses after the 17th century and originally used to distil the cordial water used for medicines or perfume. It was later used as a place to make preserves and cakes etc.

Plate 39 The great staircase designed by George Webster with the carved animal crests on the newel posts photographed c. 1870
(author's own collection)

On the first floor, opposite the landing, was the oak bedroom, which was associated with stories of murder and the supernatural. In 1842, the room contained a richly carved oak Tester (four-post) bedstead, dating from the fifteenth century. With turned and carved feet pillars and moulded cornices, it was covered in antique yellow brocade and silk, with a deep bullion fringe and drapery and green Parisian pendants. It was believed to be the bed in which King Richard III slept on the eve of the Battle of Bosworth in 1485. A traveller in the Lake District during the 1830s pasted an old news cutting into his handbook[9] which described the history of the bed. Below it, the traveller had written: *'This bedstead is at present at Mr Braddell's* (sic), *Conishead'*. According to the article, the bed came originally from the Blue Boar Inn in Leicester, where Richard III had slept the night before the battle. The King's men had carried the bed in procession towards Bosworth, but after the King's death the following day, the bed was stripped of its rich hangings and left at the inn. For years the bedstead remained a royal relic and passed from each successive tenant, until it came into the possession of Thomas Clarke and his wife Agnes during the latter half of the sixteenth century. It was said that Agnes Clarke discovered a hoard of money, believed to be part of the King's treasure chest, under a false base in the bed. The couple kept it and it made their fortune. After her husband's death, Agnes was robbed by men staying at the inn and then murdered by her maidservant after endeavouring

> *'... to cry out for help, upon which her maid thrust her fingers down her throat and choked her.'*

For this crime, the maid was burnt at the stake and her accomplices hanged at Leicester.

It is not known how the Braddyll family acquired the bedstead or what happened to it when the family finally left Conishead. We know, however, that the Blue Boar Inn

[9] Cumbria Record Office, Barrow in Furness.

Plate 40 Stained glass window by William Wailes above the great staircase
(photograph by the author)

Plate 41 Drawing for a design on the great staircase by George Webster, 1839
(Cumbria Record Office, Barrow - courtesy of Mrs S Ritson)

Plate 42 Drawing for a design on the great staircase by George Webster, 1839
(Cumbria Record Office, Barrow - courtesy of Mrs S Ritson)

was demolished in 1835 so it is possible Thomas Braddyll purchased the bed for his new house from the sale of the contents.

Other pieces of furniture in the room included rich yellow brocade and silk furniture and a gentleman's oak wardrobe and cabinets with glass frames made from carved oak. The elaborately carved wall panelling dating from the seventeenth century had been removed from Samlesbury Hall near Preston. In 1679, a Thomas Braddyll of Portfield, bought Samlesbury Hall from the financially crippled Southworth family for the sum of £3,150. Over the next two hundred years it was leased to local handloom weavers and their families. In 1834, whilst re-building Conishead, Thomas Braddyll decided to convert the decaying Samlesbury Hall into an inn, to be known as the 'Braddyll Arms'. During the conversion, oak panelling and a chapel screen were removed from the hall

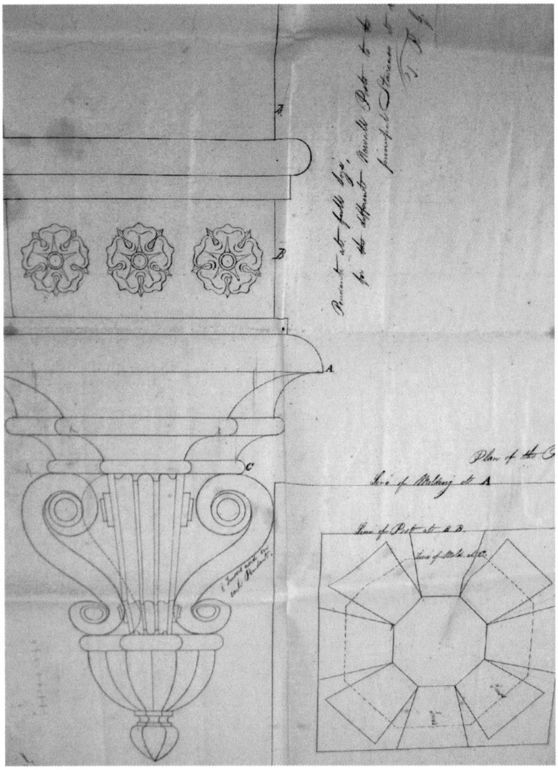

Plate 43 Drawing for a newel post on the great staircase by George Webster, 1839

(Cumbria Record Office, Barrow – courtesy of Mrs S Ritson)

Plate 44 First floor landing and great staircase *(photograph by the author)*

Plate 45 The 17th century fireplace in the oak room (photograph by the author)

Plate 46 The chapel screen in the hall which Thomas Braddyll brought from Samlesbury Hall, Lancashire (photograph by the author)

Plate 47a,b,c Details of 17th century oak carvings in the oak room originally from Samlesbury Hall, Lancashire
(photographs by the author)

and brought to Conishead under the supervision of James Atkinson, Thomas's steward. Atkinson later claimed that during the dismantling of the panelling the ghost of Thomas Southworth appeared, warning him that if he removed the part carved with the Southworth name, he would never see Conishead again. It would also *'not be long with the Braddylls'*. The steward was superstitious enough to heed the warning. The following day he

> *'decided to cut out the carved screen from the terrier saying in excuse to myself that Mr Braddyll would not care to have Southworth's name in his new house ... That is the reason why the old passage screen was left at Samlesbury Hall, whilst the chapel screen and oak panelling were removed to Conishead to decorate Mr Braddyll's new mansion...'*[10]

Because there was insufficient panelling to cover the walls at Conishead, plaster reproductions were made and painted to give the appearance of carved oak. Dating from 1623, the oldest panel depicted the three figures of 'Faith', 'Hope' and 'Charity'.

In each corner of the Oak bedroom the plaster ceiling depicted the arms of the Braddyll, Dodding, Dixon and Sandys families, and at the centre, the arms of the Richmonds, Vaux, Lowther and Cliffords. Hand-polished stone, embedded with tiny fossils, framed the early Victorian cast iron fireplace and various family portraits were displayed around the room.

Adjoining the Oak bedroom was a drawing room with a marble mantelpiece made from Florentine mosaic, and a plaster ceiling bearing the crests of the Braddyll and Richmond families.

Nearby rooms included one known as the point lace bedroom. It was intended to be decorated with point lace made by the women of the

[10] *Stories of Samlesbury* by Robert Eaton, 1927 (Cumbria Record Office, Barrow)

Braddyll family. There was an adjoining dressing room, but Jopling noted that these rooms were unfinished.

By 1848, the Chintz bedroom had been furnished with a Brussels carpet, a Spanish mahogany washstand and wardrobe, and a raised Indian Japanned cabinet, and another dressing room, contained a Spanish mahogany wardrobe, a washstand and couch bedstead.

The Decca bedroom, furnished with Decca furniture lined in blue silk and sea green chintz curtains, was possibly Thomas Braddyll's room. The long list of furniture in this room featured in the 1850 Bill of Sale[11], suggests its grand proportions. Items included a gentleman's oak wardrobe, a Brussels carpet, a polished oak bookcase, six oak framed chairs, several 'easy' chairs, a Grecian carved sofa and an oak *'conversational couch...* (with a) *chess table in* (the) *centre'*, gilt framed cabinet, an octagonal oak table, an oak writing table, a sofa table, a Buhl and mother of pearl inlaid chess table, and a Louis XIV style fire screen. Here was also displayed (in 1848) a *'beautiful sculptured female bust by Nollekens'*, probably the one depicting Thomas's mother Jane Braddyll which Jopling had noted in the morning room six years before.

Further bedrooms included the State bedroom, perhaps where Queen Adelaide slept when she visited Conishead, during the early 1830s; the Oriel bedroom (which presumably was the room that looked out of the oriel window at the east front of the house), two other dressing rooms, two water closets and a bathroom. Another room, later known as the ladies' drawing room, boasted a marble mantle-piece ornamented with Wedgwood plaques.

A small stained glass window depicting a copy of Murillo's 'Nativity' lit the upper staircase.

Above the organ gallery and cloisters, the west wing included five further bedrooms and a lady's bedroom, dressing room, bathroom, water closet and a boudoir, twenty-seven by sixteen feet (described in 1848, as having *'handsome carved doors in white and gold and costly statutory marble chimney pieces'*). These rooms may have been occupied by Thomas Braddyll's wife, Frances.

Another bedroom and dressing room were situated in what was known as the Lancaster Tower, on the south west corner,

Plate 48 The Lancaster Tower spiral stairway
(photograph by the author)

[11] Catalogue of Effects of Sale (house contents of Conishead Priory) 1850 – Cumbria Record Office, Barrow (Z/3477)

which had winding stone stairs connecting the different floors and giving access to the south terrace. Above the vestibule were four servants' rooms, a housemaid's closet, a storeroom and another water closet.

Towards the west wing there were four menservants' bedrooms, and near the tower a further four bedrooms for visitors and servants, a water closet and up a flight of stairs near the kitchen six bedrooms for female servants.

The upper floor consisted of the Yellow Velvet bedroom, twenty-four feet square with an adjoining dressing room.

There was also a bathroom and closet; two further bedrooms, another *'splendid'* room with a dressing room, two bedrooms and a water closet.

A 'Green bedroom', also had an adjacent dressing room, followed by four further bedrooms, a bathroom, another dressing room and a water closet. Nearby, there was a bachelor's bedroom and closet.

Another room, on the upper floor of the north wing, thirty feet by thirty-six with beamed ceiling and dome, leading to a copper and lead lantern tower, was later used as a billiards room. All floors throughout the house were of polished wood.

Moving to the outside of the house, Jopling focused on the south front with its stained glass conservatory, Gothic style vestibule, anteroom and bay windows, flanked by two domed minarets. In the lower parts of the south wall, sandstone blocks carved with a diamond and rose pattern from the medieval Conishead Priory, had been built into the structure of the new house.

The eastern side of the house had an elegant pillared porch with an arched and embossed ceiling. Carved with the arms of the Braddyll, Dodding and Sandys families, further decoration included plaster figures of a swineherd, butcher and farmer, monks and musicians.

A panelled octagonal vestibule led into the corridor and cloisters, with an oriel window above, and outside a fountain stood as the central focus of the east lawn. The oriel window at Conishead bears a strong resemblance to the window of a first floor office at Paddington Station in London, designed and built between 1852 and 1854, collaboratively by Sir Matthew Digby Wyatt (Philip Wyatt's cousin) and Sir Isambard Kingdom Brunel.

Charles Jopling's book included an engraving of the view of the south and east front of the house in 1842, illustrating the elegance of the turrets, spires topped with stone crosses, mountain cats, unicorns, badgers, and the ornamental strap-work chimneys, which framed the skyline. Although the roof area was less visible, no expense had been spared on decoration. Viewed from above, gargoyles could be seen intermingled with fine sculpted heads of medieval ladies, gentlemen, monks and nuns. As well as these ecclesiastical touches, the roof tops and chimneys were Tudor in style, probably influenced by Hampton Court Palace, where Thomas and Frances Braddyll had lived in a grace and favour apartment.

Plate 49 The south front and conservatory (photograph by the author)

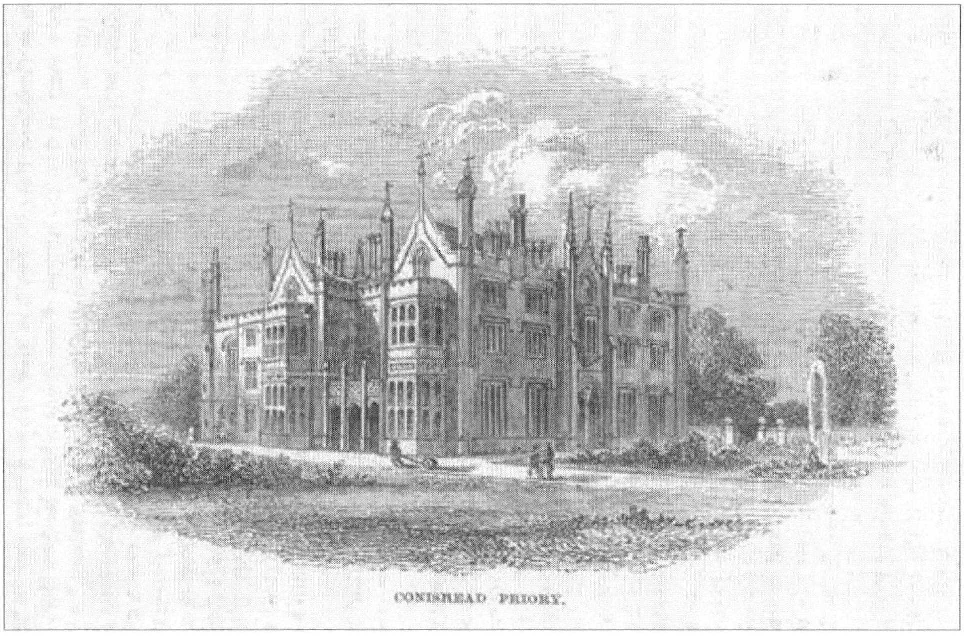

Plate 50 The south east aspect of Conishead Priory c. 1842 from Charles Jopling's 'Sketch of Conishead Priory' (Conishead Priory archives)

Plate 51a,b Hampton Court Palace and Conishead Priory. The Braddylls had a grace and favour apartment at Hampton Court and this may have influenced the design for Conishead (author's own collection)

Plate 52 The turrets and chimneys of Conishead Priory (photograph by the author)

The courtyard at Conishead Priory had standing room for six carriages, a six-stall stable, a loose box and two harness and saddle rooms with lofts and rooms above. An adjoining building, built in the Gothic character of the main house, with a turreted tower, Saxon windows and a turret clock in the centre, was to be used for baking and brewing. A continuous roof covered a barn, cart house, stabling, and carpenter's shop and there was a dairy, piggery, several other outbuildings and a large, walled, kitchen garden. This was entered through a Grecian-style portico, and was at one time, looked after by fourteen full-time gardeners.

Thomas Braddyll's ostentatious landscaping ideas for Conishead matched his ambitions for the house. In 1844, he commissioned George Webster to build a bridge over a stream in the grounds, forty feet long to be built of limestone *'with rough faces (something like the walling of Bardsea Church)'* and *'natural faced rock stone'*. Webster's drawings show that it was decorated with scrollwork and ball-topped stone pillars at each end.

At the foot of the Sycamore Avenue (marking the site of an old 'Red Lane' across Furness) in the southern boundary of the grounds, a cottage was built for Thomas's wife and daughters as a secluded place for writing or sewing. Approached through a picturesque stone arch, covered with ivy and topped with ornamental chimneys, and surrounded with syringa bushes, it was known as the Ladies' Cottage. After the Braddylls left Conishead, it was used for a time to house a collection of fossils and

Plate 53 The Ladies' Cottage c. 1900
(Conishead Priory archives)

Plate 54 The Grotto or icehouse on Hermitage Hill
(photograph by the author)

archaeological finds, including glazed tiles and fragments of gilt coffin plates from the foundations of the original priory and church.

Further fashionable landscaping features included a grotto (*'inviting to seclusion and peaceful meditation'*), a tunnelled subway leading to an ornamental lake full of trout, a Swiss fishing cottage and a Gothic style alcove.

New varieties of seeds and plants were being collected from abroad at this time and the Braddylls were quick to latch on to this horticultural development. The sides of the house opened onto terrace walks, eight-hundred feet in length, with lawns and grounds displaying shrubs, tulip trees, cedars, magnolias and foreign oak. The Cedars of Lebanon, which flourished in the grounds and the old 'wishing' oak, were believed to date from the time of the original priory's founding in the 1100s.

The east front terrace was laid out with flower gardens, fountains and vases. Pleasure gardens of around seventeen acres, a flower garden in front of the conservatory, the new American Garden and the old American Garden provided winding walks, plantations of rhododendrons, rare and plentiful specimens of tree and flower and beautiful views. A woodland path led to the beach from where the Braddylls and their friends and visitors could enjoy the panoramic view of the wooded slopes of the

Plate 55 The Hermitage c. 1900 *(author's own collection)*

Plate 56 The Hermitage today *(photograph by the author)*

Cartmel Fells, the picturesque Chapel Island and the low-lying shores of Morecambe Bay.

A Bill of Sale for the house later described the surrounding grounds, which formed part of the estate to the north:

> *'On top of a beautiful knoll in the park is a secluded Hermitage, with a painted window of 'The Annunciation' and near to this spot are the remains of a castle and circular Tower embosomed in Ivy, Rookery, Ice House, Keeper's residence and Kennels; the whole surrounded by the Park and rich lands containing together four hundred and twenty-four acres, and nine perches.'*

The *'circular tower embosomed with ivy'* was a folly built to resemble a ruined castle. Octagonal and turreted and complete with cross shaped arrow slits, which Thomas commissioned for the wooded hill to the north of Conishead Priory, it was known as Hermitage Hill. Jopling called the Hermitage nearby

> *'a pretty secluded retreat, with everything in perfect keeping. It possesses a habitable apartment and a chapel'.*

Cruciform in design, the building was constructed from large limestone blocks. The entrance porch was accessed through a high, pointed archway, above which stood a carved niche, probably intended for a statue. This led into the 'habitable apartment' measuring fifteen feet, nine inches by nine feet, nine inches, which had five windows, fitted with iron casements and wooden shutters and a narrow fireplace against the south wall. There was also a 'chapel', seventeen feet, four inches by seven foot, eight inches with a stone altar and three windows, including a nineteenth century stained glass window depicting the Annunciation. It was a strange building, a combination of dwelling and chapel, perhaps intended as a private family retreat for meditation and prayer. However, local information from the early twentieth century conveys a more interesting probability. A Dr Fell of Barrow in Furness remembered from his father that from about 1820 to 1840, Thomas Braddyll retained an old man from Bardsea as the Hermitage's resident hermit, complete with uncut nails and hair.[12] There is no mention of the Hermitage before Jopling's visit in 1842, so it is possible the old

Plate 57 The North Lodge c. 1900
(Ulverston Heritage Centre)

[12] From an article written for the *Transactions of the Cumberland and Westmorland Antiquarian and Archaeological Society*, 1902.

hermit originally dwelt in the Grotto, a cave-like structure nearby, hewn out of the limestone rock, which was a popular feature of eminent gardens from the eighteenth century.

In 1895, the Hermitage was described as 'much dilapidated' and by 1902, had become a 'mossy cell', where the remains of a massive, broken red sandstone cross and part of an old wooden bedstead were the only evidence of habitation. Over a hundred years later, the place is little more than foundation stones. The stained glass window, with its centre painting depicting the Annunciation was miraculously saved intact and sold at auction in 1972 for £10.

Tradition had it that along with the hermit, Thomas Braddyll kept a tame lion at Conishead in a building known in 1847 as the Dog Kennel; however there is nothing to verify this. The census for 1841 shows that the Conishead Priory gamekeeper Thomas Willman and his family were living in the estate's north lodge (built in the style of a castellated keep and tower) on the main road between Ulverston and Bardsea. It was known as the Kennel House and, ten years later, as the Dog Kennel. By 1861, it was referred to as the Lodge, then as the Middle Lodge and finally the North Lodge. Whatever the truth behind the stories regarding the hermit and the lion, they added to the mystery and glamour of Conishead created by Thomas Braddyll in the construction of his 'Paradise of Furness'. The hermitage, tower and grotto were part of his vision for a landscape which mirrored the style of the fashionable homes in England at the time, with their follies, mausoleums, Grecian temples and romantic ruins. By 1847, Sylvan's *Pictorial Handbook to the English Lakes* was announcing

> *'the present worthy proprietor allows the public to view the collection of pictures etc. twice a week (Wednesday and Friday) and the beautiful grounds are open to the inspection of strangers every day except Sundays'.*

With the exception of several unfurnished rooms, it seemed that finally, after fifteen years, Thomas Braddyll's monumental dream had been realized. Unfortunately, it had cost him approximately £140,000, a sum twice the original estimate.

Seven

'THE NOBLE AND SPLENDID MANSION'

1847–1850

The refurbishment of Conishead Priory by Thomas Braddyll in the early part of the nineteenth century resulted in a house of magnificent proportions and ostentatious decoration. It soon became known as one of the finest properties in the North of England. With Thomas's huge investment it seemed the family was at last committed to becoming resident in Furness. He began to take a keen interest in the history of the place and found enjoyment dabbling in minor archaeological excavations around the area, assisted by the local vicar. The glory of Thomas Braddyll's Conishead was, however, short-lived. Since inheriting the house and surrounding estates in 1818, he had worked tirelessly to create a property that would be the pride of North Lancashire, but he had begun the project in debt, and by the early 1840s, as the buildings and grounds were nearing completion, he found himself in severe financial difficulty. Tens of thousands of pounds had been invested in the reconstruction of Conishead and the cash was running out.

At the time, Thomas's chief business interest was in the burgeoning mining industry in the North East. Unfortunately, his precarious Durham mining enterprise was fraught with tensions between the co-owners. Correspondence from the time reveals arguments over finances between Thomas, Lord Londonderry and the Earl of Durham. From his Haswell home, The Lodge, Thomas grew frustrated in his inability to secure a successful mining operation, but stood his ground when faced with opposition by the Earl of Durham and Lord Londonderry. He made it known to them that he

> *'...was as good and probably better in birth and breeding as any (bloody) Durham coal owner that ever drew breath!'*

Thomas formed the Hetton Coal Company along with five co-Directors Thomas Rawsthorne, William Green, John Burrell, Matthew Forster and Percival Forster and on 1 March 1831, under the guidance of William Smith, commenced the sinking of the South Hetton Colliery, the first within the boundaries of the Easington district and the

Plate 58 Conishead Priory c. 1845 not long before it was put up for auction
(artist unknown – Conishead Priory archives)

Plate 59 South Hetton Colliery near Durham during the 19th century
(author's own collection)

first colliery in Durham to draw coal up the shaft in cages. At the same time, Thomas commissioned the construction of a waggon-way to transport the coal from South Hetton Colliery to Seaham Harbour, enabling it be shipped to markets in the south and the Continent. By 1833, the 'Braddyll Railway' (known locally as the 'Yellow Brick Road') was completed.

On 5 August 1833, after many setbacks, one of which required the construction of one of the largest and most powerful steam engines in the world to solve the problem of pumping water from a depth of 876 feet, Thomas Braddyll's South Hetton Colliery, described in the local news as *'a colliery on the most stupendous scale'*, was officially opened. A local paper noted

> *'a great concourse of people assembled at Seaham, to witness the first shipping of the first coals. W Green of Durham, Esq as one of the owners, addressed the people, amidst the most deafening cheers. The workmen belonging to the company and to Lord Londonderry, were regaled at the several public houses in the village ...'*

The inhabitants of the neighbourhood went on to enjoy a band of music and a 'fat roasted bullock'. The opening of the colliery brought with it increased employment for local men, and by the 1840s over 643 were working for Braddyll's company. As the colliery village expanded, Thomas Braddyll granted a site for a chapel and burial ground which were constructed in 1837, at an expense exceeding £1000, towards which Braddyll's company had 'liberally' contributed.

A year after opening the colliery at South Hetton, Thomas's mining company began sinking another shaft. Access to this new seam at Murton however was difficult, taking much longer than expected with unforeseen complications caused by quicksand and explosions. The colliery, when it was officially opened, was the most difficult and expensive undertaking of its kind on record.

By 1842, Thomas was applying for loans with which to support his mining ventures and the work at Conishead. He applied to borrow large sums of money, as much as £40,000 and £62,000 from Petty and Postlethwaite, his bank in Ulverston, and mortgages were taken out against his Bardsea and Samlesbury estates and other properties, in an effort to sustain his losses.

A letter from John Buddle, a leading mining engineer, replying to an enquiry from John Parkinson of Lincoln's Inn Fields, London, to whom Thomas had applied for a loan of £12,000, reveals the state of affairs:

> *'...I know Col. Braddyll personally, but know little of his private affairs. The general opinion... is that he has greatly embarrassed himself, by building an enormous house, at Conishead Priory in Lancashire where he resides. He holds some shares in the South Hetton Colliery, but I do not know to what extent and is also I believe proprietor of part of the royalty. One pit has been working for seven years and another new Winning or Plant...is now being made,*

and may probably commence the working of coals in twelve months, and grow to maturity in 3 years – when it holds out a fair prospect of being a good and permanent colliery.

But it has, and will, from extraordinary difficulties encountered in the sinking, cost an enormous sum of money; and altho' it may ultimately prove a profitable concern, yet per se, I should not consider it valid security, for a loan of any considerable sum of money. I do not know anything of Col. Braddyll's landed property, but have been informed that it is heavily mortgaged.'[1]

In 1846, having exhausted all other sources of finance, Thomas was forced to sell South Hetton, Murton Pits, Cleator Hall and Burneside Hall. An agreement for the

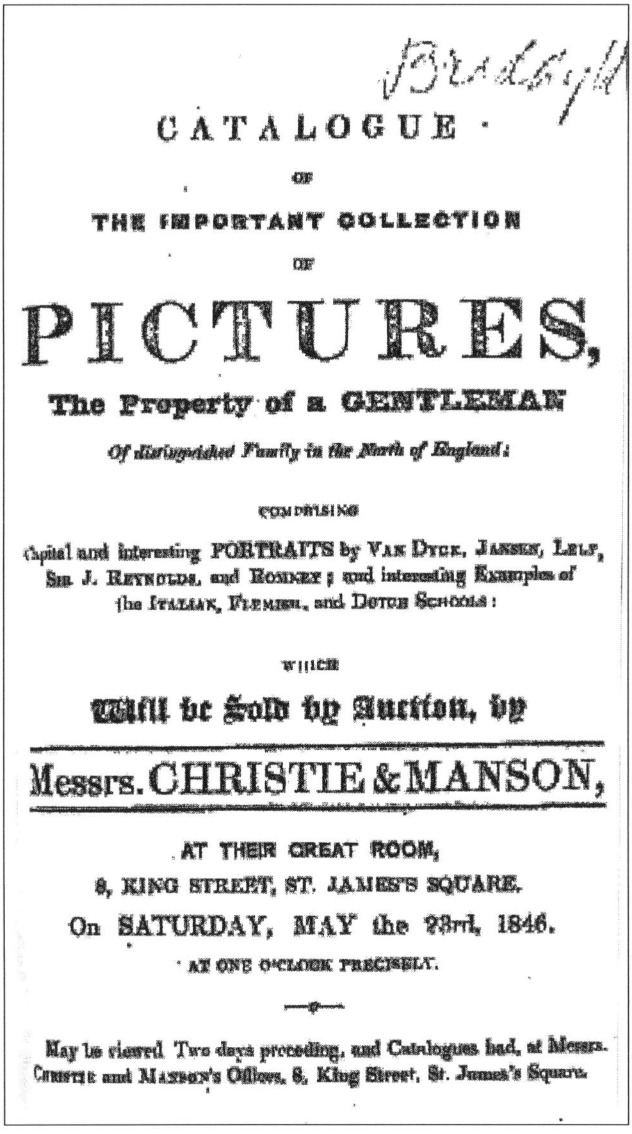

Braddyll

CATALOGUE

OF

THE IMPORTANT COLLECTION

OF

PICTURES,

The Property of a GENTLEMAN

Of distinguished Family in the North of England;

COMPRISING

Capital and interesting PORTRAITS by Van Dyck, Jansen, Lely, Sir J. Reynolds, and Romney; and interesting Examples of the Italian, Flemish, and Dutch Schools:

WHICH

Will be Sold by Auction, by

Messrs. CHRISTIE & MANSON,

AT THEIR GREAT ROOM,
8, KING STREET, ST. JAMES'S SQUARE.
On SATURDAY, MAY the 23rd, 1846,
AT ONE O'CLOCK PRECISELY.

May be viewed Two days preceding, and Catalogues had, at Messrs. Christie and Manson's Offices, 8, King Street, St. James's Square.

Plate 60 Front cover of the sale catalogue of the Braddylls' art collection, 1846

(Conishead Priory archives)

[1] Letter from John Buddle to John Parkinson, November 1842 (NCBI/JB1038) Durham County Record Office.

re-organisation of the South Hetton Coal Company was drawn up in August 1847, and twenty-two of the thirty-two shares owned by Thomas were divided between his five fellow Company Directors at a nominal price of £4,226 13s. 5d. per share. The Haswell Coal Company bought his Haswell home, and several of his other holdings were taken over by the Pemberton family of Hawthorn Tavern near Seaham, the previous owners of Monkwearmouth (Pemberton Main) Colliery. The sale of the pits, however, was not enough to cover Thomas's debts. He had no choice but to begin selling off his inheritance. In March 1846, Thomas prepared to sell part of his collection of paintings hanging at Conishead in rooms still unfinished. A few personal family paintings were conveyed for safekeeping to his eldest son Edward, who was living with his family at 'Summer Hill', near Spark Bridge.

On Saturday 23 May 1846, at the auctioneers Messrs Christie and Manson in London, the Braddyll paintings went under the hammer. They included works by Lely, Van Dyke, Rubens and Titian and, what would have been a loss of great sentimental value, the portraits of Thomas's father and mother by Reynolds and several other portraits of his mother and wife[2]. The collection, admired only four years previously by the writer Charles Jopling, was scattered around the country, never to return to Conishead.

In June 1846, Thomas executed a Deed of Trust for the benefit of his creditors and a suit was brought in Chancery in which his wife Frances, on

Plate 61 Wilson Gale Braddyll by George Romney, 1781, one of the paintings dispersed by the auction of 1846 (private collection)

[2] The Braddyll family's copy of the catalogue is particularly touching. Each painting is annotated with the selling price and the name of the new owner, and beside the entry for Reynolds's family portrait, a newspaper cutting was glued to the page:

> *'The Braddyll Family – finely grouped in a landscape whole-length. This very important and beautiful picture, the great gem of the collection was purchased direct from the Braddyll family in 1846, has never been engraved and is in the most perfect state of preservation – exhibited at Manchester'.*

Alongside, in fine copperplate handwriting, a member of the Braddyll family (possibly Thomas's wife) poignantly noted: *'Cut out of some paper… some time ago to shew him how cruelly our Pictures had been undersold'.*

behalf of herself and the other creditors were the Plaintiffs and Trustees of the Deed. His nephew Thomas Henry Sutton Sotheron, his uncle Richard Greaves Townley and cousin William Gale Townley were the defendants. Bankers Petty and Postlethwaite intervened, claiming equitable security in the Braddyll properties for loans made by their firm. They brought a suit against Thomas Braddyll, Thomas Rawsthorne of Lancaster (one of Braddyll's partners in the South and East Hetton Coal Companies), Thomas Henry Sutton Sotheron, Richard Greaves Townley, William Gale Townley, and Thomas's sons Edward Stanley Bagot Richmond Gale Braddyll and Clarence Braddyll and his wife Frances Braddyll, as defendants. The two suits were joined as Braddyll v Sotheron and Petty v Braddyll. Thomas's creditors foreclosed and by Order of the Court of Chancery dated 23 July 1847, all his remaining holdings and estates were put up for sale by public auction.

On 7 August, *The Preston Guardian* announced that the Right Honourable Henry Labouchere, MP, President of the Board of Trade

> *'is the purchaser of the Conishead Priory estate, late the property of the Braddyll family. The right hon. gentleman, we understand, intends making the noble mansion his occasional residence. This change of the property strengthens the Liberal influence in North Lancashire, - the late proprietor having been a staunch conservative, the new owner being a firm liberal and an influential member of the present government'.*[3]

A week later, however, the newspaper was forced to rescind its announcement:

> *'We understand that the report of the purchase of Conishead Priory by Mr Labouchere is not correct. The right honourable gentleman had been viewing the property, and hence the rumour originated'.*[4]

There also arose the problem of the proposed building of Trinity Church at Bardsea, for which Thomas had donated the land and George Webster had drawn plans. In 1843, against an estimated cost of £1,200 the project had gone ahead. Thomas Braddyll had promised to *'endow the chapel with sums'* (the interest of which was to be used for Clergymen and repairs) and offered stone and sand from the Conishead estate to be used in the building of the church. On 20 October 1843, in his absence, his six-year-old grandson, Henry John Richmond Gale Braddyll had the honour of 'officiating' at the laying of the foundation stone, but it was discovered that the site had not been conveyed before building commenced and it fell into the hands of Braddyll's creditors. Mr Thomas Petty of Well House, a member of the committee for the building, purchased it at auction in London. However, Mr Petty died before the church was completed and it was eventually opened by license on Sunday August 13th 1848, after Rev Edmund Petty spent four years overseeing the completion and handsomely endowing it 'at his own

[3] *The Preston Guardian*, Saturday 7 August 1847

[4] *The Preston Guardian*, Saturday 14 August 1847

Plate 62 Elford Hall, Staffordshire (now demolished) home of the Howard family, where Frances Braddyll died in 1848
(author's own collection)

expense'. The church was finally consecrated in 1853. A report in the local news noted that the church carpet near the communion table was a gift of the Misses Braddyll (Thomas's four daughters):

> *'...the border being exquisitely worked by these ladies, who although no longer living in the neighbourhood, have not ceased to feel a warm attachment for, and interest in the place.'*

The hapless Thomas Braddyll was beset by further tragedy when, on 8 January 1848, his wife Frances died from influenza at Elford Hall, near Lichfield in Staffordshire, the home of her cousin the Honourable Mary Howard. A window in the church at Bardsea was later erected in her memory.

In August 1848, still recovering from the loss of his wife and most of his property, Thomas heard the news of a sudden explosion in the West Pit of his former Murton Colliery. Sixteen men, including a twelve-year-old boy were killed and several others seriously injured. Almost one hundred men were working in the mine at the time, and they would have all suffocated but for one miner's presence of mind. He led the survivors safely to a second shaft from where they were rescued. Although mining carried high risks and many accidents occurred before and after, it was a tragic ending to Thomas Braddyll's enterprise.

Towards the end of the year there had still been no buyer for Conishead, so on 17 October 1848 at 2 pm, the Priory and the whole of the Braddyll estates were auctioned in five lots at The Bull in Preston by Messrs Hoggart, Norton and Oakley. The Particulars of Sale described Conishead as:

'a distinguished and important property, situated near Ulverston and Furness Abbey in the Lake District, about twenty miles from Lancaster and surrounded by a most luxuriant park, beautifully undulated and adorned with fine noble Oak, Sycamore and other forest trees. The mansion is of a singularly elegant Gothic structure, designed by Wyatt, the eminent Architect ... The bay of Morecambe forms for a considerable extent the eastern boundary. Chapel Island, belonging to the estate, is an object of great interest ... The Priory possesses accommodation for a family of distinction. The bedrooms are numerous, of fine proportions, airy and lofty ... The rooms on (the ground) floor consist of the north drawing room ... the blue drawing room ... the saloon ... opening to a conservatory; dining room ... breakfast room ... library, gentleman's dressing room, bath room, etc ... The servants' and detached offices are commensurate with the general arrangement ... an ornamental summer house and grotto opening to a lake, at the termination of which is a Swiss fishing cottage and in a secluded part is a hermitage with a painted window of the Annunciation, the remains of a castle and circular tower ... a rookery and icehouse...'

A local man, Myles Kennedy, made an offer of £30,000 but Thomas's debts were in excess of £35,000, and he could not accept. As neither man was prepared to bargain, there was no sale.[5]

On the 19 and 20 October, a second auction took place, dividing the estates into forty-eight lots. The venue for the sale was The Braddyll Arms in Ulverston. A week after the auction, the local newspaper reported on the progress of the sale:

'The principal part of the Conishead Priory Estates we understand is still on the market, not having been disposed of at the sales last week; but we are glad to learn 'The Cottage at Dragley Beck' (part of the estate) was purchased by a gentleman of this town, who has since considerately offered it to John Barrow, Esq., who, in signifying his acceptance of the offer, observed that he was very glad to become the proprietor of the little cottage in which his father (Sir John) was born. We trust therefore, that no apprehension need now be entertained that the spirit of pseudo-improvement will be allowed to alter the original condition of the humble cottage in which the celebrated and venerable Baronet first saw the light.'

By January of the following year, Hoggart, Norton and Oakley were announcing that the

'...beautiful property (Conishead Priory)*...extending over upwards of 1,100 acres was not disposed of at the sale in October last, and that they are now authorised to offer the noble and splendid mansion and grounds at a price infinitely below the cost, either with the whole of the surrounding lands, or any portion a purchaser may require.'*

The situation was desperate. In October 1849, an anonymous reader wrote to the *Ulverston Advertiser* suggesting a possible role for Conishead:

[5] Instead, Kennedy built his own mansion, Stone Cross near Ulverston, which finally amounted to just over £44,872.

'Sir,

It has been thought by the highest authority in Church and State, that a new college is highly necessary in the North of England, to consist of an extensive range of buildings as a collegiate establishment, similar in character and possessed of the same amount of talent in literature, theology etc... and devoted to the same high and holy purposes as the time-honoured Universities of Oxford and Cambridge....

A few months ago the rumour reached here that Conishead Priory was likely to be fixed upon for the above purpose and I hailed with pleasure the gratifying intelligence. Rumour now fixes upon Birkenhead and if that place be chosen we lose what, to this town and neighbourhood, would be of the highest importance. Birkenhead is none can deny ...a fitting place for such an institution; but the Priory is no less so, with its lordly mansion, its luxuriant groves, it's refreshing and healthy situation, its marine and mountain scenery, unrivalled in beauty and extent. ...At Conishead Priory and the adjoining grounds, Nature has been bountiful. She has done that for the scenery, which even the most consummate art can only imitate, but never rival.

I trust those whom it most concerns will not let such an opportunity pass, but use their exertions in the proper quarter, so that the Priory may be purchased, with such portion of the adjoining ground as may be required for the college; and afterwards dispose of the remainder in suitable lots for gentlemen's villas. Could a railway communication be obtained, there is no fear of the result.'

It would be some years before a 'railway communication' was obtained and another century before Conishead became a place of study.

On 23 August 1850, the house and estate were put up for auction at the Auction Mart in London, once again without success.

Meanwhile, in an effort to raise some cash, Messrs Hoggart, Norton and Oakley arranged for the contents of Conishead to be sold separately on site. Between 16 and 28 September 1850, with Mr Norton presiding as auctioneer, the Braddyll's *'costly and magnificent furniture manufactured by Gillow'* including beds, dining tables, chairs, writing tables, couches, ottomans and japanned cabinets, were auctioned. Included in the sale were the Wilton, Axminster and Brussels carpets, chandeliers, Parisian clocks, alabaster vases and figures, Indian screen, *'and other numerous effects'*. The Bill of Sale for the furniture reveals the extravagant interior of Conishead. Fifty bedrooms had been fitted with beds described as 'four-post', 'tent' and 'Arabian', with velvet, Indian chintz and satin furnishings. Mention is made of the *'ancient furniture of the old oak bedchamber*[6] *... and a magnificent cabinet, richly carved representing the Four Seasons...toilet tables, marble top wash-hand stands and china fittings. '*

Also on sale were the suits of armour, which once stood in the hall and corridors, as well as *'warlike implements, a choice collection of elegant Sevres, Dresden, old Chelsea and*

[6] The Richard III oak bedstead sold for £105.

enamelled china ...richly cut glass, a finely executed marble figure of Purity, excellent table and bed linen, consisting of about 90 damask table cloths, etc...'

An auction of the Braddyll's library of 4,000 books took place. The final lot consisted of the entire liquor collection of the Braddyll's cellar.

The sale attracted a huge number of people, some intending to purchase and others merely attending out of curiosity[7]. On 19 September 1850, the local *Ulverston Advertiser* described the event:

'As might have been anticipated the sales of furniture at the Priory have occasioned no small amount of excitement in this usually quiet locality. Coaches have run daily from Ulverston to the busy scene of the auction and the roads have glittered continually with the equipages of those who have been induced to attend ... the fine weather, with the value of the articles to be disposed of have drawn together daily an assemblage surpassing in numbers and respectability any concourse of the kind assembled on a similar occasion in the neighbourhood ... Conishead Priory had recently been offered for sale; but ... it has not yet been disposed of ... The hall ... recalls forcibly to the mind of the visitor the festive board, the noisy and exuberant revelry, the hunting horn, the broadsword and the battle-axe of the ancient English Baron ... The cloisters ... here it were an easy task to ... fancy to cause the beautiful Gothic arches to echo softly to the tread of Monks and to see in the dim and mellow light ... the gliding figures ... with tongues hushed in a lasting silence, save when they mingled in the holy chant...'

The sale of the house contents realised £8,500. The romantic descriptions of Conishead in the local newspaper, however, still failed to attract buyers, and the Bardsea Estate, Bardsea Hall, and 137 acres adjoining the Conishead Priory Deer Park were the only lots sold[8].

After enjoying only ten years residency in their 'Paradise of Furness', a bankrupt Thomas Braddyll, his youngest son Clarence and his three unmarried daughters, Frances, Margaret and Sarah left Conishead Priory for good. The distress the family experienced can only be imagined. Forced to leave behind their home for strangers to pick over, it was a tragic, if predictable close to a chapter in Conishead's history.

The Braddylls moved first to Surrey, before finally making their home at Woodcote House in the rustic and secluded village of Lillington on the outskirts of Leamington Spa in Warwickshire. Here the family retained two female servants and a lady's maid, a far cry from the days when the family had employed an army of servants at Conishead.

[7] A Mr Townley (probably Thomas Braddyll's uncle or cousin) purchased 66 lots at the house content sales, and it is possible that he was buying back the most important pieces of the Braddylls' collection (including the 'Epistle of St Augustine' manuscript and a Waterloo medal) in order to return them to the family.

[8] Thomas Braddyll's cousin, William Gale of Lightburn House, Ulverston, purchased the lots for £27,171. With his purchase of Bardsea Hall, William Gale brought the house back under the Wilson/Gale's family's ownership and when he died in 1866, he and his wife Cecilia Isabella Losh were able to pass Bardsea Hall to their son Henry Richmond Houghton Gale.

In July 1862, Thomas Richmond Gale Braddyll died and was buried in the church of St Mary Magdalene, Lillington. During his life, he had been widely known as a 'liberal and kindly man' and *Soulby's Ulverston Advertiser* was generous in its remembrance of him:

> *'Our readers will perceive, in our obituary of today, the demise of T R G Braddyll, Esq., of Leamington, and late of Conishead Priory, near this town. Colonel Braddyll was the representative of one of the most ancient families in the North of England, and which through marriages, was connected with most of the best families in this and neighbouring counties. ... The Braddyll family have long been known in this neighbourhood for their generous hospitality and almost unlimited benevolence. Colonel Braddyll expired in the bosom of his family, at Woodcote House, Leamington on the morning of Thursday last in his 85th year and was interred at Leamington yesterday.*
>
> *We believe that Colonel Braddyll was the last survivor of all who sat to Sir Joshua Reynolds for a portrait.*
>
> *We may state here that it was the intention of many of the tradesmen of Ulverston to have shown their respect for the memory of the deceased by partially closing their shops on the day of the internment, but they were unable to do so for want of information respecting the date of the funeral, which only arrived in Ulverston this morning. We understand, however that the family vault, in the Parish Church, will be placed in mourning.*
>
> *Since writing the above, a letter has been received from E R G Braddyll, Esq., thanking the tradesmen of Ulverston on behalf of himself and the family for the compliment they had intended paying to the memory of the deceased.'*

Thomas's children erected a memorial stone above the Braddyll family vault in St Mary's Church, Ulverston, and the people of Ulverston donated funds for a stained glass window. Situated in the south east end of the church, it depicts the conversion and preaching of St Paul, with a brass plate beneath inscribed: *'This window was erected AD 1866 by the townsmen of Ulverston to the memory of the Braddylls of Conishead Priory'*.

Thomas's eldest son, Edward Stanley Bagot Richmond Gale Braddyll, who would have inherited Conishead on the death of his father, was the only one of Thomas's children to marry. Once described as a gentleman of 'brilliant talents', Edward Braddyll, Captain of the Furness Troop in the Lancashire Corps of the Yeoman Cavalry, and a Deputy Lieutenant for the County of Lancaster, had been heavily involved in politics. It was an activity, which almost cost him his life. In the General Election of 1832, Edward stood with Sir Hedworth Williamson 7th Baronet and Hedworth Lambton as a Tory candidate for the Northern Division of Durham. During an election speech, open insults were exchanged between the men and Russell Bowlby, a South Shields candidate, who described Edward Braddyll as

> *'a chicken newly hatched, which the pious clucking hen, Mother Church, was invited to shelter under her dingy wing'.*

Edward Braddyll charged Williamson with 'wilful misinterpretation' after Williamson referred to him as a *'nominee of the Marquis of Londonderry'*. Heated correspondence ensued and Williamson and Bowlby were challenged to a duel by Braddyll, who was acknowledged at the time as one of Britain's deadliest shots with a pistol. The two men accepted the challenge and Edward Braddyll found himself with separate duels on his hands, both to be fought on the same day. An account of the event was recorded a year later by John Sykes in the *Historical Register of Remarkable Events*:

'1832 (Sept. 27) – About seven o'clock in the morning, a duel took place in Offerton Lane, near Herrington, Durham between Mr Russell Bowlby, a candidate for South Shields, and Mr Braddyll, a candidate for the Northern Division of the county of Durham, in consequence of expressions used by the former in a speech at South Shields, and which had been commented on by Mr Braddyll in a speech at the same place. Mr Braddyll was attended by G P Irvine, Esq., and his antagonist by Captain Bowlby. Mr Braddyll, after receiving Mr Bowlby's fire, discharged his pistol in the air. Mr Bowlby then stepped forward and declared his regret that he should have uttered expressions painful to the feelings of Mr Braddyll, and the latter gentleman, in consequence of this acknowledgement, declared his sorrow at having commented in the tone he did, on those offensive expressions. The parties then left the ground.

The same day, soon after twelve o'clock, another hostile meeting took place at the sign of the Hare and Hounds, on the Sedgefield road, between Sir Hedworth Williamson, bart, and Mr Braddyll, rival candidates for the Northern Division of the county of Durham. This duel arose out of expressions purporting to have been used in the speeches of the parties against each other. Sir Hedworth Williamson was attended by John Fawcett, Esq., and Mr Braddyll by William John Bankes, Esq., MP. The parties each fired twice, when Sir Hedworth, sanctioned by his second, agreed to the following: - "I am sorry to have used a term which has been offensive to Mr Braddyll's feelings, and which has been received in a sense in which I never intended it." The parties then shook hands, and left the field.'

Having survived the absurd and perilous custom of duelling, Edward went on to marry Sophia Hulton[9] in 1836 and raise a family.

Thomas's youngest son Clarence remained in Lillington with his spinster sisters until his death in 1865. Frances Braddyll died in 1876, and her sisters Margaret and Sarah

[9] Sophia was the daughter of William Hulton, High Sheriff of Lancashire and Chairman of the Committee of Lancashire and Cheshire Magistrates, and his cousin Maria (nee Randle Ford) of Hulton Park, near Manchester. It was through this work, dealing with the unrest sweeping the new industrial towns, that William Hulton became involved with the Peterloo riots in 1819. It was to haunt him for the rest of his life. He dealt severely with the working class, particularly when he arrested and had executed three men and a twelve-year-old boy, accused of arson in a textile mill. He also had a worker transported to Australia for seven years after he was found guilty of 'administering unlawful oaths'. Hulton read the riot act on St Peter's Field in 1819, and sent in the Manchester and Salford Yeomanry to make arrests. During the event, eleven people were killed and over four hundred injured, in what became known as the 'Peterloo Massacre'. Afterwards, William found himself severely criticised for his handling of the situation and for covering up the true number of people who lost their lives. As a result, he chose not to accept nomination for a Tory seat in the House of Commons, fearing a campaign of abuse.

lived for another nineteen years at Woodcote House, both dying within months of each other in 1895, at the great ages of eighty-seven and eighty-four.

It was the end of a momentous era in Conishead Priory's history. An epitaph to the Braddyll family by Francis Evans in his history of Furness and Furness Abbey read:

> *'The Braddylls of the present day are not only revered by the inhabitants of the neighbourhood on accounts of their ancient origin and great respectability, but much loved on account of their generosity, charity and kindness.'*

It was an epitaph to be proud of.

Eight

'THAT CHARMING PLACE'

1850 – 1878

When the Braddyll family departed Conishead Priory they left behind their magnificent Gothic home to an uncertain future. The household staff was dispersed except for the widowed housekeeper Mary Beck and her son James, who worked as an agricultural labourer on the estate. Their presence ensured that the house, and what was left of its contents, remained secure. The head agricultural labourer, Robert Stalker and his family, stayed on at the Priory Lodge to maintain the grounds and a local man, John Duke, took care of the livestock[1].

In June 1851, an Order was made transferring ownership of Conishead Priory to Ulverston bankers George Shaw Petty and William Postlethwaite, mortgagees of the real estates of Thomas Braddyll, to whom he owed a considerable amount of money. It took a year to find a buyer. In September 1852, *Soulby's Ulverston Advertiser* announced:

> *'Messrs. Petty and Postlethwaite have sold this delightful residence, with its picturesque and extensive grounds to H W Askew Esq., of Minard Castle, Argyleshire, who intends, we are informed, removing thither shortly. We may now congratulate our townsmen on the prospect of having so distinguished a family residing in our neighbourhood'.*

Henry William Askew had purchased Conishead, 800 acres of land and the nearby farms of Gascow and Sandhall for £56,000.

Born in Kent in 1808, Henry Askew was a Magistrate and Justice of the Peace for Cumberland, Lancashire and Argyll. The son of Rev Henry Askew of Greystoke, near Penrith and his wife Anne, he had graduated from Emanuel College, Cambridge with a

[1] In July 1851, Duke was mentioned in the local newspaper, the *Soulby's Ulverston Advertiser*, when he was involved in an astonishing incident at Conishead:

> *'On Monday John Duke, the hind at Conishead Priory, was attacked by an ox in a most savage and desperate manner, and in all probability would have been gored to death had not a young horse come to his rescue. The generous animal hearing the cries of the man fell gallantly to work with his teeth, biting the ox wherever he could get a hold. The fury of the ox being thus diverted from Duke, who lay on the ground, gave him time to escape. We need scarcely add that the young horse received no injury, being too fleet for the savage beast.'*

Plate 63 The clock tower commissioned by Henry William Askew in 1853
(photograph by the author)

Bachelor of Arts degree in 1832.[2] He married Lucy Heber Percy, the second daughter of the Rt. Rev Hon. Hugh Percy, Bishop of Carlisle, and they had five children: Charlotte Elizabeth, born in 1836; Emily Mary in 1837, Frances Louisa[3] in 1845, Henry Hugh[4] in 1847 and Edmund Adam[5] in 1849.

The Askews owned Minard Castle in Argyll, Scotland, Glenridding House at Ullswater and Middleton Hall, but on the acquisition of Conishead these houses were sold. Middleton Hall, a late fourteenth century manor house, near Kirby Lonsdale, was practically dismantled and Henry Askew transferred the ancient oak panelling from the

[2] Henry William Askew was mentioned, along with a fellow student, in a letter of the previous year from Charles Darwin to Professor John Henslow (a friend of Darwin who had taught him botany at Christ's College, Cambridge and encouraged the future famous scientist to study geology) *'...You must be very busy; for if Messrs Askew and Darnell have not got some fresh brains in the vacation, they will give you some trouble ...'* (Letter from Charles Darwin to Prof John Henslow, 1831 -The Darwin Correspondence Project)

[3] The three daughters of Henry William Askew never married.

[4] After a troubled adolescence spent in the navy, Henry Hugh Askew joined the 6th Dragoon Guards and went on to raise a family in Berkshire.

[5] Edmund Adam Askew followed his paternal grandfather's example and took the cloth. After gaining an MA at Trinity College, Cambridge, he was made a Deacon in 1873 and following several posts, he became rector of Greystoke, where his grandfather had served. He and his wife Mary Penelope had six daughters and two sons, and they remained at Greystoke until his death in 1901.

Plate 64 The blue drawing room at Conishead Priory, c. 1860 (Ulverston Heritage Centre)

Plate 65 The dining room at Conishead Priory, c. 1860 (Ulverston Heritage Centre)

guest hall to Conishead for additional decoration in the oak bedroom and for fireplaces and ceilings throughout the house.[6]

When he moved into Conishead Priory, one of Henry Askew's first undertakings was to commission additional work to the west side of the house. A large stable block and a garden cottage were erected, together with a clock tower and bells.[7]

Two photographs taken between 1850 and 1860, during the time of the Askews, show how the blue drawing room and the dining room were furnished. Photographed from the position of the bay window, the walls of the blue drawing room are shown covered from ceiling to dado rail with large tapestries. As Charles Jopling makes no mention of the tapestries during the Braddylls' residence, it seems likely they were brought to the house by the Askews who nonetheless acquired a number of furnishings which remained unsold after the sale of the house contents.[8]

The photograph of the dining room shows the dark oak linen-fold panelling and black marble mantelpiece from the time of the Braddylls. The oil paintings on display are not recognisably those described by Jopling in 1842. The portrait of Queen Elizabeth I by Zucchero, which the Braddylls placed above the mantelpiece, is no longer there, and instead, a full-length portrait of a gentleman, possibly an Askew ancestor, has taken its place.

At Conishead, the Askew family employed a housekeeper, seven female servants, a cook, a footman, a governess, a coachman, a groom, three gardeners, and a game-keeper, William Atkinson who lived in the North Lodge (formerly known as the Dog Kennel House). Agnes Stalker, the widow of the Braddylls' former agricultural labourer remained at Conishead, where she continued to live at the Priory Lodge and was employed as gatekeeper for the estate.[9]

In keeping with the tradition begun by the Braddylls, the house and grounds of Conishead were opened for tourists on Wednesdays and Fridays, and Henry Askew and his wife became known in the area for their generosity. *Soulby's Ulverston Advertiser* frequently referred to their charitable acts:

'H W Askew Esq., of the Priory, has we understand, forwarded to the Rev S Robertson, curate of St Mary's, the sum of £10 to be distributed in coals and blankets among the deserving poor

[6] *Transactions of the Cumberland and Westmorland Antiquarian and Archaeological Society* (1911)

[7] A sandstone shield carved with the date 1853 and the arms of the Askew and Percy families, decorate the clock tower.

[8] Two display cabinets in the photograph look similar to the furniture designed for Thomas Braddyll by Gillow and Co. A gilt and upholstered chaise lounge and armchair stand near the fireplace, close to an octagonal table and chairs and amongst a collection of boxes, candlesticks and vases, a small bust stands beneath a glass dome. It is possible that this is the bust of Jane Braddyll by Nollekens mentioned by Jopling in 1842, which was once in the morning room.

[9] On the day of the 1861 census, Henry Askew and his wife and family, with the exception of their third daughter Frances Louisa, were absent from Conishead. They were staying at their rented London residence, 8 Southwick Crescent, a wealthy area near Hyde Park with their housekeeper, two maids, cook and footman, leaving eighteen-year-old Frances at Conishead, in the company of her private governess Isabella Runciman and the five female servants.

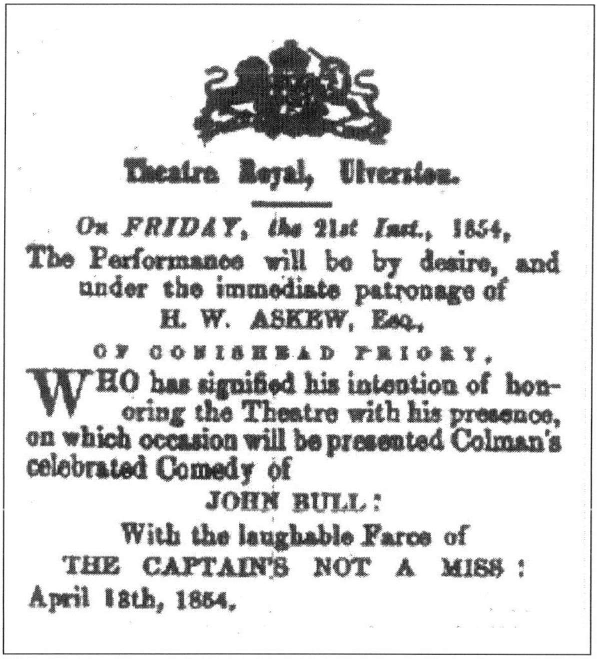

Theatre Royal, Ulverston.

On FRIDAY, the 21st Inst., 1854,
The Performance will be by desire, and under the immediate patronage of
H. W. ASKEW, Esq.,
OF CONISHEAD PRIORY,
WHO has signified his intention of honoring the Theatre with his presence, on which occasion will be presented Colman's celebrated Comedy of
JOHN BULL:
With the laughable Farce of
THE CAPTAIN'S NOT A MISS:
April 18th, 1854.

Plate 66 Detail from a Theatre advertisement, 1854 in Soulby's Ulverston Advertiser for a play patronized by Henry William Askew

(author's own collection)

of Ulverston. Mrs Askew has also forwarded to the rev. gentleman, a quantity of clothing for some poor old people, that they may not have the trouble of walking to the Priory to receive these very seasonable gifts'.

The family also donated books to the National School in Ulverston and bequeathed money to help build the Infant Day and Town Bank Sunday School through yearly subscriptions. When the Sunday School was completed in 1854, Henry and Lucy's eldest son, seven-year-old Henry Hugh Askew laid the foundation stone, a duty which *'he had discharged in a most admirable manner.'* In his speech, Henry William Askew thanked the committee of the school

'for their kind consideration in suggesting that my little boy should officiate at this interesting ceremony, and I beg to assure you that it has been the very greatest satisfaction to me that the first public act of this little fellow should be the laying the foundation-stone of an Institution which is I trust, under Providence, destined to confer a great and lasting benefit upon the town of Ulverston.'

During the Crimean War of 1854 and 1855, Askew regularly contributed subscriptions to Ulverston's Patriotic Fund for the soldiers and their families and in January 1855, a Patriotic Banquet was held in the dining room at Conishead in aid of the Crimea Patriotic Fund.[10]

[10] The large number of guests included the Rev Richard Gwillym and his wife of Ulverston, and other patrons, who joined Henry Askew, his wife and daughters, beneath a banner inscribed 'Inkermann', 'Alma' and 'Balaclava'.

Plate 67 The earliest known photograph of Conishead Priory, c. 1855
(Ulverston Heritage Centre)

Askew's patronage of the local Theatre Royal in Ulverston was also well recounted, and the family's presence usually guaranteed a full house. By 1854, the number of people attending the theatre had declined. *Soulby's Ulverston Advertiser* reported

> *'attendances* (were) *far from numerous, but the performances were in every way respectable. ...Tomorrow evening the performances will be by desire and under the patronage of H W Askew Esq., of Conishead Priory, when a "bumper" house is expected.'*

One evening at the Theatre Royal a near fatal accident occurred during an acrobatic performance. The Askew family were seated on the front row when the acrobat missed his hold and went flying over the orchestra pit and collided with Henry William Askew. The impact was so great that Henry was rendered unconscious. Thomas Salmon, the clarinet player in the orchestra (and Ulverston's Town Crier) immediately leapt to Askew's aid and

> *'with untiring effort, managed to restore* (Henry) *to consciousness again without any permanent injury'.*

No mention however was made as to the fate of the unfortunate acrobat.

The Askews were obviously respected and their involvement in the life of Ulverston added to their popularity. During the Whitsuntide holiday of May 1858, a group of visitors, described as 'hardy sons of toil', enjoyed their holiday travelling by cheap rail from Preston for a day out in Ulverston. They visited The Hoad (Sir John Barrow's Monument) and then:

pursued their way to Conishead Priory, the grounds of which ... were kindly thrown open to them by Mr Askew, and which favour they seemed greatly to enjoy.

Askew also indulged the children of Ulverston's Sunday school, day school and workhouse with annual day trips, and in 1857, paid for them to spend the day at Furness Abbey. In August 1861, he arranged for the workhouse children to spend a day in Grange over Sands.

As well as being Patron of the Ulverston Cricket Club, Patron of the Infants' School in Church Walk, Ulverston, and on the Committee of the 'North Lonsdale Agricultural Society', [11] Henry was a local Magistrate. A common problem for large estates was poaching and Conishead Priory was no exception. In his role as Magistrate, Henry often dealt with the offenders. In 1859, seven men were summoned to answer a charge of trespassing in the grounds of Conishead Priory in search of mushrooms. *Soulby's Ulverston Advertiser* described how

'Mr Askew, who withdrew from the bench during the hearing, said he did not wish to inflict any penalty but merely wished to prevent a recurrence of the trespasses, and if they would pay the costs he would withdraw the informations, which was agreed to...'

This leniency was symptomatic of Askew's charitable nature. He was an advocate for the abolition of capital punishment and in April 1858, chaired a lecture given by the County Court Judge at the Victoria Concert Hall in Ulverston on the subject.

There were other incidents which Henry brought to the attention of the Magistrates. One evening he risked serious injury returning home to Conishead when his carriage was almost upturned by a pile of stones in the road. They had been left in his path following excavation work by a local highway surveyor who had left no lights or signs in place to warn oncoming traffic. Not wishing to press a conviction on the man, Henry stated that he merely wanted to bring the dangers to the attention of the public:

'he hoped it would be a warning for the future, to all parties similarly circumstanced not to endanger the lives of the public for want of a stricter attention to their duties...'

He also showed concern over the increasing practice of turning horses and donkeys out on to the lanes and highways in the neighbourhood of Ulverston at night, including his own pastures at Conishead. He thought the surveyors

'ought to have notice of such proceedings, and in neglect of their impounding all such animals, informed that they were liable to be convicted. The act of turning animals into the highways

[11] Askew's legendary *'thoroughbred, short-horned bull'*, 'Sir Charles', was shown at the Society's shows and in 1856 won first prize, but a year later was reported to be *'too low in condition for either the red or blue ribbon'*. In 1859, along with other wealthy subscribers including the Duke of Cavendish of Holker Hall and William Gale of Bardsea Hall, Henry donated £5 towards a Challenge Cup for the North Lonsdale Agricultural Society. Each year at the Ulverston Horticultural Show, he showed and won first prize for his flowers, fruit and vegetables grown in the Hothouses and Vineries in the Conishead Kitchen Garden.

at night was not only illegal, but (especially in the case of donkeys) dangerous'.

During his time at Conishead, Henry sold and rented out parts of the Conishead estate. He also sold cattle and timber from the estate which was regularly offered for public auction, particularly for the attention of the local ship builders, millwrights and railway contractors.

In 1863, the people of Ulverston must have been saddened to learn that after a residency of only eleven years, the Askews had decided to move from the area. To his friend John Sawrey of Broughton in Furness, Henry complained of a number of ailments which had been afflicting him, including asthma and gout.[12] Of the Lake District air he wrote: *'this heavy, damp atmosphere kills me.'* Once when his attendance was required at a local Magistrates meeting, he had been forced to submit his apologies:

'I cannot get my boot on yet. ...This gout is a troublesome customer – and as I rarely take wine or spirits or eat rich dishes it is doubly vexatious...'

A few days later he was still *'a prisoner from gout'* and had

'contrived to catch cold in my eye, when wandering in the Hothouses and it is swelled up like an incipient haystack! I should like to show you the Vineries ...before I go south ...'[13]

Perhaps Henry's ill-health made him mindful that in the event of his death, his family would be left with a large estate to manage. What is evident however is that Askew was now anxious to move south to a place more congenial for his health.

In May 1865, Askew's friend John Sawrey sent a copy of the Bill of Sale[14] of Conishead Priory to Joseph Feilden of Whitton Park in Blackburn. Evidently, Feilden was not interested although in his reply to Sawrey he added:

'Nothing would please me more than to possess that charming place...'

The Bill of Sale described Conishead Priory and gardens with the stables, coach houses, and new clock tower, as well as a private gas works. Contradicting Askew's conviction that the area was unhealthy, it boasted that the house and grounds

'enjoy(s) the highest salubrity of climate and has facility of immediate railway communication with every part of the country. It is Freehold of inheritance and Tithe-free and confident belief exists that rich veins of iron ore run through its strata.'

The solicitors commissioned to sell Conishead were Francis Yarker and Alan Backhouse Salmon of Ulverston, Frederic Broadbent of Bolton le Moor, Lancashire, and Thomas Johnston of Gray's Inn, London.

12 Letter from Henry W Askew to John Sawrey – undated c. 1860s (BD/Broughton/19/30/4) Cumbria Record Office, Barrow

13 Letter from Henry W Askew to John Sawrey (BDTB/24/1/7) Cumbria Record Office, Barrow

14 Bill of Sale for Conishead Priory – 1 May 1865 (BDKF/145/22) Cumbria Record Office, Barrow

Harwood del[t]. Lizars sc.

CONISHEAD PRIORY.

Published by D. Atkinson, Ulverston.

THIS pre-eminently distinguished RESIDENTIAL PROPERTY, delightfully situate on the Western shore of MORECAMBE BAY, within two miles of Ulverston—comprising splendid modern-built Mansion in the early English and Baronial styles of Architecture, erected from designs by the late eminent Architects, P. F. WYATT and GEORGE WEBSTER, Esquires, with grand entrance hall, prospect towers, and stately corridor; magnificent suite of commodious entertaining rooms, decorated in the sumptuous taste of the Elizabethian era; noble staircase, with gorgeous stained glass windows; music gallery, boudoir, and numerous state and other bed-rooms, with dressing-rooms, baths, &c.; range of kitchens, pantries, store-rooms, and all requisite inferior domestic offices; court-yard with stables, coach-houses, clock tower, and all suitable out-offices; private gas-works; extensive lawns, avenues, and terraces with parterres and fountains; flower gardens, with conservatories; kitchen gardens, with vineries, peach-houses, &c., in full bearing; arboretum, with alcove, grotto, and aquarium; beautifully undulating park, of rich fertile soil, studded with timber trees of every variety and of all ages, of healthy and luxuriant growth; fine quadrangle of farm buildings and bailiff's residence; keepers' lodges; fish ponds; hermitage; and the romantic CHAPEL ISLAND, with remains of antique oratory: also several MOST DESIRABLE FARMS, of yearly increasing value, containing in the whole eight hundred acres and upwards of arable, meadow, pasture, and wood land, of quality equal to that of the most reputed feeding lands in England, and valued at above £1,700 per year (the timber being valued at nearly £15,000),

IS NOW ON SALE BY PRIVATE TREATY,

and if not disposed of by the middle of next month, will be offered to public competition, in London.

THE DOMAIN presents an illimitable number of building sites of the most picturesque description, and possesses an abundance of building materials: enjoys the highest salubrity of climate, and has facility of immediate railway communication with every part of the country. It is Freehold of inheritance and Tithe-free, and confident belief exists that rich veins of iron ore run through its strata.

For terms and further particulars, and cards to view, apply to THOMAS JOHNSTON, Esquire, Solicitor, 5, Raymond Buildings, Gray's Inn, London; FREDERIC BROADBENT, Esquire, Solicitor, Bolton-le-Moors; FRANCIS YARKER, Esquire, Solicitor, Ulverstone: or MR. JOHN BURTON, Auctioneer and Accountant, 38, Avenham Lane, Preston.

CONISHEAD PRIORY, ULVERSTON, May 1st, 1865.

Plate 68 A Bill of Sale for Conishead Priory, 1865

(Cumbria Record Office, Barrow - courtesy of Mrs S Ritson)

Yarker and Salmon notified Broadbent and Johnston of Askew's terms. Not all the land was to be included in the sale, as some had been 'ear-marked' by a local ironworker, Henry William Schneider. There was also the problem of whether Chapel Island would be sold with the priory. Whatever the final agreement, Yarker and Salmon stressed that Henry Askew was not inclined to negotiate. The house, outbuildings and fixtures, including all the fire grates except the dining room grate and one bedroom grate were valued at £12,000.

In November 1865, Yarker and Salmon received a letter from Broadbent, on behalf of a prospective buyer:

'...With reference to your letter I should be glad to know whether you have any offer to make relative to the house and garden either with or without a portion of the land. If you could come to some agreement upon the subject it might facilitate the preliminaries of our scheme...'[15]

A letter sent between solicitors in December 1865 shows little progress had been made:

'...I am sorry to say I think your letter is quite at variance with what I expected from your Mr Salmon's promise when he left me on Tuesday. As I understood, you wish to make an offer in two or three distinct forms instead of which you write saying in effect that you adhere to your original proposal to purchase a "picked" part of the estate...

You must therefore excuse my saying that if you have no offer to make the matter had better be at an end ...'[16]

Three months later negotiations were still continuing, with Henry Schneider now party to the issue.

In February 1866, Yarker and Salmon received a letter from Thomas Johnston in London:

'Dear Sirs

Conishead Priory

I have seen Mr Askew today and learn from him the negotiations, which had passed with you relative to a franchise of part of this estate.

Mr Askew is at this moment open to an offer for this, or the whole of the estate and if your client wishes to buy this at the only favourable opportunity he may have.

If you send me an offer at once for the part previously proposed for and pointed out by Messrs Cass and Broadbent, or for the whole, containing the highest price your client will give, I will give you a decisive answer.

[15] Cumbria Record Office, Barrow (BDKF/145/34/5)

[16] Ibid

Mr Askew has another proposal, but I have advised him to give your client the opportunity before communicating with the other party'.[17]

In the meantime Henry Askew wrote to Alan Backhouse Salmon:

'...I send a plan of the Priory estate and should be obliged if you will mark in ink the line proposed by Mr Schneider. I know the rivulet and stream are fixed upon for the source, to near the top of the fishpond – but I don't know the exact line, nor do I know the line through Gasgow or where it meets the lane by the Deer Park.

Mr Johnstone (sic) had an offer yesterday for the house and some land – but much less than Mr Schneider requires. I expect to hear tomorrow morning in reference to Sir H O Houghton or possibly tonight, but it depends whether he is in London. He offered £75,000 once for the whole and his agent has since written to me that had I asked £80,000 at Lancaster he would have bought it ...'[18]

It may have been the last line in the final paragraph in the Bill of Sale, concerning the rich veins of iron ore, which attracted the Barrow in Furness entrepreneur Henry William Schneider. In September 1867, Askew agreed to lease Conishead to Schneider and his wife for a year and a half, furnished, at £800 per annum. The Article of Agreement gave the Schneiders the rental of Conishead Priory, including the furniture, fixtures and fittings, together with the vineries, conservatories, pleasure grounds, gardens and orchards, fishponds, stables, coach houses, barns and other outbuildings, gas works and conveniences, and the fishery on Conishead sands. Schneider, his stewards and servants were also given the right of sporting, either by hunting, coursing, fishing or fowling on the Conishead, Sandhall and Gasgow estates, which also belonged to Henry Askew. During his tenure at Conishead, Schneider agreed to perform all parochial and other offices, which came as a result of residing in the house. He also had to maintain the premises in tenantable repair and condition excepting the main walls, roofs and main timbers, and keep the glass, windows, bells, locks, fastenings, fixtures and household furniture in good repair. The agreement further stipulated that at all times he must keep the vineries, hothouses, conservatories, gardens and grounds in proper and ornamental order and cultivated, manured and managed according to approved methods of gardening and keep the walks and roads in good order and condition. The vines, fruit trees, bushes, plants and shrubs were to be carefully preserved, pruned and managed, and not be cut down or removed – *'except such as shall be dead or decayed'*[19]. With this agreement signed and sealed, Conishead Priory welcomed its new tenant and the Askews decamped south.

[17] Cumbria Record Office, Barrow (BDKF/145/34)
[18] Cumbria Record Office, Barrow (BDKF/145/34/3)
[19] Cumbria Record Office, Barrow (BPR2/M/10)

A young Schneider had arrived in Barrow in Furness in 1839 to speculate in the iron industry and begin exploring for iron deposits at Whiterigg iron mine near Dalton[20]. During the early half of the eighteenth century, Whiterigg had been central to the rise of the iron ore industry in the area, and an ancient road across Furness via Conishead (which archaeological evidence has suggested may have been constructed by the canons of Conishead) was used to transport large quantities of the iron ore for shipment. This road through Conishead Bank gradually became stained with the deep red haematite ore and became known locally as Red Lane. By the time Thomas Braddyll began re-building Conishead, the road had been abandoned and was overgrown. Cobbles from part of the old lane were taken up and used for building walls in the grounds of the new Conishead Priory.

Schneider rented Conishead Priory from Askew until 1870, when he moved into a new home, Belsfield, overlooking Bowness Bay. By 1871, with the house empty again, the Askews returned temporarily to Conishead, while they continued the search for an alternative home where Henry Askew might *'buy additional land for shooting – heaven – that is the thing I want'*.

When he did find his ideal property, it was Burwood Park, an eighteenth century mansion house in Walton on Thames, Surrey. Eager now to sell Conishead for a good price, he looked on Henry Schneider as a prospective buyer. However, letters sent to and via his solicitors reveal Askew's growing exasperation and irritation over the matter. His daughters' illness did not help matters.

'...Mr Schneider did not come yesterday, being apprehensive of the chicken pox, which two of my daughters have had and one recovering from. Mr Schneider was not singular in his apprehension, for Lord and Lady Amherst who were to have arrived on Thursday have this morning declined coming with their daughter from the same cause.'[21]

Henry Schneider wrote to his solicitor -

'...I think the best plans now will be to let any questions of my buying the Priory go to sleep for the present – after thinking well over the matter ...the house is the great drawback on account of its size and ...the estate ought only to be bought at a trifle over the value of the land. ...'

He went on to admit that his offer was *'so much below Mr Askew's'* and he did not think *'it looked too wise to give him his asking price.'* Schneider thought that continuing negotiations

[20] Schneider took over the Whiterigg mine and other ore deposits and, in1850, discovered a large wealth of iron in the area. He went on to construct blast furnaces at Barrow in Furness and by 1876, they formed the largest steelworks in the world. Schneider became a foremost industrialist of the late Victorian age and, with Sir James Ramsden, the first Lord Mayor of Barrow in Furness, founded the Barrow Haematite Iron and Steel Company. Schneider became Chairman of the Barrow Steel Works; he was a shareholder in the Furness Railway, was elected the third Mayor of Barrow from 1875 to 1878 and a street in Barrow was named after him.

[21] Cumbria Record Office, Barrow

Plate 69 William Gradwell
(author's own collection)

Plate 70 William Park
(author's own collection)

'would probably only make him (Askew) *angry. The best way therefore will be to let the whole matter drop for the present.'...*[22]

At last in 1874, for an overall sum of £77,500, Henry Askew sold part of the Conishead estate to two buyers, William Park, a builder from Barrow in Furness and John Poole of Woodburne and Poole Solicitors in Ulverston.

In a letter to his friend Sawrey, Henry Askew wrote that John Poole intended to rent out land on the estate with the right to kill rabbits:

'...he will also have the house (unfurnished) from the 15th October – paying £500 on the 1st October for the lot, which will enable me to discharge the Gardener etc here. I understand that he also wishes to cut down trees here – these for building sites and views – to which I have consented provided he pays down £20,000 of the purchase money first – to secure me.

Between ourselves, I believe he is a damned scoundrel! For he has lied as fast as a decent horse can gallop and I have in consequence declined holding any communication with him'.[23]

[22] Ibid
[23] Cumbria Record Office, Barrow

John Poole went on to sell a large part of the Conishead estate for £19,546 to one of Barrow's major builders, William Gradwell, who owned the Brickworks near Sandhall. The land was to be used for quarrying to source limestone for the North Lonsdale Iron Works. Poole gave Gradwell permission to build a single-track railway on which a locomotive would circulate daily hauling quarry materials from the quarry towards Bardsea, across the public highway to other parts of the estate. This development was met with public outcry. Conishead Priory's neighbour, Henry Richmond Houghton Gale of Bardsea Hall registered an objection, arguing that the direct road to Bardsea Hall crossed the Conishead estate and was a public highway. He was successful and permission to build the railway was refused. The quarry gradually fell into decline, forcing Gradwell to sell his interest in it. Conishead Priory was left empty and neglected for the next three years.

Henry Askew finally managed to unburden himself of Conishead Priory in 1878, when the house and 150 acres of land was sold for £77,500 to a firm of Edinburgh and Dundee speculators. It had been on the market for twelve years. After three hundred years as a family home, a very different chapter in the history of Conishead Priory was about to begin.

Nine

'THE RESTFUL RIVIERA OF THE NORTH WEST'

1878 – 1929

Towards the end of the nineteenth century the expense of maintaining an extensive property on the scale of Conishead Priory was becoming prohibitive for any family, however wealthy. Even the successful Barrow businessman, Henry Schneider, withdrew his interest following a temporary residence there. For several years the priory's future remained uncertain, until a company of Edinburgh and Dundee speculators decided Conishead was an ideal place to establish a Hydro.

During the nineteenth century, hydrotherapy, the 'water cure', became established as an effective and popular treatment for ailments relating to the nervous system and circulation. It offered patients respite from arduous remedies such as emetics, purgatives and bleeding that were universally prescribed at the time. Under the supervision of a doctor and staff, hydrotherapy involved a regime of cold-water showers and baths, wrapping in wet sheets for hours, washing and soaking different parts of the body, rubbing, massage and the 'douche', a special shower from which a fall of icy water fell from a great height. Patients seemed to benefit from the treatment, although cures were not instantaneous and required weeks and months of regime before results were observed. Thousands of people tried this alternative therapy and it increased in popularity when prominent figures including Alfred Lord Tennyson, Florence Nightingale, Charles Dickens and Charles Darwin publically endorsed it. A leading man in the medical profession of that time, Dr James Gully of Malvern, had established hydropathic institutions in Britain and it was in Malvern where Darwin took the treatment and later brought his daughter Annie[1].

By 1891, there were sixty-three hydros in Britain; twenty were in Scotland, with Conishead Priory the only one in the North West.

The syndicate which purchased Conishead in May 1878 comprised ten Edinburgh subscribers for £14,000 worth of shares at £100 each. By the following October a

[1] In 1849, after three months of hydrotherapy treatment Darwin wrote:
'Physiologically, it is most curious how the violent excitement of the skin, produced by simple water, has acted on all my internal organs. I mention all this out of gratitude to a process which I thought quackery a year since, but which now I most deeply lament I had not heard of some few years ago.' (*Annie's Box* by Randolph Keynes, 2001)

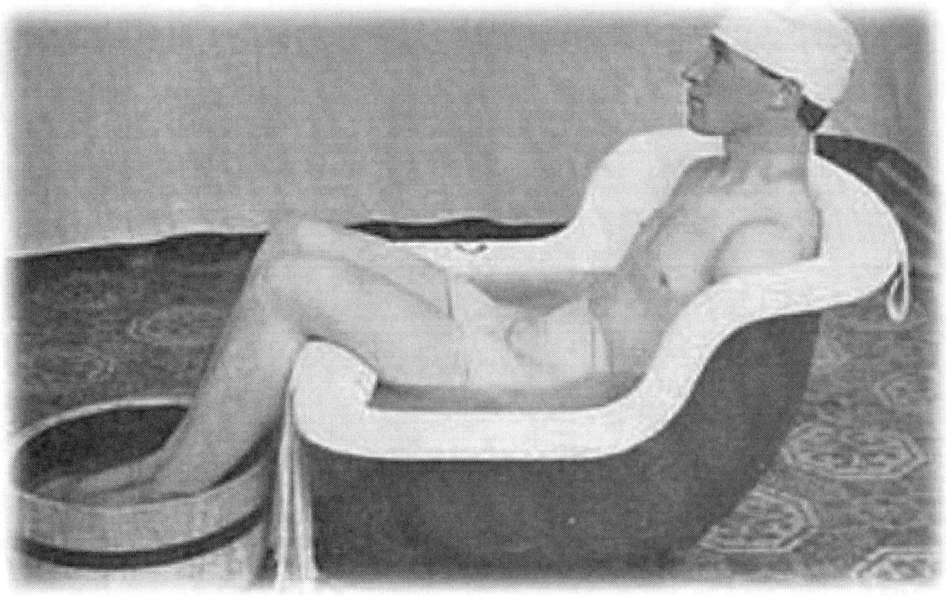

Plate 71 The Sitz Bath, c. 1900
(author's own collection)

further fifty-two shareholders from the East of Scotland had invested in the enterprise[2]. The investors raised £32,500 which, with additional borrowing, was more than enough to finance the necessary alterations. It was managed by a wealthy jute merchant and temperance affiliate, Alexander Moncur from Dundee (who was made Director of the 'Conishead Hydrotherapy Hotel'), and Andrew Philp, a temperance hotelier. William Cornford Philp (Andrew Philp's son) was engaged as the qualified hydropathic doctor. With its temperance leadership, it was noted by the *Lake Chronicle* that

'intoxicating liquors are neither supplied or permitted in the place.'

The *Ulverston Mirror* for September 1878 reported:

'The enterprise is to be carried out by a company principally composed of Edinburgh gentlemen – some of whom have already had experience in connection with such institutions in Scotland, which have had considerable success. ...There will be accommodation provided for 150 to 200 people, and sea water is to be conveyed in pipes to the building, so that the Priory will have the inestimable advantage over most other hydropathic establishments of providing facilities for indoor sea bathing, by means of which even the most delicate and infirm and the most nervous persons will be able to enjoy this luxury with the least exertion and with perfect privacy and immunity from alarm ... it will involve no impairment of the beautiful architectural features of the place; but this will remain the same noble and magnificent structure, to be admired by strangers as one of the most imposing ornaments and

2 The company's solicitor was Richard Greenwood from Kendal.

Plate 72 The lower ground floor location of the Turkish and treatment baths
(photograph by the author)

objects of interest in this charming district ... we see no reason why the Priory Hydropathic Establishment should not become as famous as, or more than, that at Malvern or any other in the United Kingdom.'

Conishead Hydro was designed to be both a summer and winter retreat. A large part of the refurbishment involved the installation of Turkish, Russian, vapour, medicated, sea and fresh water baths, along with a larger number of conventional baths, showers, and a central heating system that would provide a summer temperature inside the house throughout the year.

Shortly before Conishead opened, Dr William Philp produced a brief advertisement for the new Hydro:

'Directors have the highest medical authority for stating that the situation is one of the best in the kingdom for a Hydropathic Establishment both for a Summer and Winter residence ... The interior in no sense yields to the exterior for elegance of design and splendour of decoration. The elaborate oak carvings and splendid glass staining cannot be surpassed'.

It is interesting to note that Conishead's former owner, Henry William Askew had taken exactly the opposite view and regarded the location as damp and hazardous to his

Plate 73 The ladies' writing room, c. 1880, formerly the oak room
(Conishead Priory archives)

health. A tendency towards hypochondria *is* noticeable in his correspondence, however. Mannex's *Directory of Furness and Cartmel* for 1882, stated:

> *'...The extreme salubrity of the atmosphere, the sheltered situation of the Priory, and the beautiful walks and drives in the vicinity render it peculiarly adapted for such an establishment. The grounds in connection with the Priory extend to 150 acres, about 16 of which are beautifully laid out in gardens and shrubbery, and include excellent croquet and tennis lawns and a fine bowling green ... The establishment at present is only fitted for the accommodation of 150 visitors, but is capable of adaptation for double that number. There are all the usual appliances for Hydropathic treatment – Turkish, Douche, Spray, Plunge, and Sitz baths, with the advantage of a copious supply of fresh and salt water.'*

The Braddylls' former blue drawing room, which looked out on to the south lawns, became a recreation room where a raised stage with painted wings was erected for theatricals, and the oak floor was regularly polished for dancing.

The former morning room or saloon, with its conservatory along the southern side of the house, was converted into a second dining room. The oak bedroom became a ladies' writing room and the billiards room in the west wing, with its lantern ceiling and two large billiards tables, was open to residents from 10 am until 10.30 pm, except on Sunday, when gaming was not permitted, and the room was used for smoking. The spacious organ gallery above the hall was ideal for concerts. What was once the Braddylls' north drawing room was transformed into a larger library and reading room to accommodate the large number of visitors. The floorboards of the cloisters were replaced with a more durable concrete floor and a suite of Turkish and treatment baths

Plate 74 The corridor leading to the cloisters, c. 1890
(Conishead Priory archives)

Plate 75 The former Conishead Priory railway station house
(photograph by the author)

was installed around the boiler house on the lower ground floor, reached at the end of the cloisters through an arched portico. The west wing remained the quarters of the domestic staff, and the laundry facilities for washing, drying, ironing and sorting clothes were situated in the basement.

Amongst the outdoor activities provided were fishing, sea bathing, bowling and croquet. There were grass and gravel tennis courts, and golf on a private course within the priory grounds, situated between the station house and the beach, but *'strictly confined to visitors'*. At the nearby village of Bardsea, boating and bathing facilities were developed.

On 3 April 1879, Conishead Priory Hydropathic and Winter Residence was officially opened. Proceedings began at 6 pm with a speech, dinner, fireworks and a ball, which continued until 2 am the following morning.

The Chairman, Robert Lockhart of Kirkcaldy, made a speech in which he *'expressed the hope that in a year or two the institution would become as profitable as it was useful'*.

Three months later, a Scottish financial journal noted

> *'All who have visited this place since its recent opening will agree with us that in the beauty of its surroundings and the interest of the district it has no superior amongst such establishments. The visitors who have thronged to it from the busy towns of Lancashire and Yorkshire owe a grateful feeling to the enterprising Scotsmen who have so successfully utilised the 'white elephant' of Conishead.'*

The daily routine at Conishead Hydro was laid out in a list of general regulations. A bell sounded a morning call at 8.00 each day. Breakfast at 8.30 was followed by prayers in the drawing room. Dinner was at 1.30, tea at 6.00 and supper (just after prayers) at 9.15. A bell was rung throughout the corridors a quarter of an hour before each meal and a gong sounded a second time at the commencement of each meal. No house servants were expected to be on attendance after 10.00 pm, unless there was sickness. Alcohol was prohibited, although smoking was permitted in the smoking room. Visitors' dogs were not allowed indoors, although accommodation was provided for them in the stables.

'Board, Lodgings etc.' was charged at £2.12.s 6d. per week. Additional terms were listed for visitors' male and female private servants, for children under the age of twelve, the use of private parlours, and fires in private rooms and bedrooms. These terms also included

> *'the use of the Reading Room and Library, and all other charges. Gratuities forbidden. Stabling provided for Visitors' horses on moderate terms. An excellent laundry is attached to the Institution...'*

The gas was turned off from the public rooms at 10.30 pm each evening and visitors were obliged to turn off their gas and retire by 11.00 pm *'so that perfect quiet may be maintained throughout the corridors and rooms'*.

Immediately after prayers in the morning, Dr Philp could be found in the consulting room. Patients were instructed to assemble in the reception room and were seen in the order in which they presented themselves. The introductory consulting fee was 10s. 6d. However, no additional fee was charged during the residence of the visitor. Clergymen and medical men received free consultations.

The summer season ran from 1 April to 30 September. During that time, ordinary, fresh, seawater, plunge, spray, douche and sitz baths were available every weekday for both men and women, from 6 am until 8 am, 11 am until 1 pm, and 3 pm until 5 pm. The Turkish, Russian, vapour and medicated baths were also available every weekday but these sessions were segregated and accessible for a longer period of time for men:

'Gentlemen: 6 – 8 am and 3 – 5 pm (Summer season)
7 – 8.30 am and 3 – 5 pm (Winter season)
Ladies: 11 am – 1 pm (Summer and Winter season)'

On Sundays only, hot, cold and ordinary spray baths were permitted for men and women in the morning from 7.00 am until 8.30 am.

In 1880, Dr Philp wrote *A Guide to Conishead Priory and the Surrounding District*[3], using Charles Jopling's book as his source of information. In his guide, Philp described the only approach to the priory at that time, via the North Lodge with

'a long avenue of stately trees. The drive winds round the base of the Hermitage Hill, which is to the right, while a lovely bit of water of considerable length stretches itself on the left. The house stands in the centre of a lofty plateau, sloping gently to the bay, and is an imposing edifice of palatial dimensions.'

Philp believed that the hall occupied the site of the north transept of the ancient church, and noted that the suits of armour had gone and the niches were empty. The cloisters were furnished with velvet-cushioned recesses, which *'offer a grateful repose'*. He described the great staircase with its balustrade and railings as 'unique', and where the carved figures of two mountain cats, symbolic of the Gale family crest, were originally positioned, they *'have been replaced by more useful ornaments, viz., two handsome gas brackets.'*

Behind the gallery was the ladies' drawing room,

'the large windows of which overlook the Bowling green and the Tennis ground, and in the distance may be descried the opposite shores of Morecambe Bay, the silvery waters gleaming through the foliage ... The whole house has been re-decorated and painted by Mr Campbell T Bowie, to whose excellent taste and judgement the Company is indebted for the harmony maintained between the architectural features, decorations and colouring.'

[3] *A Guide to Conishead Priory and the Surrounding District* by Dr Philp (Resident Physician) 1880, published by John Bartholomew, Edinburgh (Conishead Priory Archives)

Plate 76 The Conishead estate gardeners and labouring staff, c. 1890 (Conishead Priory archives)

Philp's description of the gardens mentioned the old Red Lane, (mistakenly attributing it to the Romans) and the Braddylls' Ladies' Cottage:

> '...*the path leads through the glorious avenue of sycamores, their leafy arch forming a roof of perfect symmetry. This walk is of great antiquity, having been at one time part of a great Roman highway, which led from Coniston Bank, through Low Furness to the Duddon Sands. In more recent times it was known as the 'Red Lane' because of the tinge it took from the iron ore carted along it to be shipped at Conishead Bank; and on turning up the soil the tinge is still distinctly visible. At the foot of the sycamore avenue nestles a picturesque cottage, known as the Ladies Cottage, and used at one time as a museum* ...'[4]

Dr Philp stayed only briefly at Conishead Priory before moving to his father's hydro on Bute. He was succeeded by thirty-one-year-old Dr Thomas Marshall from Edinburgh, who came to live at Conishead with his wife and son. Over the next twenty years, most of the senior house staff would be from Scotland. The head manager was a young Scots bachelor, Francis Grant, who was assisted by a thirty-nine-year-old unmarried housekeeper, Christina Thompson.

[4] Unfortunately, the Ladies Cottage was demolished during the early half of the 20th century. Today, all that remains of the cottage are three limestone steps, easily missed and almost hidden beneath a covering of moss and leaves.

By 1881, they had been joined by Peter Milne the house porter who lived with his wife in the South Lodge, at the main entrance to the priory. There was also William Bladen, the night porter; Robert Redpath, head bath attendant; James Smith, a bathman; Cordelia Higham, the telegraph clerk; and Rose Ann Johnstone, the cook (referred to as 'the Cusiniere'). The head gardener, Charles Milne (brother of the house porter) lived with his wife in the Gardener's Lodge (formerly the gamekeepers' Dog Kennel and the North Lodge), and three young gardeners, James Adam, John English and John Stackhouse assisted him.

The 1881 census shows that the domestic employees consisted of twenty-three indoor staff, attending sixty-two guests staying at the Conishead Hydro. Most of these people were from the iron and textile industries: merchants, master weavers and factory owners. Three families, a number of shopkeepers, two students and three retired businessmen from Warwick, Bradford and Dublin, were also receiving the water treatment.

To cope with the increased number of visitors, the Conishead railway station and two miles of branch line of the Furness Railway running from the Plumpton Junction near Ulverston to Conishead was opened on 27 June 1883. Work on the line had begun before the syndicate purchased Conishead and took nine years to construct. A single passenger train conveyed people to Conishead from Ulverston each day at noon, and after a six minute wait, made the return journey.[5] The single platform of the Priory Station and the red-bricked station buildings had been constructed in 1882 from designs by the Lancaster Architects Austin and Paley. There were toilets, women's and general waiting rooms, a ticket office and the Station Master's house, where Matthew Brockbank from Ulverston, lived with his wife and children.

By 1891, there had been a managerial change at Conishead. Isa Wright, a twenty-four-year-old Scots woman had been appointed the manageress of the Hydro, assisted by John Stainton, the house porter; a cashier Jessie Martin; a female bath attendant Annie O'Hara; the male bath attendant, Robert Redpath (who had been the attendant from the early 1880's), and the cook, Maria McLean. An unmarried army of thirty-two indoor staff including waitresses, scullery maids, housemaids, washers, pantry maids, laundresses and linen maids who hailed from Scotland, Ireland, Wales, Westmorland and Yorkshire ensured the efficient running of the establishment. There was also a waiter, a female upholsterer, a 'boots' boy and office and kitchen boys. The previous head gardener, Charles Milne, had left the estate by 1891, and was succeeded by Alexander Grant who moved into the Priory Lodge with his wife and daughter.

5 This service remained in place until March 1916, when it was withdrawn from lack of use when the popularity of hydropathic establishments waned. The line was later used for transporting minerals. It served as a railway connection for the North Lonsdale Ironworks, which had opened in 1874, and later for Glaxo, who used their own diesel locomotive on the line until 1994.

Plate 77 The lounge, c. 1890, formerly the hall
(Conishead Priory archives)

Plate 78 The lounge, c. 1890, formerly the hall, looking towards the organ gallery and chapel screen
(Conishead Priory archives)

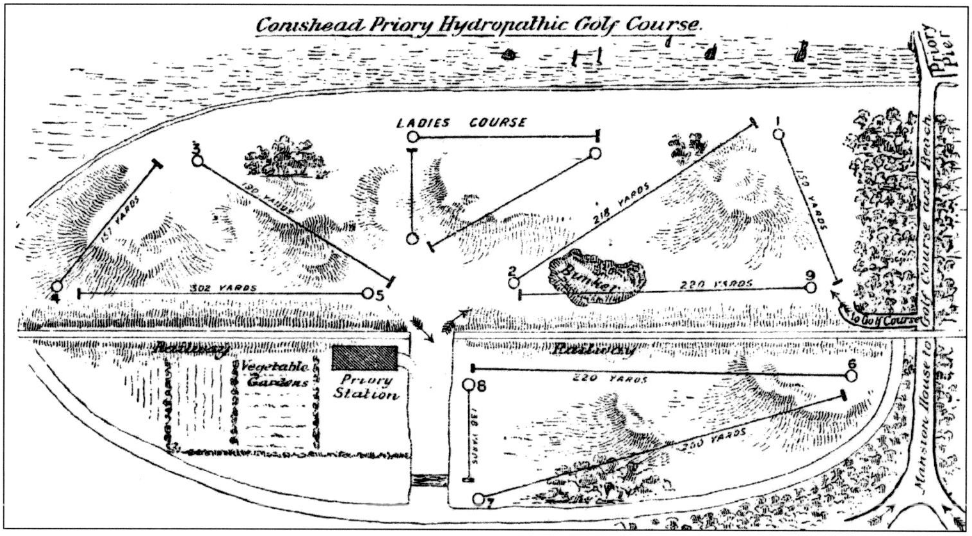

Plate 79 The Conishead Hydro golf course, 1907 *(Conishead Priory archives)*

Three young Scottish gardeners, Andrew Alexander, John Lyall and William Mounsey, who at the age of sixteen was the apprentice, lived in one of the priory cottages in the quadrangle known as the Priory Bothy. A drover, Richard Staunton from Urswick, also lived in the Bothy and looked after the livestock.

Forty-five visitors were staying at Conishead on the day of the 1891 census, including woollen merchants and a significant number of textile manufacturers, a ship owner, a clergyman, a civil engineer, a retired dyer, an iron works manager, two nurses and five families. Five visitors lived 'by their own means'.

A booklet entitled *Souvenir of Conishead Priory,*[6] printed in 1895, advertised Conishead as the 'best centre for the Lake District' and listed the weekly tariff. For the winter season between 1 October and the 31 March, an adult was charged £2.12s.6d. per week, the same price as when the Hydro was first established in 1878. Children under the age of twelve paid £1. 8s. with servants charged at the same rate. The summer season, between 1 April and 30 September, was more expensive. Adults were charged £3.3s. and children and servants £1. 15s. There was a special reduction of 5 per cent for visitors on further residence after one month. Meals taken outside the Dining Room or *'for private family'* were charged 1/- and for single visitors, each meal, 6d. The reader was further informed of:

'Single meals at Table d'Hote – Breakfast 2/6, Lunch 2/6, Dinner 3/6, Plain Tea 1/6, Meat Tea 2/6.

Lawn Tennis Courts, Bowling Green and Golf Course within the grounds.

Stabling, with Carriage and Cycle accommodation.

[6] Conishead Priory Archives

Visitors leaving are requested to give Two Days' Notice at the Office.
Baths and Massage - Fresh and Sea Water, Plunge, Spray Wave, Douche and Sitz Baths, Turkish, Russian, Vapour and Medicated Baths.
Massage Treatment – Dry, Wet or Oil – under Medical Advice and Superintendence for Ladies and Gentlemen at a charge of 2s. each time or 10s. for 6 times'.

The booklet included extracts from local guides and newspapers, praising the virtues of the Priory as 'The Paradise of Furness'. An extract from the *Christian World* described how:

'you make your way along lofty corridors – all built in the Gothic style, with painted glass windows shedding everywhere a dim religious light – to library, or dining room, or reception

Plate 80 A marquee in the grounds of Conishead Hydro, 1906 *(author's own collection)*

Plate 81 Conishead Hydro staff, c. 1912
(author's own collection)

rooms, or amusement rooms; or ascend a massive staircase landing in a organ gallery, whence you have a fine view of the interior below; or to the drawing rooms and other apartments, all in the grandest state, and fitted up with all the "resources of civilisation"... The connoisseur will be charmed with the handsome oak panelling, and magnificently carved mantelpieces and fretted ceilings, everywhere meeting his eye. Higher up are the bedrooms, which are neat and airy ... Can there be a jollier place for invalids than Conishead Priory? I think not. And truly we are all invalids, and treated accordingly. The rule of the house is to rise early and go to bed betimes.'

The *Bradford Observer* was less poetic and more practical:

'The appliances for hydropathic treatment comprise Turkish, douche, spray, plunge and sitz baths, upon the construction of which the best skill has been employed and visitors have the advantage of either fresh or sea water, or both, hot or cold. The Turkish bath is heated by steam, which induces a temperature of the highest without producing in the patients an over-oppressiveness or stifling feeling'.

The booklet included a series of interior black and white photographs, displaying the hall (used as the lounge), with its organ gallery, a plethora of aspidistras, cane furniture and plush velvet couches. Photographs showed the corridor draped with curtains at each side of the archways and decorated with side tables, sofas and an umbrella stand. The ladies' writing room (formerly the oak bedroom) displayed a decorative frieze of Arts and Crafts style wallpaper above the oak panelling.

The dining room was photographed with two rows of tables arranged with napkins and silver plated cutlery, engraved 'Conishead Hydro', and the recreation room (originally the blue drawing room) contained a painted stage front and stage set complete with a piano and aspidistra.

A review from *The Manchester City News* in July 1900 enthused:

'The old Monks rarely made any mistakes in selecting a site and the hydro today is reaping the benefit of an enviable position ... There are ... quadrangular courts, octagonal towers, oriel windows, domed minarets, stained glass windows, clock towers and all the magnificence of architecture ... Sufficient is it to say that the Priory possesses all the elegancies of a lordly mansion, all the quietness and dignity of a church and all the comforts and conveniences of a first-class hydro ... Thanks to the enterprise of the Furness Railway Company, it is possible to explore all the country by means of combined day tours at a very cheap rate. There are nearly thirty of these tours arranged for railway, gondola and coach, with ample time for lunch and they fit so well that in the majority of cases you reach Conishead in time for dinner if you choose.'

By 1901, the manager of Conishead Hydro was Scots born Peter Keiller and the 'bathman' was John William Pawson from Yorkshire, who also lived-in with his wife. Frances Garrett, a single woman of thirty-four from Portsmouth worked as the 'bathmaid'. There were instances of sisters working as domestic servants, housemaids, linen, hall and pantry maids. However, staff numbers had fallen during the last ten years. Only twenty members of staff were listed as working indoors, a decrease reflected in the number of visitors at the time, when only twenty-four, chiefly consisting of couples and single people, were resident at Conishead on the day of the 1901 census.

The 1911 census showed a further decrease, with only five male and nine female visitors in residence, attended by a household of twenty-one members of staff under the management of Edinburgh-born Thomas McNair. A Head Coachman, an Overseer and four gardeners were also employed. It appears that at the dawn of the twentieth century, popularity for hydrotherapy was gradually waning.

During the First World War, when many large mansion houses were appropriated for use as military hospitals, Conishead remained open to those in need of hydropathic treatment, as well as catering for wounded soldier's convalescence. When the war ended in 1918, the management of the Hydro looked at ways of rejuvenating the establishment. After four years of world conflict, people were looking for places of rest and recuperation where there was an emphasis on fun and recreation.

In 1922, a programme of investment was suggested and a general refurbishment took place. The golf course was extended to eighteen holes (*'It is now one of the finest in England and is becoming very popular'*), a garage was built for 110 cars and a Tennis Tournament on two hard and five grass courts became a major feature from 29 August to 4 September each year. Visitors could also indulge in pleasure boating, fishing, badminton, dancing, bowls, clock golf, croquet, billiards, library, table tennis and sea bathing. Consequently, numbers rose from 7,487 in 1924 to 12,480 in 1925 and as a result Conishead was awarded four-star classification by the Automobile Association.

In 1922, a young lady, staying at Conishead with her parents and sister, described the spacious surroundings in a letter to her future husband:

> *'...Conishead looks just lovely and the green seems greener than ever it did before...I have been given the largest bedroom here, which seems ...positively ridiculous! ...just for a lark... I stepped it the other night from wall to wall and it was 16 strides!! And when I want anything by the bed & then walk back to the dressing table I am positively tired! There's also a lovely comfy couch to lie on, two large chairs and a round table in the middle of the room with writing materials ... It is a lovely, restful sort of a room.'*[7]

In 1925, the Scottish syndicate who owned Conishead Hydro decided to sell up. The house and grounds were sold for £15,000 to a partnership consisting of a Rev Dr John George Gibson and a Dr John Wishart from Newcastle. Initially, there were problems:

> *'at one stage it appeared as if the whole scheme would fall through. By May 1926, only £3,875 of the purchase price had been paid over and the old Company was retaining receipts from*

[7] Extract courtesy of Dr David Cross

the operation to cover the deficit. Dr Wishart's relationship with Gibson (who had the funds) had, in his words, become strained. But they must have patched things up and Conishead passed into their hands, the word 'Hydro' being dropped from the title.'

The new owners formed the 'Conishead Priory Company Ltd', and converted Conishead into a high-class, four-star holiday hotel, advertising it as *'the restful Riviera of the North West'*, catering for conferences, weddings, parties and associations.

Improvements carried out during 1926 and 1927 included easier access for 'motor traffic'. The drive and roadways on the estate were re-laid using eight hundred tons of material from the quarry on the estate. Two lifebuoys were installed at the beach for bather's use, the lake was cleared, waterfalls constructed, trout re-introduced and three 'rustic' bridges built. An avenue of a hundred beech trees was planted along the north side of the west drive and a plantation of ash trees were laid down in the old golf field. A motor workshop was added to the garage, a 'cosy corner' established near the manager's house and the Ladies' Cottage and Swiss fishing chalet were renovated. A thousand books were added to the library, and bedrooms and bathrooms were painted and refurbished. A new cloakroom for women was installed on the first floor and single twin beds had replaced double beds in many of the rooms.

During the previous few years, tennis had become a major feature at Conishead and a week in August each year, weather permitting, the high point of the season arrived when the two hard tennis courts were host to the increasingly popular tournament. Players from North Lancashire and the Lake District arrived at Conishead, and a famous tennis celebrity was invited to open the proceedings for a small fee and a few days free accommodation.

A visitor, who remembered these halcyon days, recalled the high spirits of some of the male players who readily frequented the local bars in Ulverston, the day before the games commenced:

'Their antics and high spirits could strain the hospitality of their dignified hosts at Conishead. As the afternoon, and the drinks wore on their behaviour became more outlandish. Finally the landlord...his patience exhausted, called up the hotel (Conishead) *begging the Manager to please send the old ten-seater Ford wagon to pick them up. They drove down the Priory Road singing raucous songs and whistling at any of the local girls they passed along the way'.*

A grandstand was erected for the local gentry on the eastern terrace and a marquee was brought over from Cartmel to act as a committee room and serve sandwiches and champagne. The Ulverston Town Band supplied the music, beginning with the National Anthem, and a local dignitary opened the tournament. Play continued each afternoon until 5.00 pm when the guests retired to the house to bathe and dress for dinner. The final day of the tournament saw the championship playoff, when the victors received the silver challenge cups, before the Ulverston Band closed with the National Anthem once more.

Plate 82 A tennis tournament at Conishead, c. 1926 *(Conishead Priory archives)*

On the last evening, a Tournament Ball was held in the hall and makeshift dance floors were laid out on the eastern terrace and the lower part of the Priory Lake. The guests danced to orchestral music and many of the unmarried, younger generation took to the floor by the side of the lake, with their gramophone and ukuleles. They danced illuminated by a chain of multi-coloured Chinese lanterns, sustained by generous quantities of champagne and sandwiches served in the Swiss fishing chalet. Long remembered were the

> *'peals of girlish laughter...mingled with the deeper voices of their men friends and many a romance began... Many of the walks around the Priory's lovely grounds were named by the younger set – 'Honeymoon Lane', 'Kissing Bridge', 'Lover's Lane' and a tunnel under the road at the lower end of the lake - ...the 'tunnel of love'.*

The 'younger set' joined their parents in the hall by 10.30 pm and the festivities came to a resounding close with a firework display at 1.00 am. This annual event revived something of the communal atmosphere established by the Braddylls and Askews, and Conishead echoed once more with the sound of music and dancing.

Sadly, however, Conishead's prominence as the 'restful Riviera of the North West' was coming to an end:

> *'Some improvements were undertaken, electric lighting, new bathrooms and a five valve wireless, a dance band engaged and there was a last Indian summer or two, with the tennis week a highpoint. But it could not be made to pay and Conishead was purchased in 1929 for £35,000 by the Durham Miners for use as a convalescent home. It had made its jubilee, but only just.'* [8]

[8] *The Business of Hydrotherapy in the North of England* by Alastair J Durie, 2002.

Ten

'THE DURHAM MINERS' RITZ'

1929 – 1976

By 1929, it became evident from the steadily decreasing visitor numbers that Conishead Priory's life as a hydro and hotel had run its course. The house and grounds were offered for sale.

The Durham Miners' Association, the largest miner's Trade Union in the United Kingdom, had been considering the provision of a convalescent home for injured and sick miners since 1924. The Association's affiliates were impressed with what they saw at Conishead:

'It is a very beautiful property, well equipped and in the centre of a large and well wooded estate. I could conceive of no centre better for convalescent properties, as it is on the edge of Morecambe Bay, well sheltered and amid beautiful scenery.'

Following swift negotiations between the Coal Owners' Association and the Durham District Miners' Welfare Committee (on behalf of the Durham Miners' Association), Conishead was purchased for £35,000. The Association also 'inherited' an on-going archaeological excavation of the original priory and church which had been instigated by Conishead's previous owner, Dr John Wishart, and supervised by Archaeologist P V Kelly, who recorded:

'...the turf of the tennis lawn had become weedy and poor and several large stones were beginning to show through, Dr Wishart of the Conishead Priory Co. decided to re-turf it, and at that same time to make an effort to trace the foundations known to be there.' [1]

The excavation commenced on 2 October 1928 and continued, despite inclement weather, until the end of the year:

'I have ... through the courtesy of the new owners, been permitted, from time to time, to examine the walls in the basement, whilst they were stripped of plaster, during the

[1] *Transactions of the Cumberland and Westmorland Antiquarian and Archaeological Society* 1929 (article by P V Kelly), Kendal Local History Library

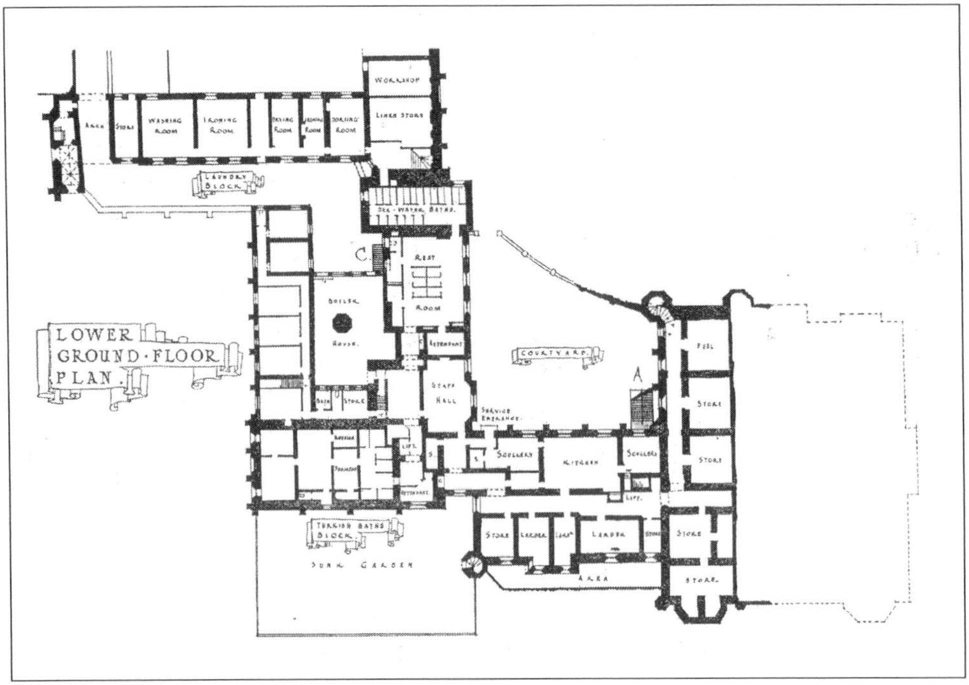

Plate 83 A plan of the lower ground floor of Conishead Priory, 1929 (Conishead Priory archives)

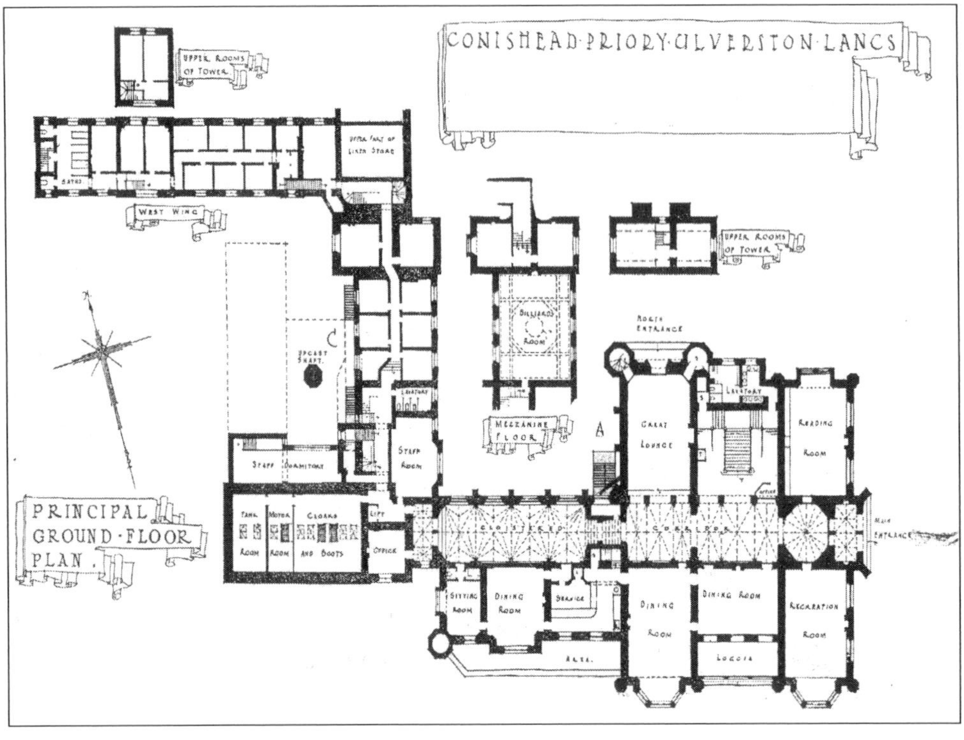

Plate 84 A plan of the ground floor of Conishead Priory, 1929 (Conishead Priory archives)

alterations necessary to convert the house into a convalescent home, and I am convinced, after close examination, that a good stretch of the south wall, for 4 or 5 feet upwards from the foundations, is of medieval date ... There was also found when the plaster was removed, in one of the walls, a brick oven, 4ft wide and about the same depth and 2ft high, with a very flat arch, slightly domed. This oven, which has since been built up, belonged however, I think to the first house built on the site after the dissolution ...

With the change in ownership of this property, it is sincerely hoped that the Durham Miners' Welfare Committee will consider the desirability of handing over the small plot containing the foundations of the church to the Nation, so that these newly recovered remains of a religious house in our district, which most people had given up as lost for ever, may be properly displayed and preserved for future generations.' [2]

Sadly, Kelly's hope was unrealised. The Durham Miners' Welfare Committee did not allow the 'small plot' to be given over to the nation. Instead, when the excavation came to an end the site was re-covered and the ancient foundations left buried beneath the south lawn of the house.

The Welfare Committee engaged a prominent Durham Architect, W Arthur Kellett, and £22,000 was spent on making the necessary alterations and modifications. Great credit was given to the architect and contractor *'for the efficient manner in which they have carried out the extensive alterations'*. The fabric of the house was strengthened and renewed in places but the historic architectural features were left undisturbed. Several wings adjoining the main building were re-arranged and the Co-operative Wholesale Society equipped the bedrooms with furniture. An electric lift, a suite of Turkish baths, seawater baths, changing and rest rooms were established and the cold rooms in the basement were lined with cork. An annual sum of over £10,000 raised from investments by the Committee, would be spent on the upkeep of the house and estate.

A small guide book from this time described further work undertaken:

'The kitchen apartments have been re-arranged and an electric lift facilitates the prompt serving of meals. There is an entirely re-modelled laundry equipped with modern electrically driven machinery. All the bedrooms are fitted with lavatory basins with constant hot and cold water, and there are bathrooms on each floor. A self-acting electric passenger lift serves all four floors and electricity is utilised all over the building to the fullest possible extent.

The new system of (steam-powered) central heating ensures a comfortable temperature even in the remotest wings. The water supply and drainage have been completely renewed, and the sanitary arrangements generally are of the most efficient type ... The completion of the necessary and very extensive scheme of reconstruction has converted the mansion into one of the finest Convalescent Homes in the Kingdom. It provides the maximum of comfort

[2] *Transactions of the Cumberland and Westmorland Antiquarian and Archaeological Society* 1929, Vol 30 (article by P V Kelly – 11 September 1929)

and convenience, and standing, as it does, in the midst of lovely surroundings and in a singularly healthy climate, it offers unrivalled opportunities of recuperation to those who are unfortunate enough to need the health-giving environment, which the Home affords.'

On 23 August 1930, Conishead Priory was opened as the 'Durham Miners' Welfare Convalescent Home' by Alderman Thomas Taylor of Chipchase, Northumberland (President of the Durham Coal Owners and Chairman of the Durham Coal Miners Association) and James Robson (Chairman and Joint Secretary with Reginald Guthrie of the Durham Miners' Welfare Committee).

The Welfare Committee published an illustrated souvenir[3] of the newly opened home with a brief description of the history and their purchase of Conishead. The Joint Secretaries, Guthrie and Robson wrote:

'The old Priory will in future serve an entirely different purpose than affording pleasure to a few people seeking a holiday. Bracing air, fine scenery and quietude will help to restore to health those of the miners who fall victims to accidents in our mines, or ill health. It has sheltered the religious devotions of thousands for centuries and has witnessed the religious and civic struggles of the past and is now to be devoted to gathering under its healing wings those who are seeking the restoration of their health lost through accidents in our mines and other causes ...'

In the souvenir publication the architect Arthur Kellett described how

'The rooms on the upper floors are attractively planned but possess few features of architectural importance, with the exception of the Oak Room, the walls of which are covered with carved figures and panelling of intricate detail ...

The kitchen apartments have been re-arranged and are now cheerful well-lighted rooms where food may be prepared under the most hygienic conditions. An electric lift communicates with the Servery above, facilitating the prompt service of meals ...

The new system of central heating is designed to ensure a comfortable temperature in the remotest wings of the building ...

An effect of warmth and cheerfulness is obtained by the bright colouring introduced into the scheme of internal decoration.

Every endeavour has been made to provide the maximum comfort and convenience, so that the triple alliance of an attractive Home, beautiful natural surroundings and a healthy climate may continue to form ideal conditions for recuperation.'

Conishead Priory, which opened with a hundred beds, was soon able to accommodate up to a hundred and seventy patients. A convalescing miner initially stayed for a week but this was later extended to a fortnight. He applied to his Lodge Secretary for a place and names were chosen by ballot. He would then travel from Bishop Auckland to

[3] *Illustrated Souvenir of the Durham Miners' Convalescent Home* 1930 (private collection)

Ulverston by train and in later years by bus. In certain circumstances financial assistance was provided. On arrival at Conishead, miners handed their admission card to the Matron, were taken to their room and shown where to put their belongings. A rules and regulations booklet was given to every newcomer:

> *'Patients are requested to remember that the Convalescent Home with it's beautiful internal decorations, gardens, grounds, lake etc... has been acquired for the special purpose of assisting them in regaining their lost health...by taking the utmost care of the premises and the existing fixtures of the Home, and they are also requested to avoid damaging the furniture and equipment, which has been provided for their use and comfort. By doing so they will guard and conserve every feature for the enjoyment of Convalescent patients who will in due course follow them ...*
>
> *Patients should be out of doors as much as possible during the daylight but are not allowed out of the grounds after supper ...*
>
> *The Kitchen Gardens may not be visited by patients without special permission from the Superintendent ...*
>
> *Gambling, swearing or improper conversation or literature to which objection may be taken shall not be allowed in the Home ...*
>
> *The cutting of sticks, flowers, fruit etc... or the doing of other damage to the grounds or plantations belonging to the Home or elsewhere in the neighbourhood is absolutely forbidden ...*
>
> *Each patient must bring with him a change of underclothing, indoor shoes, brush and comb and shaving requisites. The change of underclothing should be clearly marked with the patient's name with marking cotton or marking ink ...*
>
> *Boots must not be worn on any of the upper floors and patients are expected to put on slippers before going upstairs – the object being to keep the Home clean and as far as possible minimise the labour and at the same time ensure quietness while the residents are indoors.'*

A Durham miner recuperating at Conishead in 1933 wrote home:

> *'...The change here is doing me a world of good, plenty of good food and the air is fresh and feels lovely. Having long walks in all directions, going to Lakes on Wednesday, Turkish baths on Thursday. Every day has some fresh outing.'*

Others described it as *'a grand place'* with beautiful surroundings. Another convalescent miner sent home word that:

> *'I go to bed at ten and get up at seven when the bell rings and breakfast is at half past eight. It is a nice place here, plenty of rooms to go in over the fires. When I want a bit of a lay down on the couch I take the rug over and have a good sleep. There is about a hundred and fifty in this time, a good few short.'*

It was also a place for good food: *'You will not know me when I come home. I am like a big brewer just eating and drinking'.*[4]

Convalescing Durham miners found themselves surrounded by an array of antique furnishings left by the Braddylls whose financial ruin had, ironically, been partly due to speculation in the Durham coalmines. There was the 'Brinsmead' baby grand piano, situated in the lounge (formerly the hall), patterned Axminster and Turkey carpets, old oak dining chairs and tables, various carved mahogany and rosewood dining tables, a Victorian walnut drop-leaf side table, a Victorian mahogany 'Tambour' topped writing desk, a mahogany 'chiffonier', mahogany hall chairs, sideboards, an upright rosewood piano, barometer, various clocks and chandeliers. There was also a pair of bronze figures in armour, a cast iron figure of the Sphinx, a marble figure of 'Beatrice' on a black pedestal base, which stood at the bottom of the great staircase, the Braddylls' marble figure of 'Purity' on the great staircase landing, and a large sixteenth or seventeenth century oil painting of a lady and three gentlemen, which was placed over the mantelpiece in the dining room. A huge gilt-framed mirror on a marble and gilt base, which hung in the main corridor at one end of the cloisters reflected the light and gave the impression of a never-ending corridor. A Durham-made carpet stretched the length of the entrance vestibule to the end of the cloisters.

Mr and Mrs John Birbeck were placed in charge of the convalescent home as Superintendent and Matron[5]. Thomas Braddyll's former study, situated at the far end of the cloisters became John Birbeck's office, while his wife occupied Thomas Braddyll's dressing room, adjacent to the original old library. The old library became the Birbeck's dining room. The former breakfast room was used as a still room or servery, where food was brought up on the dumb-waiter from the kitchen below, and then prepared for serving in the main dining room next door. The former morning room or saloon became a second dining room and seating was extended through to the conservatory. The oak room was used for the Durham Miners' Welfare Committee meetings, and was generally out of bounds to the miners although they were allowed entry, with permission, to admire the ancient carvings.

Outdoor staff maintained the house and grounds and a team of gardeners supplied the house with vegetables and fruit from the old kitchen garden. Cattle, poultry and pigs gave fresh milk, eggs and bacon. Workhorses were kept in the stables to plough the land.[6]

[4] Souvenir pottery was commissioned for the Durham miners to purchase as a reminder of their stay. Crown Devon Pottery produced orange and cream lustre ware from tea sets with plates and beakers, to biscuit barrels, plates, rose bowls and trinket boxes, carrying an image of Conishead Priory together with the legend *'Happy Memories of Conishead Priory'* and *'Ye canna whack it'*.

[5] By 1932, Mr and Mrs Birbeck were in charge of 32 indoor and 32 working outdoor staff.

[6] During the Second World War, a young porter at Conishead remembered how the wife of the Priory Railway Stationmaster, Mr Newby, who loved visiting the horses in the stables, suffered a terrible accident on one such visit and was maimed for life.

Plate 85 The second dining room, c. 1930, formerly the morning room *(courtesy of Mrs S Ritson)*

Plate 86a,b A Crown Devon Jug, c. 1930, produced for the Durham Miners as a souvenir of their stay
(photograph by the author)

Plate 87 Superintendent John Birbeck
(Conishead Priory archives)

Plate 88 Matron Birbeck
(Conishead Priory archives)

Indoor maids dressed in a brown uniform. Head maids wore green, and were paid a weekly wage of eleven shillings and three pence. Bedroom maids could expect to earn ten shillings and three pence per week. The Matron's personal maids were paid twelve shillings.

A maid, who worked at Conishead in 1932, recalled how bread was delivered daily from the local Co-operative Wholesale and an inventory was taken every fortnight in the kitchen and stillroom. Each patient's bedroom was inspected daily by the Sister or Matron. The maid recalled how she started as a bedroom maid with nineteen beds on the top floor of the house, then moved to the second floor and was made the Assistant Matron's personal maid. Later she applied for the post of kitchen maid and was offered staff dining room maid. She then worked as a store maid, followed by a time as assistant cook, before being eventually promoted to Head Cook, when her wage was more than the Assistant Matron at £2 ten shillings a week.

A fourteen-year-old school leaver who was employed as a domestic maid in 1936, earned twelve shillings and six pence per week, working under strict rules and conditions. The hours of work were long and unsociable. Work commenced each morning at 7.00 and continued, with a meal break, until 9.00 pm on a Monday, Wednesday and Friday, until 4.00 pm on a Tuesday and until 2.00 pm on a Thursday and Saturday. Sundays were no exception, the working day starting at 7.25 am until 10.00, followed by a four-hour break, then a return to work from 2.00 pm until 9.00 pm. The days were ruled by a timetable announced with bells and gongs.

Plate 89 Domestic staff at Conishead, c. 1930 *(Conishead Priory archives)*

Plate 90 Kitchen staff at Conishead, c. 1930 *(Conishead Priory archives)*

Plate 91 The domestic staff and nurses' accommodation built in 1933 (Conishead Priory archives)

During the 1930s, a journalist visiting Conishead reported on the 'Durham Miner's Ritz':

> *'The Priory has two schools of patients – those who say unhesitatingly they are perfectly satisfied with the Home and those who say that things are just a bit too strict! The patient isn't required to make his own bed. All he has to do is to turn the coverings down and one of the thirty maids makes it ready for the next night's rest. The day has fifteen hours – the night has nine ... In easy chairs and on couches (in the Lounge) were miners lying in all the queer positions of somnolence. It was a tribute to their lunch and to their contentment ... The rattle of dominos in the Recreation Room by very young miners did not fit in with the sunshine outside, though on a wet day the Recreation Room is a very desirable haven, and so must be the Library and Reading Room. The number and variety of periodicals seemed rather inadequate for 150 men ... Of food ... there is no maximum ... You may have two big plates of savoury dinner ... breakfast is just as adequate as all the other three meals.'*

The house was closed during the Christmas period for spring-cleaning, when furniture was shrouded in white sheets to prevent dust from settling. No miners were admitted for three weeks before and the three weeks after Christmas.

In 1933, a large accommodation block was built in sandstone and Lakeland slate with thirty-four bedrooms for domestic and nursing staff, and two pairs of semi-detached three bedroom cottages nearby were located in the park at the foot of the Hermitage Hill, overlooking the estuary.

Plate 92 Graves of the dogs and cats belonging to Conishead Priory near to the site of the Ladies' Cottage
(photograph by the author)

Plate 93 A group of Durham miners convalescing at Conishead, c. 1950
(Conishead Priory archives)

The domestic staff entered the house by a separate entrance and were forbidden to fraternise with the miners. This strict rule was, however, overlooked on one occasion with Matron Birbeck's permission. In 1934, a twenty-seven-year-old miner, Arthur Robinson, recovering from a colliery accident, fell in love with twenty-two-year-old Mary Torrance the head cook. On the day before he was due to leave Conishead after a two-week stay,[7] the Superintendent John Birbeck brought Mary to the dining room

[7] Mary had started work at Conishead in the late 1920s, first as a chambermaid and then as an assistant cook, before her promotion to head cook.

Plate 94 The Durham miners' library at Conishead, c. 1950, formerly the north drawing room
(Conishead Priory archives)

so the miners could thank her for the Christmas dinner. Arthur would later tell a friend that on seeing Mary he immediately received 'a bolt from the blue' and decided he would marry her. Panicking that he would not get the chance to see Mary again before he left Conishead, he sought permission from the Matron to speak with her. The following morning the Matron took him down to the kitchen and introduced him to Mary. This short meeting at Conishead would eventually lead to marriage.[8]

At the outbreak of the Second World War in 1939, Conishead was commandeered as an emergency hospital for air-raid victims from Barrow in Furness.[9] Large red crosses were painted on the entrance gate pillars and sandbags placed against the doors. Only a short time before war was declared, the house and the staff quarters had been re-decorated and a scheme had been approved by the Durham Miners' Welfare Committee to develop and 'beautify' the 160 acres of grounds over a five-year period. In 1938, £4,644 had been allocated for the purpose, bringing the total grants for the Conishead up to £447,646[10]. It is not known whether this five-year ground programme ever went ahead.

The Superintendent, John Birbeck, conscious of the potential danger of bombing, made enquiries with Abbott and Company, a stained-glass manufacturer in Lancaster, regarding the nineteenth century Willement and Wailes stained glass windows in the hall and above the great staircase. Abbott and Company inspected the windows and reported:

[8] Recollection with kind permission of the family of Arthur and Mary Robinson

[9] It was not until May 1942 that the first air raid victims were admitted from Barrow and the surrounding area.

[10] In the same year, 3,257 miners were accommodated at Conishead.

'The windows are excellent examples of their period. Their present day value is approximately £2000. The painting has perished in parts...and this is particularly evident in the staircase window. It is caused by a defect in the original firing of the glass, the temperature not having been high enough to allow of the paint fusing itself into the surface of the glass. We do not recommend that the defective parts be repainted, as they will probably not further deteriorate ... The whole of the large lower lights to the windows are in very urgent need of re-leading'.[11]

After months of preparation, which included the construction of five self-contained wards or 'huts' in the corner of the field to the north of the main house to accommodate two hundred patients, the Durham Miners' Convalescent Home became Conishead Priory Emergency Hospital. A complete telephone exchange for the hospital was situated in the main entrance and a woman was employed full time at the main door and front hall. Her duties included washing and cleaning the floor the full length of the hall each day.

Superintendent John Birbeck and his wife continued to manage the staff of seven nursing sisters, and St John and Red Cross nurses for each ward. Senior Medical staff were billeted in Bardsea and Ulverston. Every room and several corridors in the main part of the house were converted into wards with accommodation for between three hundred and four hundred patients. Conishead Priory became the largest Military Hospital in the North West. Operating theatres were assembled and installed with the latest X-ray machines and a resident Chemist dispensed medicines on site.

A young man who worked as the porter during that time recalled that

'several times ill or injured German Officers, held prisoners of war and interned at Grizedale Hall in the Rusland Valley, would be brought to the hospital for treatment. Their stay was brief and they were returned to the prison camp as soon as was possible.'

The majority of the patients were servicemen of all ranks stationed in the district, and were provided with the standard convalescent's uniform of light blue suit, white shirt and red tie.

The scope of treatment at Conishead was gradually extended to fractures, with modern rehabilitation treatment available for these and other injuries. There was a physiotherapy department with three masseuses, an Army Physical Training Instructor, two Occupational Therapy Instructresses and an Army Educational Corps Instructor.

Patients arrived at Conishead through the north door where the entrance hall had been made into the main reception area. Here they were assessed and allocated to the various areas. The seriously injured were placed in the main part of the house and the walking wounded sent to one of the newly constructed wards with a glass veranda, in

[11] Cumbria Record Office, Barrow

the field overlooking the lake. A mortuary was located in the west wing of the house.[12]

The memories of a Red Cross nurse who escorted an injured soldier to Conishead for a night during the war, described the Matron Mrs Birbeck as a martinet who demanded that after each meal all staff and patients should stand whilst she and the sisters *'swept'* out of the dining room:

'This was also the signal that all other ranks had to be finished too. It was too bad if you had only just managed to get started. A nurse had to jump up and open the door.'

The nurse recalled that on her arrival at Conishead, an administrative oversight on the part of the hospital authorities resulted in her having no bed for the night:

'So it was decided that I sleep in the Nurses' sick room, which was up in the battlements in a turret. They showed me to my room, which was reached by a double flight of stairs merging into one, at the top of which sat a ... little organ ... the nurses' kitchen (was) *right next door to the bedroom; it was a funny place to have a kitchen but it was a great comfort to hear them pottering about all night ... When the Red Cross had omitted to provide lodgings for me in Ulverston, they also omitted to provide me with refreshments. The result of the mix up was that the nurses had to chip in with their meagre rations ... and they were meagre in the extreme ... I at once offered to help with such menial jobs as cutting bread for the hospital meal, making beds etc. but Matron would have none of this and sent her knitting to me. This I at once sent back, no doubt to her displeasure.'*

On another occasion, the Matron snubbed a convalescing soldier after they crossed on the great staircase. Out of bounds for patients, Matron had caught him descending the stairs and rebuked him

"You are not supposed to be on those stairs, soldier".
He had replied, "What's good enough for your dogs is good enough for me".[13]

The matron's strict discipline caused two nurses to leave Conishead after only a few months. Throughout their time at the Priory they pitied the soldiers, who endured the cold rooms and corridors and *'put the plug in the sink to keep the draught out'*.[14]

During the Allied invasion of Western Europe in 1944, the hospital staff was augmented by medical students from Manchester and nurses from hospitals nearby, although Conishead was called upon to treat small numbers only.

At the end of the war the staff at Conishead continued to care for the sick and injured from neighbouring Service Units, as well as casualties from the theatres of war whose homes were nearby so that relatives could visit during their course of treatment. From

[12] In recent years the former mortuary has served as living accommodation for residents.

[13] The Birbecks' dogs were loyal and popular with the staff and patients and after their deaths were buried in the grounds, near the Ladies Cottage. Small headstones mark the final resting places of these faithful friends: Lucifer who died in 1932, Rufus in 1948 and Gen during the 1950's, as well as a number of cats who were resident there over the following years and up to the present day.

[14] *The North West Evening Mail*, 24 October 2008.

October 1940 to August 1945, a total of 8,000 in-patients received treatment at Conishead. As an emergency hospital, the house finally closed its doors on 31 January 1946.

The red crosses on the entrance pillars, the last indications of its role as a hospital for war casualties, were painted over and in April 1946, the Durham Miners returned, resuming their occupancy for a further twenty-six years[15]. A new Superintendent and Matron, Mr and Mrs Selden-Lyddall took over from the Birbecks, and each year more than 2,800 recuperating miners came and went, playing bowls and croquet on the lawns and reading magazines and books ranging from Punch to Dickens in the library.

In 1952, a journalist from the *Durham Advertiser* shared his experience of the miner's convalescent home:

'Conishead Priory provides health and recreation of mind and body. ... As the present Matron says "Only the best and the very best is good enough for this happy breed of men". And so it is. The Priory is their retreat, their interlude from the grim job they daily undertake. Pride of possession is plainly seen in their faces, their approach and their demeanour. And individual forgetfulness or excess evokes from the men themselves the sternest rebuke. Many are the occasions I join the groups in the corridor or cloisters and listen. I find a variety of subjects are intelligently discussed ranging from racing to religion, politics to pigeons, sport to sociology'.

Four years later, Jessica Lofthouse wrote about the *'good-humoured "Geordies" one passes in Ulverston streets or hobnobs with on Bardsea-bound buses; brown skinned men in cloth caps and best suits...'* who stroll along the avenues of rhododendrons and azaleas and play bowls on immaculate lawns[16].

By the early 1960's, the Durham Miners' Convalescent Home was under the management of Superintendent and Matron Colin and Agnes Graham. An updated rules and regulations leaflet was produced:

Patients are requested to refrain from excessive drinking and the use of improper language, and to behave courteously at all times to the Superintendent, Matron and Staff, and also to their fellow patients.

You must be very punctual in returning to the Home at night. The last bus leaves Ulverston at 10.00 pm and leaves Bardsea at 10.10 pm. ... The main doors are closed at 10.20 pm and re-open at 7.00 am. ... Baths may be used at any time between 5.30 pm and 9.30 pm. ... Patients should not gossip with the Staff or interrupt or delay them at their work. ... A Captain and Vice-Captain are elected by the patients each fortnight. Duties are to assist in the organising of competitions and other social activities. The Captain will act as a liaison between the Superintendent and the Patients.'

15 In 1945, the Durham Miners' Association became the Durham Area of the National Union of Mineworkers, and is now the North East Area of the NUM.

16 Lofthouse, Jessica *The Curious Traveller* (1956)

The following regulations were to be strictly observed:

'Patients must be on the premises at meal times unless special permission is given.

Early morning tea is served on the corridor from 7.15 am until 7.45 am. Tea must not be taken to Bedrooms.

Meals will be served punctually at the following times: -

Breakfast	*9.00 am*
Dinner	*12.30 pm*
Tea	*4.30 pm*
Light Supper	*7.30 pm*

On leaving bedrooms, patients must see that their rooms are left tidy. Blankets and sheets to be folded and left on chair at foot of the bed, so that beds can be well aired before being made by staff.

Patients must keep their clothes in the appointed places, and on no account leave them about the rooms or on their beds. Each patient should have a pair of slippers. Boots must not be worn in bedrooms.

Any patient bringing intoxicating liquors into the Home, or found at any time in a state of intoxication, will be instantly dismissed from the Home.

Patients must note the position of Fire Escapes from their Bedrooms, also noting the situation of Fire Extinguishers and Fire Alarm Switches.

Smoking is prohibited in the Dining Rooms, Bedrooms, Bedroom Corridors and all rooms off Bedroom Corridors. This is an important precaution against Fire. Any patient contravening this Rule will be liable to instant dismissal.

Patients must not enter any room other than those provide for them, except by permission of the Superintendent or Matron and may not remain in their bedrooms during the day unless by special permission.

Patients must retire to their bedrooms by 10.30 pm. Lights must be out by 10.45 pm and conversation discontinued.

Relatives and friends may visit the home any day between 2.00 pm and 4.00 pm. Tea cannot be provided for visitors.

The Superintendent may dismiss any patient who contravenes any of the above regulations, or who is guilty of improper behaviour or obscene language. His conduct will be made known to the Management Committee and to the Welfare Committee, Lodge or Branch, as the case may be, on whose recommendation he was admitted.'[17]

In October 1965, the Durham Miners welcomed a new Matron and Superintendent – Selina Gray, a nursing sister from the Durham Mines Brandon Pit House and her husband Alexander, formerly a costing department employee in the Durham

[17] Conishead Priory Archives

Plate 95 Matron and Superintendent Selina and Alexander Gray, c. 1965 (courtesy of Mrs S Ritson)

coalfield. The number of staff employed had diminished since the war and by the 1960s Superintendent and Matron Gray were managing a team of nine dining room maids, two cooks, fifteen cleaners, one seamstress, one laundry maid, one engineer, two porters, one head gardener, six gardeners, two masons, one joiner, a painter and a registrar/book keeper. Superintendent Alexander Gray took an interest in the history of the house and was happy to respond to occasional letters from researchers regarding the Dodding and Braddyll families. He kept meticulous reports of the work carried out each week in the kitchen garden and grounds and produced monthly reports for the Durham Miners' Welfare Committee on the general running of the home, with notes on patients and staff.[18]

In 1967, the Superintendent's report included an architect's inspection which noted

> *'The present furniture has served the Convalescent home for about 30 years and is naturally shabby and largely outdated in use and appearance. In particular the bedrooms tend to be drab and cheerless whereas they could contribute to the patient's well-being by bright and comfortable furnishings'.*[19]

[18] Extracts from collection of archive material deposited by Mrs S Gray of Lowood, formerly Matron of the Durham Miners' Convalescent Home on 25 May 1979, with permission of Mrs S Ritson (Cumbria Record Office, Barrow – Box Ref. BDX/53)

[19] Extract from collection of archive material deposited by Matron S Gray of the Durham Miners' Convalescent Home 1960's – 1971, with permission of Mrs S Ritson (Cumbria Record Office, Barrow – Box Ref. BDX/53)

The architect advised the removal of the stage and dais in the recreation room, which had survived from the days of the hydro, and the lounge (formerly the main hall) to continue to be used as a quiet room for afternoon rest, reflecting the religious nature inspired by the stained glass windows. Following the recommendations of the report, a programme of renewal and maintenance work was carried out. Four new radiators were fitted in the billiard room and the whole house was given a revitalising makeover. The exterior of the house was repainted[20].

The improvements maintained the fabric of the house but could not halt the decreasing number of miners arriving at Conishead. With the decline of the coal industry the need for convalescence was waning. Between 1930 and 1961, there had been over 72,000 admissions (excluding the 8,000 treatments carried out during the Second World War). In 1930, the Durham coalfield employed approximately 115,000 men. By the 1960s, this figure had dropped to 31,000, so that Conishead served chiefly as a holiday home for miners.

In February 1970, as if to signal the end of an era, the bell situated in the porch bearing the inscription '*Wilson Gale 1777*' was stolen. Superintendent Gray reported that '*The bell has little value other than historic value as part of the history of the Braddyll family*'.

Despite police efforts, enquiries were in vain and the bell was never recovered. A few months later the last of the Durham miners left Conishead and the house, related buildings and estate were put up for sale.

The Chairman of the Management Committee for the former Durham Miners' Convalescent Home commented on the forty-year association with Conishead and how they were leaving with 'sad hearts'.

> *'On behalf of the Durham Miners', he said 'I thank all the people in Ulverston and Bardsea districts who were so friendly to my comrades these past forty years'.*

The regular sight of a line of miners walking from Ulverston station to Conishead Priory would never been seen again.

In January 1971, a local newspaper announced that Conishead was on the market:

> *'For the past year or so the future of the mansion has been undecided but a decision has now been made to sell ... Handling the sale is the Carlisle firm of chartered surveyors Smiths Gore. A spokesman told the News that he could not yet reveal details of the asking price. All he could say was that the property would be on offer as a whole. The spokesman would make no comment on the rumour that the asking price would be £2 million.'*

The Smiths Gore sales brochure described Conishead Priory as

[20] The exterior of Conishead had been painted four years previously and had taken two years to complete.

> *'a magnificent Victorian Gothic Mansion, set in beautiful and productive gardens and woodland, about 10.321 acres, 4.177 hectares with vacant possession'.*

It described how

> *'Certain relics of a previous mansion can be discerned in the foundations and some of the oak wainscoting of the present mansion. It was designed by P W Wyatt in the revivalist style of Victorian Gothic to have a stately and decorative external appearance with a grandiose, spacious and dignified interior. The principal rooms are well proportioned and well lit and eminently suitable for large-scale accommodation. There is excellent coal-fired central heating throughout, and the whole property has been maintained in exceptional condition ... There is much fine ornate stonework with heraldic crests, bosses, pinnacles, battlements and various other relief work. The roof is mainly local slate with much lead finishing and felted flat areas'.*[21]

The illustrated brochure gave a detailed description of each room. The still room, adjoining the main dining room, was well equipped with a dishwasher and stainless steel sink units and a service lift to the main kitchen below. On the first floor from the main landing was the former Superintendent's flat, complete with a large sitting room (over the library), two bedrooms, bathroom and kitchenette. Within the basement were storerooms and larders, cellars, an ice room and old bathrooms used as stores. A salt-water bathroom complete with six showers and thirteen baths was connected to a separate salt-water storage tanks and plumbing system. The staff dining room was also in the basement, together with the main kitchen with glazed tile walls and Terrazzo floors laid down by the Durham Miners' Welfare Association. The west wing was described as being 'an *extension to the main building in two sections providing accommodation on three floors'*. On the main floor was situated the billiards room *'with an oak beam ceiling and a dome leading to a wooden lantern'*, eighteen small bedrooms, various bathrooms and lavatories and *'a further six disused bedrooms of poor access'*.

Outside, in the main courtyard, stood a coal hopper with storage capacity for approximately five tons of coal, an engineer's shop, garages for four cars, a gardener's office and tool room, a mason's shop and store, a joiner's shop and the clock tower, with a loft beneath. From the secondary courtyard there were various stores and sheds, an old stable and the electricity board sub-station serving the Priory and the 'North Lodge' cottage.

A description of the grounds listed the American Garden, a small sunken garden, a rose garden, bowling green, a walled-in kitchen garden, a lean-to greenhouse, the lake, sewage works, outlet stream and foreshore. Also included in the sale were the staff block and three staff cottages, Chapel Island, the Priory Stationhouse, and the Priory crossing cottages, agricultural land amounting to 86.756 acres and dedicated woodland

[21] Conishead Priory Archives

Plate 96 17th and 18th century bells from Conishead Priory
(Conishead Priory archives)

Plate 97 Durham miners on the bowling green, c. 1960 in the grounds of Conishead
(courtesy of Mrs S Ritson)

of 47.076 acres. The furniture, furnishings and fittings were not included in the sale and would be auctioned separately.

Prior to the sale of 1971, there had been widespread public interest in Conishead's future. A week before the sale, a local newspaper reported that

> *'there have been numerous enquiries about its purchase from those who would like to bulldoze it to the ground and sell its marvellous fittings – priceless fireplaces, murals, stained glass...*

(and) ...*those who could see themselves making nice pickings by turning it into countless flats – all to be sold at high prices of course – but they are going to be unlucky.'*

The article assured its readers that Conishead was protected from such unscrupulous plans since it was registered as a Grade II listed building, *'under the watchful eye of the Ministry of Environment'* and therefore could not be altered or demolished. *'Failure to observe the law on this matter can lead to a swingeing fine or an indefinite term in prison'.* As a Grade II listed building, Conishead Priory was defined as *'a building of special interest, warranting every effort being made to preserve it'.*

The sale went ahead on 29 October 1971, with the estate sub-divided into lots. Conishead was bought by *'a Lancashire businessman, who wishes to remain anonymous, for about £25,000. The actual price has not been revealed, but the reserve was £25,000.'*

The new owner, a Mr Jones from Preston, Lancashire, planned to convert Conishead into a motel and restaurant, with a garden centre, holiday park and site for three hundred caravans.

An auction of the Priory's entire contents took place at Conishead between 22 and 24 March 1972. The first day's sale consisted of *'china, glass, plated ware, kitchen utensils and surgery equipment'.* Conishead's time as a hospital and convalescent home was reflected in the large amount of surgical equipment, including stretchers, blankets, sun lamps, examination couches and Avery scales. Kitchen equipment was in great supply, with thousands of pieces of cutlery and china, 'Pink and Green Hotel Duraline' ware, condiments sets, and silver and aluminium tea services.

On the second day, bedroom and bathroom items were sold, including 100 beds and Dunpillow mattresses and large quantities of towels, sheets, blankets and bedspreads, wardrobes and chests of drawers.

The final day of the auction saw the sale of items of furnishings, including some dating back to the time of the Braddylls and the hydro. There were large quantities of Turkey and Axminster patterned carpets (twelve men were needed to lift the entire Turkish carpet in the cloisters), a large collection of books from the library, and various items of fine Victorian mahogany furniture and ornaments, including a thirty-inch-high *'fine oriental blue and white vase decorated with birds and flowers'*, which sold for £80. The *'Brass Gong and Hammer on brass and oak frame'* which had sounded the call for so many mealtimes over the years, sold for £12 and the 'Brinsmead' baby grand piano fetched £54. The oldest item for sale was a large bell on a carved oak frame, dated 1604, which sold for £60, and may have been one of the bells originally belonging to the ancient Conishead Priory church. The Victorian mahogany Tambour topped desk with pull-out writing slide, which was purchased for £40, might once have been the writing place for Colonel Thomas Braddyll or his wife. An oak sideboard from the dining room was listed as:

Plate 98 The terrace walk (photograph by the author)

'a fine oak sideboard with three cupboards and enclosed shelves with frame mirror back ornately carved with birds and flowers, and the head of a deer'.

It sold for £40. These antique furnishings were listed alongside modern equipment, including refrigerators, Hobart dishwasher machine, ovens, electric mixers, Hoovers, typewriters and Gestetner duplicating machine, television, table-tennis table and Electrolux floor polisher.

The northern part of the estate, including the 1933 nurses home, was bought by Roger Fisher, who converted the nurses' home into flats, built Great Head House and developed a racehorse training centre and stables.

During the next five years, the new owner of Conishead repeatedly sought planning permission for a holiday park, but on each occasion his plans were turned down. In the meantime, the house was neglected. The roofs began to leak and the guttering became blocked, resulting in water penetration which badly affected the early nineteenth century ornate plaster ceilings and walls. The ground floor began to collapse into the cellars and vegetation thrived internally. Dry rot fungus spread, destroying much of the old woodwork and reducing many of the structural timbers to powder.

In 1976, having failed to obtain planning permission for a holiday park, Mr Jones decided to sell, but by this time the 'Paradise of Furness' was on the verge of total collapse. A purchaser with the money and vision to restore Conishead Priory sympathetically was urgently needed. The house with its rich history was in danger of being lost forever.

Eleven

FULL CIRCLE

Conishead Priory was founded as a place of spirituality and healing by a community of canons over eight hundred years ago. In 1976, another spiritual group came to Conishead, rescuing the deteriorating house and securing its future once more. History had turned full circle.

The new owners, a group of Western Buddhists of the new Kadampa tradition of Tibetan Buddhism, were looking for a place to establish a centre of learning and meditation. In 1976, they purchased Conishead for the sum of £75,000 and a year later, in 1977, invited the Venerable Geshe Kelsang Gyatso, a Buddhist Teacher from Tibet, to become the resident Spiritual Teacher. Since then Conishead has become his spiritual home and thousands of Buddhist teachings have been offered there. The Priory was initially called 'The Manjushri Mahayana Meditation Centre', but in recent times it has become known as 'The Manjushri Kadampa Meditation Centre' and is the 'mother centre' from which over 1,100 Buddhist centres have been established worldwide in the same tradition.

When the community purchased Conishead they discovered that the damage from years of neglect was more serious than had first been suspected. Immediately, a major building programme was initiated to make it structurally safe. During the first winter a group of volunteers worked up to seventy hours a week on this crucial work, with only a wood-burning stove in each room to combat the extremely cold conditions. It was no exaggeration to say that the temperature was colder inside the house than it was outside and volunteers recall the challenge of keeping bodily warm, wearing clothes in bed and daring to strip very briefly to use the old showers in the freezing basement. As well as the bitterly cold and damp conditions, those early volunteers lived with an unpleasant infestation of rats that infiltrated the bedrooms and settled on the beds of the often unsuspecting occupants. Gradually, their number was reduced and eventually eliminated compassionately with humane traps, before they were released into the open.

Plate 99 An aerial view of Conishead Priory and grounds, 1971, when the house was sold as the Durham Miners' Convalescent Home
(Conishead Priory archives)

Once the basic structure had been made safe, the community began the massive task of restoring Conishead. Tons of rotting wood, bricks and plaster were stripped away, structural beams were supported by trees felled from the Conishead woods, half a mile of internal lead guttering was ripped out and replaced with fibreglass, fungicide was injected into the walls and the remaining timbers were chemically treated. Ceilings were knocked away to treat the affected timber structure behind, roof joists were renewed and the original ornate plasterwork was carefully replaced or reproduced where necessary. Miraculously, the oak linen-fold panelling in the dining room had escaped the ravages of dry rot and the morning room/saloon too was unaffected so that it retains the most original features of any room in the house.

In May 1977, a Job Creation Grant was made in official recognition of the restoration work underway and this contributed towards the purchase of materials and the employment of tradesmen and labourers. By Christmas 1977, the treatment of the rot was almost complete.

Amidst the chaos of building work, the community straight away began establishing a programme of Buddhist study and a wide range of holistic, spiritual and meditation

Plate 100 Reproducing a plaster cast mould, c. 1980, during the restoration of Conishead Priory
(Conishead Priory archives)

courses were made available to the public. The community endeavoured to make the guest bedrooms as comfortable as possible but at this early stage in their communal life at Conishead, the rooms remained very basic. In exchange for accommodation, participants volunteered their time and abilities to help residents with the restoration work, the basic running of the house and the grounds, and the administration work required behind each programme. All were expected to make a contribution and a specific amount of work was delegated each week. The community shared meals together, and produced their own organic food from the old kitchen garden. Despite the demanding challenges, the constant and hectic workloads and difficult conditions (*'there was rubble everywhere'*), there is the sense that in those very early days the residents felt part of a tremendous community which was exciting, bohemian and liberating. It was a new adventure, and residents were to an extent unrestricted in initiating their own courses. It was a meeting of like-minded people who shared the vision of living in a spiritual community. One former resident remembered how people from all over the world were attracted to Conishead:

> *"We met really wonderful people. Everyone was trying to follow the spiritual path. It was fantastic".*

Over the years, people arrived and left with their different memories and the restoration work continued. In 1991, fifteen years after the Buddhist community

Plate 101 The massive task of restoration, 1980s (Conishead Priory archives)

Plate 102 Restoration of the great staircase, 1980s (Conishead Priory archives)

Plate 103 Architectural decoration above the north front entrance, coincidently resembling the Buddhist triskele symbol (photograph by the author)

Plate 104 The former Victorian kitchen garden and greenhouses, c. 1980 (Conishead Priory archives)

had made Conishead their home, a £500,000 appeal fund was launched for interior restoration, and by the end of 1994 over half the total had been raised by fund-raising activities and generous voluntary donations. Many of the ceilings, floors and walls were replaced and the almost derelict top floor was converted into accommodation for the community of Buddhist monks and nuns and the large number of lay students.

In July 1997, a Buddhist Temple, designed by the community's Spiritual Director, the Venerable Geshe Kelsang Gyatso, was consecrated and dedicated to world peace through meditation. Built on the site of the old kitchen garden, it functions as the main meditation hall and the location for the spring and summer festivals, which attract Kadampa Buddhists from around the world. The Temple was the first to be built as part of an on-going international project to build a World Peace Temple in all the major cities of the world and members of the public are invited to discover a sense of peace and look upon the exquisite decoration within its sanctuary. The magnificent bronze statue of the Buddha above the shrine is the largest of its kind in the West. The original kitchen garden greenhouse was also fully restored.

The year 2003 saw the community awarded a development grant by the Heritage Lottery Fund in recognition of the enormous contribution made by the Buddhist community in restoring Conishead. The grant was to assist the first phase of a £1million restoration plan for work on the exterior of the building. This involved replacing the main roofs and restoring the high stone work. The second phase entailed restoring the two 100 foot towers at the front entrance.[1] The Project Administrator at Conishead observed that

> *'by carrying out this work we will be ensuring the use of this important and beautiful public building for generations to come. This will be a great tribute to the hard work of everyone involved in firstly rescuing the building from collapse in the late 70s and 80s and since then restoring the whole of the interior'.*

A Lottery Grant was also awarded for the restoration of the greenhouse and gazebo in the gardens.

Work continues both at the house and in the grounds, and at the same time Conishead provides enjoyment, inspiration and regeneration for its many visitors. By opening the doors to the wider community and initiating tours of the house, the restoration process at Conishead Priory can be fully appreciated. The public rooms have been sympathetically restored. The elaborate mantelpieces, ceilings and oak carvings in the library, dining room, morning room and oak room have been cleaned and renovated and the great staircase and stained glass windows continue to inspire admiration. The bright, airy conservatory, which once cast stained glass colours of light upon the Braddyll family's hybrid rhododendrons, is now home to the World Peace Café.

[1] Both projects were estimated to cost approximately £2m.

If one looks close enough however, clues to Conishead's long history can still be detected; for example the small marks in the floor behind the great staircase, where a door once led to the main reception office. This was where the kiosk once stood where the Durham miners purchased their sweets, cigarettes, newspapers, postcards and souvenirs. The carved Braddyll badgers on the staircase newel posts, discovered in the cellars by the Buddhist community and restored to their original place, now carry a pendant with a Buddhist symbol instead of the Braddyll coat of arms; a fitting tribute to change acknowledging the past. The change has been gentle. If the Braddylls, the Askews and the thousands of patients who have received care at Conishead were to return today, they would find much of it instantly recognisable. When so much rich history and craftsmanship came perilously close to destruction, it is a joy to see Conishead Priory very much alive again, magnificently restored and worthy once again of its long-standing appellation 'The Paradise of Furness'.

Plate 105 Conishead's resident mouser, 2012
(photograph by the author)

Appendices

Family Tree of the Sandys, Doddings and Braddylls

*(heirs who lived at Conishead – **in bold**)*

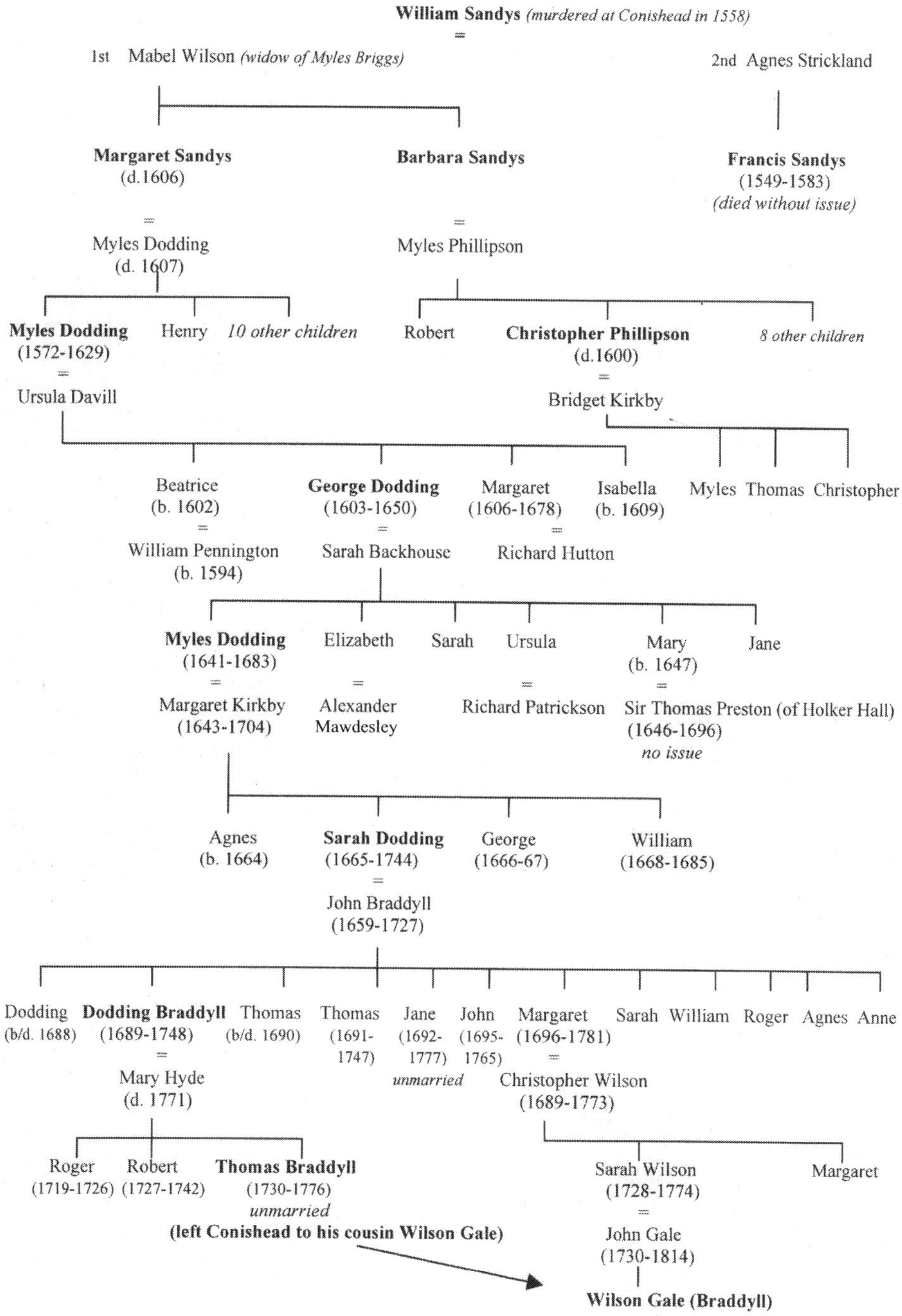

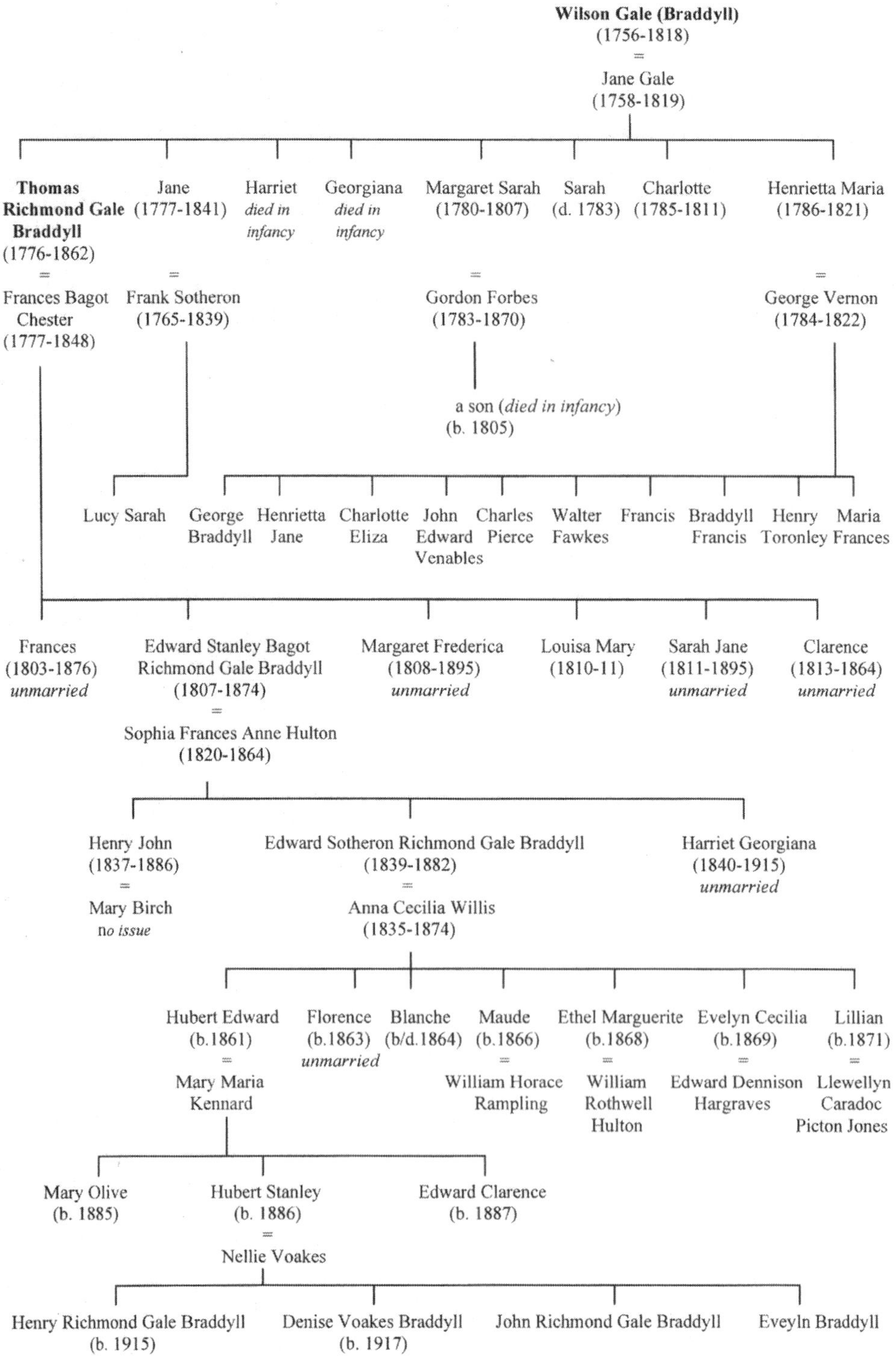
Wilson Gale (Braddyll)
(1756-1818)
=
Jane Gale
(1758-1819)
Thomas Richmond Gale Braddyll
(1776-1862)
=
Frances Bagot Chester
(1777-1848)
Jane
(1777-1841)
=
Frank Sotheron
(1765-1839)
Harriet *died in infancy*
Georgiana *died in infancy*
Margaret Sarah
(1780-1807)
=
Gordon Forbes
(1783-1870)
a son (*died in infancy*)
(b. 1805)
Sarah
(d. 1783)
Charlotte
(1785-1811)
Henrietta Maria
(1786-1821)
=
George Vernon
(1784-1822)
Lucy Sarah
George Braddyll
Henrietta Jane
Charlotte Eliza
John Edward Venables
Charles Pierce
Walter Fawkes
Francis
Braddyll Francis
Henry Toronley
Maria Frances
Frances
(1803-1876)
unmarried
Edward Stanley Bagot Richmond Gale Braddyll
(1807-1874)
=
Sophia Frances Anne Hulton
(1820-1864)
Margaret Frederica
(1808-1895)
unmarried
Louisa Mary
(1810-11)
Sarah Jane
(1811-1895)
unmarried
Clarence
(1813-1864)
unmarried
Henry John
(1837-1886)
=
Mary Birch
no *issue*
Edward Sotheron Richmond Gale Braddyll
(1839-1882)
=
Anna Cecilia Willis
(1835-1874)
Harriet Georgiana
(1840-1915)
unmarried
Hubert Edward
(b.1861)
=
Mary Maria Kennard
Florence
(b.1863)
unmarried
Blanche
(b/d.1864)
Maude
(b.1866)
=
William Horace Rampling
Ethel Marguerite
(b.1868)
=
William Rothwell Hulton
Evelyn Cecilia
(b.1869)
=
Edward Dennison Hargraves
Lillian
(b.1871)
=
Llewellyn Caradoc Picton Jones
Mary Olive
(b. 1885)
Hubert Stanley
(b. 1886)
=
Nellie Voakes
Edward Clarence
(b. 1887)
Henry Richmond Gale Braddyll
(b. 1915)
Denise Voakes Braddyll
(b. 1917)
John Richmond Gale Braddyll
Eveyln Braddyll

Family Tree of the Braddylls of Portfield and Whalley

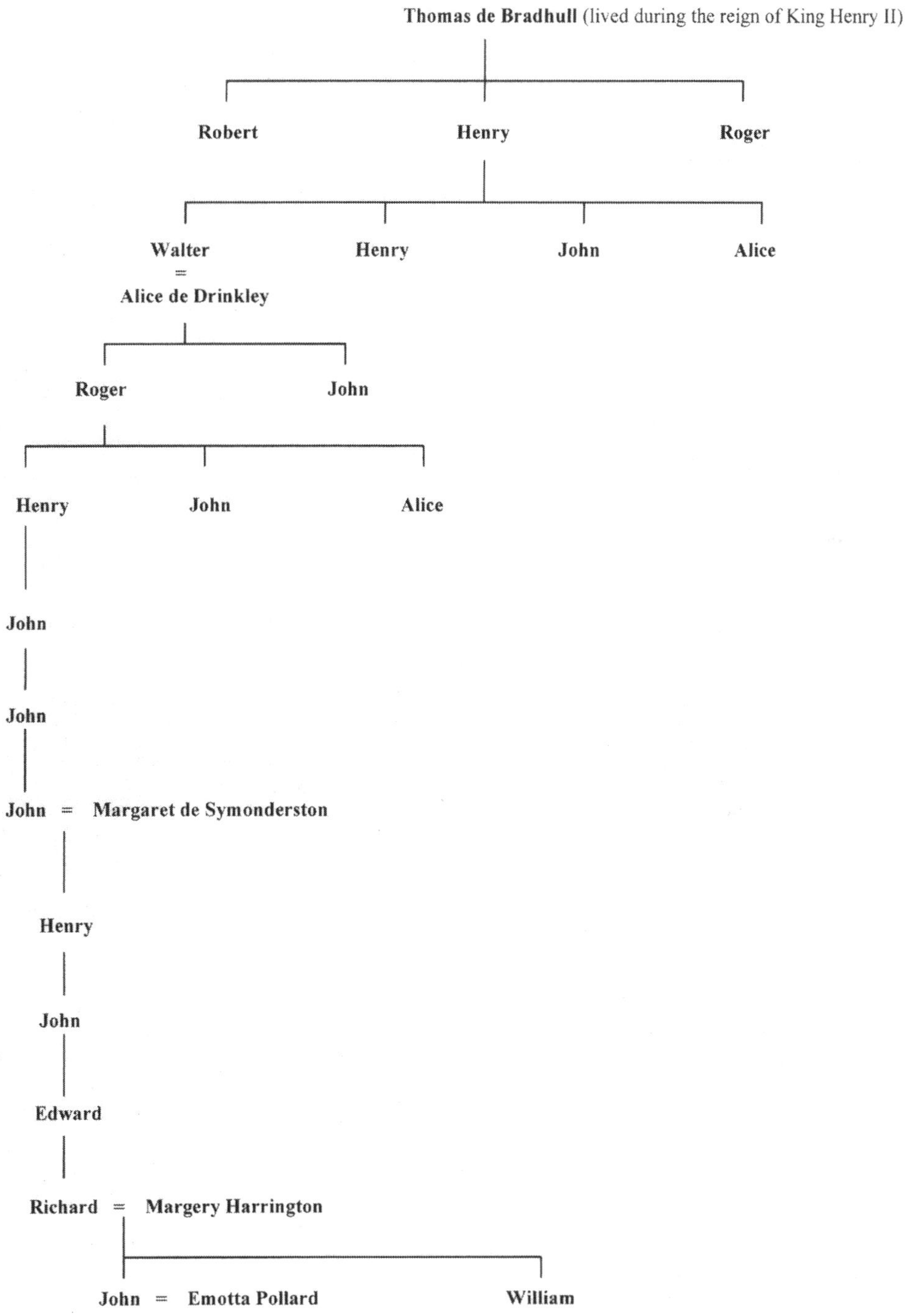

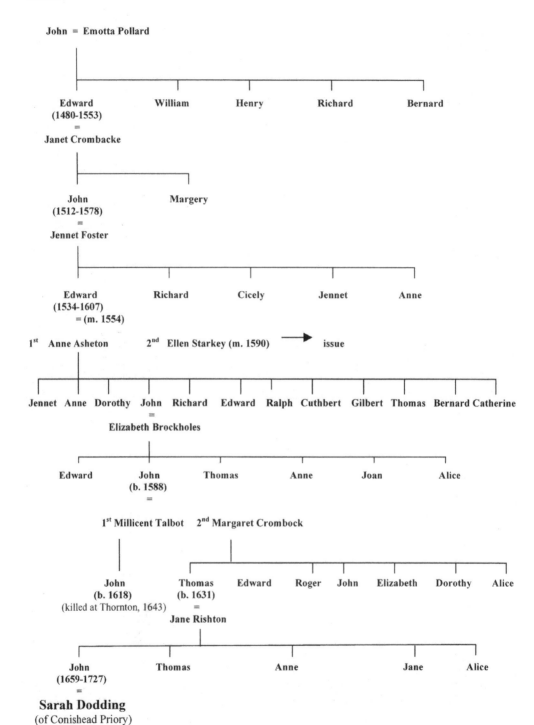

John = Emotta Pollard

Edward (1480-1553) = Janet Crombacke | **William** | **Henry** | **Richard** | **Bernard**

John (1512-1578) = Jennet Foster | **Margery**

Edward (1534-1607) = (m. 1554) | **Richard** | **Cicely** | **Jennet** | **Anne**

1st Anne Asheton | **2nd Ellen Starkey (m. 1590) → issue**

Jennet | **Anne** | **Dorothy** | **John = Elizabeth Brockholes** | **Richard** | **Edward** | **Ralph** | **Cuthbert** | **Gilbert** | **Thomas** | **Bernard** | **Catherine**

Edward | **John (b. 1588) =** | **Thomas** | **Anne** | **Joan** | **Alice**

1st Millicent Talbot | **2nd Margaret Crombock**

John (b. 1618) (killed at Thornton, 1643) | **Thomas (b. 1631) = Jane Rishton** | **Edward** | **Roger** | **John** | **Elizabeth** | **Dorothy** | **Alice**

John (1659-1727) =

Sarah Dodding
(of Conishead Priory) | **Thomas** | **Anne** | **Jane** | **Alice**

Family Tree of Henry William Askew and his Family

(Lived at Conishead 1853 – 1874)

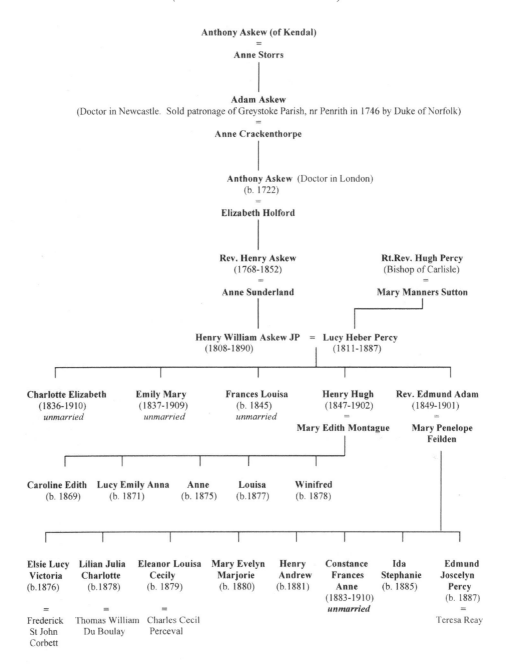

Anthony Askew (of Kendal)
=
Anne Storrs

Adam Askew
(Doctor in Newcastle. Sold patronage of Greystoke Parish, nr Penrith in 1746 by Duke of Norfolk)
=
Anne Crackenthorpe

Anthony Askew (Doctor in London)
(b. 1722)
=
Elizabeth Holford

Rev. Henry Askew
(1768-1852)
=
Anne Sunderland

Rt.Rev. Hugh Percy
(Bishop of Carlisle)
=
Mary Manners Sutton

Henry William Askew JP (1808-1890) = **Lucy Heber Percy** (1811-1887)

- **Charlotte Elizabeth** (1836-1910) *unmarried*
- **Emily Mary** (1837-1909) *unmarried*
- **Frances Louisa** (b. 1845) *unmarried*
- **Henry Hugh** (1847-1902) = **Mary Edith Montague**
  - **Caroline Edith** (b. 1869)
  - **Lucy Emily Anna** (b. 1871)
  - **Anne** (b. 1875)
  - **Louisa** (b.1877)
  - **Winifred** (b. 1878)
- **Rev. Edmund Adam** (1849-1901) = **Mary Penelope Feilden**
  - **Elsie Lucy Victoria** (b.1876) = Frederick St John Corbett
  - **Lilian Julia Charlotte** (b.1878) = Thomas William Du Boulay
  - **Eleanor Louisa Cecily** (b. 1879) = Charles Cecil Perceval
  - **Mary Evelyn Marjorie** (b. 1880)
  - **Henry Andrew** (b.1881)
  - **Constance Frances Anne** (1883-1910) ***unmarried***
  - **Ida Stephanie** (b. 1885)
  - **Edmund Joscelyn Percy** (b. 1887) = Teresa Reay

Inter-marriage of the Fleming, Lowther, Kirkby, Preston, Dodding and Braddyll Families

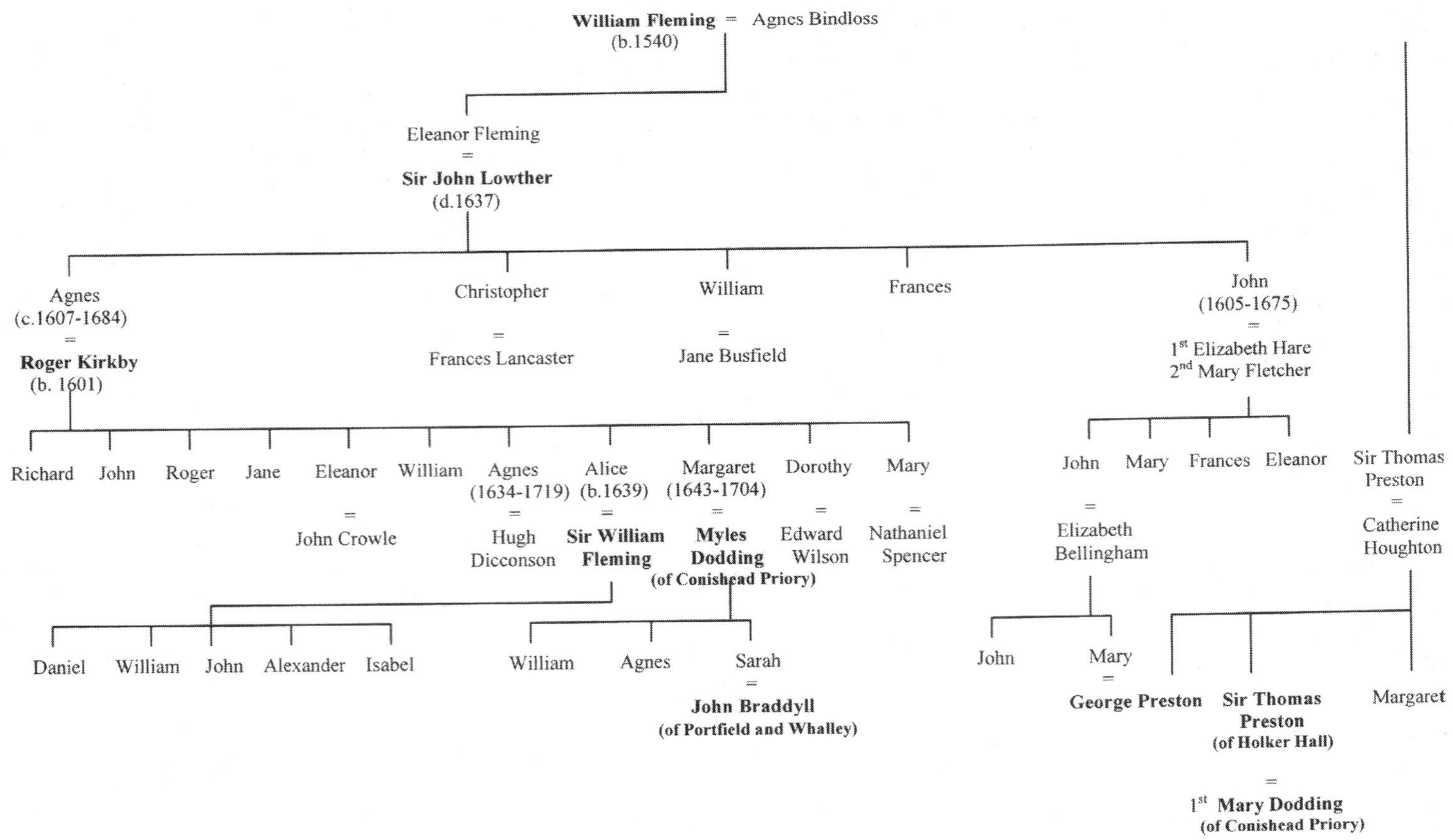

Census Return – Conishead Priory 1841

Name	Age	Employment
Thomas Braddyll	55	Independent
Frances Braddyll	60	
Frances Braddyll	30	
Margaret Braddyll	25	
(Sarah) Jane Braddyll	20	
Eliza Vernon	20	
followed by 6 female servants (names unintelligible on original census return)		
Jane Sharp	20	Female servant
Mary Kirby	30	Female servant
Maria Wiseman	20	Female servant
Dorothy Kirby	15	Female servant
Eliza Braithwaite	25	Female servant
Ralph Train	25	Male servant
William (Jennings?)	25	Male servant
Thomas Hodgson	30	Male servant
Joseph Creamer	15	Male servant
James B……..?	25	Male servant
James Haywood	30	Upholsterer
John Bi ……?	50	Cabinet maker
John Simpson	29	Male servant
Kennel House		
Thomas Willman	30	Gamekeeper

(Source: Public Record Office, London – HO 107/531/13)

Census Return – Conishead Priory 1851

Name	Status in Hhold	Marital status	Age	Employment	Place of birth
Mary Beck	Head	Widow	72	Housekeeper	Dalton, Lancs
James Beck	Son	Unmarried	38	Agricultural	Urswick, Lancs
Dog Kennel					
Thomas Willman	Head	Married	45	Gamekeeper	Tunstal, Lancs
Priory Lodge					
Robert Stalker	Head	Married	53	Agric Labourer	Grayrigg

(Source: Public Record Office, London – HO 107/2274)

Census Return – Conishead Priory 1861

Name	Status in Hhold	Marital status	Age	Employment	Place of birth
Frances L Askew	Daughter	Unm	16	Scholar	Greystoke, Cumb
Isabella Runciman	Governess	Unm	55	Private Governess	Woburn, Bedford
Mary Longmark	Servant	Unm	50	Servant	Lincolnshire
Jane Owl	Servant	Unm	31	Servant	Northumberland
Ann Teasdale	Servant	Unm	25	Servant	Shap, Westmorl
Sarah Teasdale	Servant	Unm	22	Servant	Shap, Westmorl
Mary Boyes	Servant	Unm	24	Servant	Scotland
Michael Curwen	Servant	Unm	31	Coachman	Greystoke,Cumb

Robert Utton	Servant	Unm	25	Groom	Surrey
John Jordan	Servant	Unm	26	Gardener	Scotland
Edward Anderson	Servant	Unm	21	Gardener	Carlisle, Cumb
John Thompson	Servant	Unm	26	Gardener	Scotland
Lodge (formerly the 'Dog Kennel' or 'Kennel House')					
William Atkinson	Head	Marr	31	Gamekeeper	Bowes, Yorks
(Priory) Lodge					
Agnes Stalker	Head	Widow	73	Gate Keeper	Witherslack

(Source: Public Record Office, London – RG 9/3167)

Census Return – Conishead Priory 1871

Name	Status in Hhold	Marital status	Age	Employment	Place of birth
Henry William Askew	Head	Marr	62	Landed Proprietor	Greystoke
Lucy Askew	Wife	Marr	59		Kent
Charlotte E Askew	Daug	Unm	35		Greystoke
Emily M Askew	Daug	Unm	33		Patterdale
Frances L Askew	Daug	Unm	26		Greystoke
Ann Mount	Serv	Unm	37	Housekeeper	Denton, Lincoln
Elizabeth Lill	Serv	Unm	37	Cook	Cartmel, Lancs
Jane Cook	Serv	Unm	29	Kitchen Maid	Carlisle
Jane Carr	Serv	Unm	24	Housemaid	Westmoreland
Elizabeth Wake	Serv	Unm	23	Ladies Maid	Bedale, Yorks
William Peters	Serv	Unm	37	Butler	
James Adgie	Serv	Unm	29	Footman	Walstow
Charles Nicholls	Serv	Unm	34	Coachman	Colton, Lancs
Thomas Breary	Serv	Unm	21	Groom	Ulverston
Conishead Gardeners Cottage					
Alexander Brown	Serv	Unm	26	Gardener	Scotland
Middle Lodge					
Thomas Sanders	Head	Widow	49	Labourer	Lowick, Lancs

(Source: Public Record Office, London – RG 10/4240)

Census Return – Conishead Priory Hydropathic Establishment 1881

Name	Status in Hhold	Marital status	Age	Employment	Place of birth
Francis G Grant	Head	Unm	26	Manager	Scotland
Christina Thompson	Housekeeper	Unm	39	Housekeeper	Scotland
Janet L Martin	Boarder	Marr			Huddersfield
Marion S Taylor	Boarder	Marr	44		Scotland
May S Taylor	Boarder		9		Scotland
James Keith	Boarder	Marr	32	Gas & Water Engr	Scotland
Agnes B Lennox	Boarder	Marr	50		Scotland
David Lennox	Boarder	Unm	22	BMedicine in Surg	Scotland
Gordon Lennox	Boarder		7		Scotland
Agnes B Lennox	Boarder		12		Scotland
Matilda McGregor	Servant	Unm	23	Domestic Serv	Scotland

Cordelia Higham	Servant	Unm	25	Telegraph Clerk	Cartmel
Catherine Winton	Servant	Unm	25	Domestic Serv	Scotland
James Smith	Servant	Unm	25	Bathman	Scotland
Rose Ann Johnnstone	Servant	Unm	32	Cuisiniere	Lancs
Mary J Balfour	Servant	Unm	24	Domestic Serv	Scotland
Mary J Burrow	Servant	Unm	16	Domestic Serv	Ulverston
William Bladen	Servant	Unm	43	Night Porter	Stafford
Helen Cowan	Servant	Unm	25	Domestic Servant	Scotland
Agnes Aldcorn	Servant	Unm	17	Domestic Servant	Scotland
Kate Kassels	Servant	Unm	22	Domestic Servant	Goole
Isabella Still	Servant	Unm	27	Domestic Servant	Scotland
Janet Winton	Servant	Unm	20	Domestic Servant	Scotland
Ada Walker	Servant	Unm	18	Domestic Servant	Lancs
Annie Burns	Servant	Unm	23	Domestic Servant	Ireland
Jane Veitch	Servant	Unm	25	Domestic Servant	Scotland
Janet Ferguson	Servant	Unm	19	Domestic Servant	Scotland
Agnes Barrow	Servant	Unm	23	Domestic Servant	Dalton
Elizabeth Hodgson	Servant	Unm	24	Domestic Servant	Ulverston
Margaret B Donel	Servant	Unm	15	Domestic Servant	Scotland
Jane McGregor	Servant	Unm	18	Domestic Servant	Scotland
William Stackhouse	Servant	Unm	15	Domestic Servant	Lancs
Thomas Marshall	Boarder	Marr	31	Resident Physician	Scotland
Alice Marshall	Boarder	Marr	32	Wife	Northum
Oliver Marshall	Boarder	Unm	1	Son	Scotland
Henrietta McConnel	Boarder	Marr	33		Manchstr
George Patrickson	Boarder	Unm	36		Cumbrld
Elizabeth A Frost	Boarder	Marr	48		London
John Hall	Boarder	Wid	59	Wool Merchant	Northum
Patrick Martin	Boarder	Marr	67	Retired Cloth Merc	Ireland
Wilson Waterfall	Boarder	Marr	68	Retired Bank Mangr	Warwick
Frances Martin	Boarder	Marr	60		Yorks
Edith I Sharp	Boarder	Unm	25		Lancs
Eleanor M Sharp	Boarder	Unm	19		Lancs
William H Saunders	Boarder	Unm	28	Commrc Traveller	London
Reuben Wright	Boarder	Wid	59	Retired Wool Buyer	Yorks
Fred Martin	Boarder	Marr	36	Cloth Manufacturer	Yorks
Emma Buckley	Boarder	Unm	49		Lancs
David Caruthurs	Boarder	Marr	33	Iron Merc Manufc	Cumbld
Agnes Caruthurs	Boarder	Marr	22		Scotld
Isabella Railton	Boarder	Marr	57		Cumbld
Isabella Railton	Boarder	Unm	20		Scotld
Annie Railton	Boarder	Unm	14		Scotld
Mary R Pattinson	Boarder	Unm	27		Cumbld
Theobald F Butler	Boarder	Unm	36	Iron Merchant	Ireland
Margaret A B Hall	Boarder	Unm	28		Yorks
John King	Boarder	Marr	61	Cotton Spinner	Lancs
Thomas M Rowles	Boarder	Marr	57	Wholesale Shoe	Lincolns
Isabella E Watson	Boarder	Unm	30		Lancs
John H Lace	Boarder	Unm	43		Yorks
Joseph Taylor	Boarder	Unm	22	Coachman (Domst)	Yorks
George Buchanan	Boarder	Marr	56	Iron Merchant	Demarara
Mary M Buchanan	Boarder	Unm	27		London
Patricia Bankhead	Boarder	Wid	39		Scotland
William D McLaren	Boarder	Unm	25	Student in Theology	Scotland

John P Walton	Boarder	Marr	42	Mine Owner	Cumbld
Frances M Walton	Boarder	Marr	33		London
Joseph Rhodes	Boarder	Marr	71	Iron Founder	Yorks
Grace Rhodes	Boarder	Marr	63		Yorks
William Ranch	Boarder	Unm	17	Scholar	Middlsx
John Dennis	Boarder	Marr	39	Furnace Builder	Lincoln
Rebecca Dennis	Boarder	Marr	35		Lincoln
Christopher Ling	Boarder	Marr	43	Corn Merchant	Cumbld
Sarah Ling	Boarder	Marr	36		Cumbld
William D Ling	Boarder		8		Cumbld
John R Ling	Boarder		2		Cumbld
Christopher G Ling	Boarder		5 m		Cumbld
Hannah Telford	Servant	Unm	18	Domestic Servant	Cumbld
Thomas Watson	Boarder	Marr	60	Silk Manufactuer	Lancs
Helen Watson	Boarder	Marr	56		Lancs
Robert S Aitchison	Boarder	Unm	24	Stationer	Scotland
William Blackburn	Boarder	Marr	56	Wool Carder	Yorks
Alice Watson	Boarder	Unm	21		Lancs
Isabella B Brown	Boarder	Unm	28		Scotland
Catherine B Brown	Boarder	Unm	40		Scotland
Ada J Watson	Boarder	Unm	20		Lancs
Harriette Nicholls	Boarder	Marr	63		Lancs
Conishead Priory Gardener's Lodge					
Charles Milne	Head	Marr	29	Gardener (Dom)	Scotland
Eliza Milne	Wife	Marr	32		Essex
Gardener's Cottage					
James Adam	Head (Serv)	Unm	21	Gardener (Dom)	Scotland
John English	Servant	Unm	21	Gardener (Dom)	Scotland
John L Stackhouse	Servant	Unm	18	Gardener (Dom)	Lancs
Gardener's Bothy or Cottage					
Robert Redpath	Head	Marr	25	Bath Attendant	Scotland
Betsy Redpath	Wife	Marr	25		Scotland
Isabella Redpath	Daughter		2		Scotland
Priory Gate Lodge					
Peter Milne	Head	Marr	25	House Porter	Scotland
Christina Milne	Wife	Marr	23		Scotland

(Source: Public Record Office, London – RG 11/4277)

Census Return – Conishead Priory Hydropathic Establishment 1891

Name	Status in Hhold	Marital status	Age	Employment	Place of birth
Isa Wright	Manageress	S(ingle)	26	Manageress, Hydro	Scotland
Jessie C M Martin	Cashier	S	25	Cashier, Hydro	Scotland
Arthur Young	Visitor	M(arried)	58	Woollen Merc	Nrthmbld
Sarah Young	Visitor	M	55		Kent (?)
Mary E Young	Visitor	S	21		Lancs
? ? Jackson	Visitor	S	26	Surgeon	Lancs

Robert I Roberts	Visitor	S	29	?	Lancs
Sarah A E Roberts	Visitor	S	23	Living on own means	Lancs
George E Burrows	Visitor	S	29	Woollen Mfct	Yorks
Thomas N Anderson	Visitor	M	39	Vicar	Westmld
Ann I Anderson	Visitor	M	35		Westmld
Thomas A Holland	Visitor	M	39	Living on own means	London
Thomas H Murphy	Visitor	S	54	Retired Civil Engineer	France
Peter Hudders	Visitor	Wid	72	Retired ship owner	Cumbld
Henry Euler	Visitor	M	47	Wool Merc	Germany
William J Euler	Visitor		15		Yorks
John Schofield	Visitor	M	63	Retired Dyer	Lancs
Elizabeth Schofield	Visitor	M	63		Yorks
Ellen Schofield	Visitor	S	33		Lancs
Richard Ripley	Visitor	M	58	Blue Manufc	Yorks
Lilian W Ripley	Visitor	M	27		Lancs
Florence E Ripley	Visitor	S	20		Lancs
John H Boyd	Visitor	M	61	Flax Spinner	Ireland
Anne Boyd	Visitor	M	55		Ireland
Emma S Boyd	Visitor	S	25		Ireland
Bessie Boyd	Visitor	S	22		Ireland
Arthur G Smith	Visitor	M	43	Chemical Agent	Lancs
Isabella Smith	Visitor	M	38		Yorks
Dorothy S Smith	Visitor		1		Lancs
Henry Sheerness	Visitor	M	54	Living on own means	Middlsx
Elizabeth Sheerness	Visitor	M	45		Surrey
Jane Swan	Visitor	M	50		Surrey
John Paterson	Visitor	M	37	Iron Works Manager	Scotland
Elizabeth Paterson	Visitor	M	44		Cumbld
George D Paterson	Visitor		13		Cumbld
John Paterson	Visitor		7		Cumbld
Mary S Paterson	Visitor		6		Cumbld
Matilda LeRossquot ?	Visitor	S	56	Proprietress of houses	Chn Isles
Mary E Mantell	Visitor	M	33	Wife of Hotel Proprieter	Ireland
William R Jones	Visitor	M	35	Secretary ? toAlderman ?	Lancs
Mary Jones	Visitor	M	32		Lancs
Hannah G Perks	Visitor	S	42	Living on own means	born?
Sarah Knowles	Visitor	S	21	Domstic Nurse	Cheshire
Margaret J Fell	Visitor	S	20	Housemaid	Lancs
Julia F Johnson	Visitor	S	33	Own means	Lancs
Elizabeth Gates	Visitor	S	30	Hosp Nurse	Lancs
Mary Evans	Visitor	S	45	Hosp Nurse	USA
Sarah Stewart	Upholsteress	S	26	Upholsteress	Scotland
Jessie Duff	Staff	S	36	Waitress	Scotland
Margaret A Parry	Staff	S	21	Pantry Maid	Wrehxm
Ann Lyon	Staff	S	20	Pantry Maid	Scotland
Maria McLean	Staff	S	28	Cook	Scotland
Sophia Parry	Staff	S	16	Pantry Maid	Lancs
Mary A Watson	Staff	M	29	Waitress	Staffs
Isabel Cherry	Staff	S	19	Waitress	Lancs
Sarah E Wilson	Staff	S	16	Scullery Maid	Lancs
Mary E Ward	Staff	S	20	Scullery Maid	Yorks
Hettie Ramfield	Staff	S	21	Kitchen Maid	Kent

Nellie Brew ?	Staff	S	18	Kitchen Maid	Lancs
Margaret Argo	Staff	S	20	Housemaid	Scotland
Mary McKesh…?	Staff	S	24	Housemaid	Scotland
Emily Halsell	Staff	S	17	Housemaid	Lancs
Annie Jewell	Staff	S	20	Waitress	Nrthmld
Florence Spencer	Staff	S	19	Housemaid	Lancs
Agnes A Smith	Staff	S	18	Housemaid	Lancs
Bridget Mulholland	Staff	S	27	Housemaid	Ireland ?
Annie McPhinn	Staff	S	23	Housemaid	Scotland
Eliza J Vincent	Staff	S	15	Pantry Maid	Cumbld
Mary Leeman ?	Staff	S	21	Laundress	Ireland
Annie Leeman?	Staff	S	19	Laundress	Lancs
Agnes Douglas	Staff	S	37	Laundress	Scotland
Elizabeth S McIvor	Staff	S	34	Linen Maid	Scotland
Annie O'Hara	Staff	M	45	Bath Attendt	Scotland
John Stainton	Staff	S	34	House Porter	Lancs
John J Cherry	Staff	S	39	Waiter	Westmld
George R S Rose	Staff	S	15	Office Boy	Derbys
James Storey	Staff	S	14	Kitchen Boy	Lancs
Thomas Norris	Staff	S	20	Boots	Scotland
John H Davidson	Staff	S	16	Pantry ? Boy	Monmths
Middle Lodge					
Euan Fraser	Head	M	52	Gardener	Scotland
Ann Fraser	Wife	M	50	Dairymaid	Scotland
Priory Lodge					
Alexander Grant	Head	M	34	Gardener & Overseerer	Scotland
Elizabeth Grant	Wife	M	32	Scotland	
Leah Grant	Daughter		9	Scholar	Scotland
Priory Bothy					
Richard Stainton	Head	S	49	Cattleman	Lancs
Andrew Alexander	Servant	S	22	Gardener	Scotland
John Lyall	Servant	S	20	Gardener	Scotland
William Murray ?	Servant	S	16	Apprentice Gardener	Scotland
Priory Bathman's Lodge					
Robert Redpath	Head	M	35	Bath Attendant	Scotland
Elizabeth Redpath	Wife	M	35		Scotland
Isabella Redpath	Daughter		12	Scholar	Scotland
William Redpath	Son		8	Scholar	Lancs
Herbert Redpath	Son		7	Scholar	Lancs
Elizabeth Redpath	Daughter		5		Lancs

(Source: Public Record Office, London – RG 12/3476)

Census Return – Conishead Priory Hydropathic Establishment 1901

Name	Status in Establishment	Marital status	Age	Employment	Place of birth
Peter Keiller	Head	M	34	Manager of Hydro	Scotland
Elizabeth Keiller	Wife	M	33		Scotland
William Keiller	Son		6		England

James Keiller	Son		4		England
Agnes E Keiller	Daughter		2		England
Thomas Alex Keiller	Son		1 mth		Lancs
John William Pawson	Head	M	40	Bathman	Yorks
Esther Pawson	Wife	M	41	Laundress	Glos
Samuel J Summerson	Visitor	M	49	Iron Industry	Durham
Dorothy Summerson	Visitor	M	27		Lancs
Walter Thorp	Visitor	Widower	63	Colliery Agent	Yorks
Edith Thorp	Visitor	S	22		Derby
Alex McDougall	Visitor	M	63	Master Mariner	Scotland
Florence D Jackson	Visitor	S	45		Yorks
Clara E L Grieve	Servant	S	23	Clerk	Scotland
Joseph F Hodgson	Visitor	M	49	Indept Means	Cumbld
Bessie Hodgson	Visitor	M	44		Scotland
Sarah Tweedy	Visitor	M	44		Lancs
Edith M Ellis	Visitor	S	24		Yorks
William D Ellis	Visitor	S	26	Merchant	Yorks
Mary Kleinwort	Visitor	Widow	68		Germany
Louisa Kleinwort	Visitor	S	31		London
Lizzie Dubson	Visitor	S	27	Housekeeper	Scotland
Arthur W Cole	Visitor	M	33	Draper	Yorks
Mary Cole	Visitor	M	24		Yorks
Mary Leach	Visitor	M	56		Cumbld
John Shallcross	Visitor	M	68	Retired Corn ? Merchant	Yorks
Emma Shallcross	Visitor	M	64		Yorks
Sarah Jane Sharp	Visitor	S	45		Yorks
Mary Winterbottom	Visitor	S	37		Yorks
Sarah E Saville	Visitor	S	40	Journalist	Yorks
Maud M Middlement	Visitor	S	39		Middlsx
Clara H Middlement	Visitor	S	30		Yorks
Alexander Bridgford	Servant	S	28	Hall Porter	Scotland
Thomas Buchan	Servant	S	24	Boots	Scotland
Annie M Jackson	Servant	S	19	Dom Servant	Lancs
Ellen Slavin	Servant	S	19	Dom Servant	Cumbld
Charlotte Crewdson	Servant	S	22	Dom Servant	Lancs
Mary Jane Slavin	Servant	S	21	Dom Servant	Cumbld
Mary B McLean	Servant	S	34	Waitress	Scotland
Jeannie W Gillen	Servant	S	21	Kitchen Maid	Scotland
Sarah Allen	Servant	Widow	45	Cook	Staffs
Eliza Quayle	Servant	S	23	Housemaid	Lancs
Mary Brown	Servant	S	21	Housemaid	Lancs
Margaret O'Brien	Servant	S	18	Housemaid	Lancs
Mary Quayle	Servant	S	19	Linen Maid	Lancs
Annie Farrell	Servant	S	23	Housemaid	Lancs
Annie Wilding	Servant	S	14	Hall Maid	Lancs
Mary Farrell	Servant	S	21	Laundry Maid	Lancs
Sarah J Brown	Servant	S	28	Laundry Maid	Lancs
Thomas Jones	Servant	S	16	Boots	Lancs
Jennie S(?)ottell	Servant	S	28	Maid	Wales
Frances E Garrett	Servant	S	34	Bathmaid	Portsmth

The Bothy

William Rock	Servant	S	25	Gardener	England
William Johnson	Servant	S	24	Stockman Cattle	Lancs

Peter Durham	Servant	S	16	Gardener	Scotland
Harry Walker	Servant	S	18	Gardener	Lancs
James Whiting	Servant	S	18	Gardener	Suffolk
William Gudgeon	Servant	S	21	Gardener	Lancs
Joseph B Ward	Servant	S	22	Dom Driver	Lancs
John Thompson	Servant	S	28	Coachman	Lancs
Priory Gate Lodge					
David Ferguson	Head	M	34	Joiner on Estate	Scotland
Christina Ferguson	Wife	M	35		Scotland
Margaret Ferguson	Daughter		4		Scotland
Mary Ferguson	Daughter		1		Scotland

(Source: Public Record Office, London – RG 13/4005)

Census Return - Conishead Priory Hydropathic Establishment 1911

Name	Marital status	Age	Employment	Place of birth
Manager's House				
Thomas McNair	Head	37	Manager of Hydro	Edinburgh
Janet McMullian McNair	Wife	35		Edinburgh
David McMullian McNair	Son	9		Edinburgh
Catherine Jaffrey McNair	Daug	2		Forfarshire
Amy Molyneaux	Serv	17	Domestic Servant	Ulverston, Lancs
House Staff				
Thomas Buchan	Single	33	Hall Porter	Kincardineshire
Harry William Gould	Single	23	2nd Boots	Liverpool, Lancs
Christopher Rigg Lewis	Single	44	Head Bath man	Bardsea, Lancs
George Bernard Griffiths	Single	18	3rd Boots	Garston, Lancs
Anton Meyer	Single	35	Head Waiter	Austria
Agnes Grant	Single	28	Head Bath maid	Lanarkshire
Charlotte Hannah	Single	32	Pantry maid	Penny Bridge, Lancs
Chrissie Victoria Hutchinson	Single	29	3rd Laundry maid	Westmorland
Lilly Needham	Single	19	Housemaid	Ulverston, Lancs
Mary Alice Lambert	Single	26	Housemaid	Carnforth, Lancs
Rose Lambert	Single	24	Housemaid	Ulverston, Lancs
Maggie Blake	Single	28	Housemaid	Ulverston, Lancs
Walburna (?) Cowbrough	Single	18	Housemaid	Stirling
Mary Ann Graverson	Single	18	Housemaid	Ulverston
Mary Slaven	Single	28	Head Waitress	Milburn, Cumb
Margaret Ferguson	Single	45	Cook	Fordyce, Banffshire
Hannah Denny	Single	28	Scullery maid	Dalton, Lancs
Archibald Gregg	Single	23	2nd Coachman	Barrow, Lancs
Fanny Bennett	Single	36	Housekeeper	Preston, Lancs
Alice Marion Knox	Single	23	Book keeper	Edinburgh
Harriett Briggs	Widow	56	Head Laundress	Rochdale
William Alexander MacGregor	Single	29	Gardener	Morayshire
Daniel Simpson Barrerman	Single	27	Gardener	Ross shire
Arthur Briggs Travis	Single	20	Gardener	Dalton, Lancs
Isaac Bowness	Single	48	Cowman	Crosthwaite, Westm

Alexander B Fraser	Head	35	Overseer	Forfarshire
Janet Mathieson Fraser	Wife	30		Ayrshire
John Fraser	Son	6		Midlothian
David M Fraser	Son	4		Midlothian
Martha M Fraser	Daug	1		Midlothian
William Fraser	Son	under 1		Ulverston, Lancs
Coachman's House				
John Thomson	Head	39	Head Coachman	Ulverston, Lancs
Jane Thomson	Wife	39		Grange, Lancs
Mary Thomson	Daug	1	(adopted)	Kents Bank, Lancs
Visitors staying at the Conishead Hydro				
Greeley Haigh Lougee	Visitor	42	Bank Manager	Yorkshire
Catherine Edith Lougee	Visitor	38	Wife	Bradford, Yorks
Dudley Martin Lougee	Visitor	13	Son (scholar)	Bradford, Yorks
John Greeley Lougee	Visitor	6	Son	Bradford,Yorks
Harriet Hodge	Visitor	29	Professional Nurse (Single)	Formby, Lancs
John Smart (junior)	Visitor	34	Writer to the Signet	Edinburgh
Alexandra H McCulloch	Visitor	27	Private means (single)	Liverpool, Lancs
Alice May Kendall	Visitor	31	Professional Nurse	Somerset, Devons
Helen Fenwick	Visitor	44	Private means (single)	Northumberland
Margaret Amelia Fenwick	Visitor	52	Private means (single)	Northumberland
Emily Louisa Johnson	Visitor	49	Private means (widow)	Wakefield, Yorks
Eliza Robinson	Visitor	49	Principal of Women's Hostel (Durham University) (single)	Averthorpe, Yorks
Lizzie Cowbrough	Visitor	70	Private means (married)	Yorks
Henry Cowbrough	Visitor	81	Private means (married)	Stirling

(Source: Public Record Office, London - RG/481/3/12)

Bibliography

'*Souvenir of Conishead Priory*' (c. 1890)

'*The Story of Conishead Priory*' (1950)

Ayre '*Handy Guide to Ulverston*' (1904)

Barnes, F '*Barrow and District*' (1951)

Christie & Mason *Auction Catalogue for the Braddyll Art Collection* (1846)

'*The Cumberland Pacquet*' Newspaper

Dugdale '*Monasticon Anglicanum*'

Durie, Alastair J. '*The Business of Hydrotherapy in the North of England c. 1850 – 1930*' (Northern History Vo. XXXIX 1 March 2002)

Eaton, Robert '*Stories of Samlesbury*' (1927)

Edward, Lewis '*Daniel Mendoza*' from the Transactions of the Jewish Historical Society of England

Evans, Francis '*A History of Furness and Furness Abbey*' (1842)

Ford, Rev. William '*A Description of the Scenery in the Lake District*' (1839)

Girouard, M '*Life in the English Country House*' (1978)

Girouard, M '*A Country House Companion*' (1992)

'*A History of the County of Lancaster: 'Houses of Austin Canons: The Priory of Conishead*' Volume 2 (1908)

'*A History of the County of Lancaster:* Volume 8 (Farrer and Brownbill, 1914)

Jopling, Charles. M '*Sketch of Furness and Cartmel*' (1843)

Kelly, P.V. '*Excavations at Conishead Priory*' from the Transactions of the Cumberland and Westmorland Antiquarian and Archaeological Society (1929)

Keynes, Randall '*Annie's Box*' (2001)

Layfield, Jack '*Conishead Priory and the 20th Century*' (2004)

'*Life*' *Magazine* (13 Sep 1948)

Lofthouse, Jessica '*The Curious Traveller*' (1956)

'*The North Lonsdale Magazine*' Vol 1 (1820)

'*The North Lonsdale Magazine and Furness Miscellany*' Vol 1 No 7 (1895)

Mackay, Charles '*The Scenery and Poetry of the English Lakes, a Summer Ramble*' (1852)

Mackereth's '*Year Book for 1900*'

Manjushri Kadampa Buddhist Centre '*Conishead Priory and Gardens*' (2003)

Marshall, Brian '*Lancashire's Medieval Monasteries*' (2006)

Mason R. J. '*The Income, Administration and Disposal of Monastic Lands in Lancashire from the Dissolution to 1558*' (1962)

Page R. I. '*Introduction to English Runes*'

Parson and White's '*History, Directory and Gazetteer of Cumberland and Westmorland*' (1829)

Pevsner, Nikolaus '*Buildings of England*' (1969)

Philp, Dr '*Guide to Conishead Priory and the Surrounding District*' (1880)

Salmon, William '*History of the Ulverston Canal and the Commerce of the Port*' (1849)

Schalch, Phillis '*Grandmamma's Recollections and Letters*' (1855)

Soulby's '*Ulverston Advertiser*' Newspaper

Strickland, A '*Lives of the Queens of England from the Norman Conquest*' (1854)

Sylvan's '*Pictorial Handbook to the English Lakes*' (1847)

Taylor, Angus '*The Websters of Kendal*' (2004)

'*The Times*' Newspaper

Trevelyan, G. M. '*English Social History – A Survey of Six Centuries: Chaucer to Queen Victoria*' (1944)

West, Thomas '*Antiquities of Furness*' (1774)

'*The Westmorland Advertiser*' Newspaper

Wilson, A.N. '*The Victorians*' (2002)

Index